Daniel Defoe, Henry Morley

The Earlier Life and the Chief Earlier Works of Daniel Defoe

Daniel Defoe, Henry Morley

The Earlier Life and the Chief Earlier Works of Daniel Defoe

ISBN/EAN: 9783337055936

Printed in Europe, USA, Canada, Australia, Japan

Cover: Foto ©Thomas Meinert / pixelio.de

More available books at **www.hansebooks.com**

THE PROFESSOR.

𝔄 Novel.

BY

CHARLOTTE BRONTÉ ("CURRER BELL").

AUTHOR OF "JANE EYRE," "VILLETTE," "SHIRLEY," ETC.

NEW YORK:

Carleton, Publisher, 413 Broadway.

M DCCC LXV

5

PREFACE.

THIS little book was written before either " Jane
Eyre" or " Shirley," and yet no indulgence can be so-
licited for it on the plea of a first attempt. A first attempt it certainly was not, as the pen which wrote it
had been previously worn a good deal in a practice of
some years. I had not indeed published any thing
before I commenced " The Professor," but in many a
crude effort, destroyed almost as soon as composed, I
had got over any such taste as I might once have had
for ornamented and redundant composition, and come
to prefer what was plain and homely. At the same
time, I had adopted a set of principles on the subject
of incident, &c., such as would be generally approved
in theory, but the result of which, when carried out
into practice, often procure for an author more surprise than pleasure.

I said to myself that my hero should work his way
through life as I had seen real living men work theirs;
that he should never get a shilling he had not earned;
that no sudden turns should lift him in a moment to
wealth and high station; that whatever small competency he might gain should be won by the sweat of his
brow; that, before he could find so much as an arbor

to sit down in, he should master at least half the as
cent of "the Hill of Difficulty;" that he should not
even marry a beautiful girl nor a lady of rank. As
Adam's son, he should share Adam's doom, and drain
throughout life a mixed and moderate cup of enjoyment.

In the sequel, however, I found that publishers in
general scarcely approved of this system, but would
have liked something more imaginative and poetical—
something more consonant with a highly-wrought fancy, with a taste for pathos, with sentiments more tender, elevated, unworldly. Indeed, until an author has
tried to dispose of a manuscript of this kind, he can
never know what stores of romance and sensibility lie
hidden in breasts he would not have suspected of cas-
keting such treasures. Men in business are usually
thought to prefer the real; on trial, the idea will be
often found fallacious: a passionate preference for the
wild, wonderful, and thrilling—the strange, startling,
and harrowing, agitates divers souls that show a calm
and sober surface.

Such being the case, the reader will comprehend
that to have reached him in the form of a printed book,
this brief narrative must have gone through some
struggles—which indeed it has. And, after all, its
worst struggle and strongest ordeal is yet to come;
but it takes comfort—subdues fear—leans on the staff
of a moderate expectation, and mutters under its breath,
while lifting its eye to that of the public,

"He that is low need fear no fall."

CURRER BELL.

The foregoing preface was written by my wife with a view to the publication of " The Professor," shortly after the appearance of " Shirley." Being dissuaded from her intention, the authoress made some use of the materials in a subsequent work—" Villettc." As, however, these two stories are in most respects unlike, it has been represented to me that I ought not to withhold " The Professor" from the public. I have, therefore, consented to its publication.

A. B. NICHOLLS.

Haworth Parsonage, September 22d, 1856.

THE PROFESSOR.

CHAPTER I.

INTRODUCTORY.

THE other day, in looking over my papers, I found in my desk the following copy of a letter, sent by me a year since to an old school acquaintance:

"DEAR CHARLES,—I think when you and I were at Eton together, we were neither of us what could be called popular characters. You were a sarcastic, observant, shrewd, cold-blooded creature; my own portrait I will not attempt to draw, but I can not recollect that it was a strikingly attractive one—can you? What animal magnetism drew thee and me together I know not; certainly I never experienced any thing of the Pylades and Orestes sentiment for you, and I have reason to believe that you, on your part, were equally free from all romantic regard to me. Still, out of school hours, we walked and talked continually together; when the theme of conversation was our companions or our masters, we understood each other, and when I recurred to some sentiment of affection, some vague love of an excellent or beautiful object, whether in animate or inanimate nature, your sardonic coldness did not move me. I felt myself superior to that check *then* as I do *now*.

A 2

"It is a long time since I wrote to you, and a still longer time since I saw you. Chancing to take up a newspaper of your county the other day, my eye fell upon your name. I began to think of old times; to run over the events which have transpired since we separated; and I sat down and commenced this letter. What you have been doing I know not; but you shall hear, if you choose to listen, how the world has wagged with me.

"First, after leaving Eton, I had an interview with my maternal uncles, Lord Tynedale and the Hon. John Seacombe. They asked me if I would enter the Church, and my uncle the nobleman offered me the living of Seacombe, which is in his gift, if I would; then my other uncle, Mr. Seacombe, hinted that when I became rector of Seacombe-cum-Scaife, I might perhaps be allowed to take, as mistress of my house and head of my parish, one of my six cousins, his daughters, all of whom I greatly dislike.

"I declined both the Church and matrimony. A good clergyman is a good thing, but I should have made a very bad one. As to the wife—oh how like a nightmare is the thought of being bound for life to one of my cousins! No doubt they are accomplished and pretty; but not an accomplishment, not a charm of theirs, touches a chord in my bosom. To think of passing the winter evenings by the parlor fireside of Seacombe Rectory alone with one of them—for instance, the large and well-modeled statue, Sarah—no; I should be a bad husband, under such circumstances, as well as a bad clergyman.

"When I had declined my uncles' offers they asked

me 'what I intended to do.' I said I should reflect. They reminded me that I had no fortune, and no expectation of any, and, after a considerable pause, Lord Tynedale demanded sternly 'whether I had thoughts of following my father's steps and engaging in trade.' Now I had had no thoughts of the sort. I do not think my turn of mind qualifies me to make a good tradesman; my taste, my ambition does not lie that way; but such was the scorn expressed in Lord Tynedale's countenance as he pronounced the word *trade*— such the contemptuous sarcasm of his tone, that I was instantly decided. My father was but a name to me, yet that name I did not like to hear mentioned with a sneer to my very face. I answered then, with haste and warmth, 'I can not do better than follow in my father's steps; yes, I will be a tradesman.' My uncles did not remonstrate; they and I parted with mutual disgust. In reviewing this transaction, I find that I was quite right to shake off the burden of Tynedale's patronage, but a fool for offering my shoulders instantly for the reception of another burden—one which might be more intolerable, and which certainly was yet untried.

"I wrote instantly to Edward—you know Edward —my only brother, ten years my senior, married to a rich mill-owner's daughter, and now possessor of the mill and business which was my father's before he failed. You are aware that my father—once reckoned a Crœsus of wealth—became bankrupt a short time previous to his death, and that my mother lived in destitution for some six months after him, unhelped by her aristocratical brothers, whom she had mortally offended by her union with Crimsworth, the ——shire manufacturer. At the end of the six months she brought me into the world, and then herself left it without, I should think, much regret, as it contained little hope or comfort for her.

" My father's relations took charge of Edward, as they did of me till I was nine years old. At that period it chanced that the representation of an important borough in our county fell vacant. Mr. Seacombe stood for it. My uncle Crimsworth, an astute mercantile man, took the opportunity of writing a fierce letter to the candidate, stating that if he and Lord Tynedale did not consent to do something toward the support of their sister's orphan children, he would expose their relentless and malignant conduct toward that sister, and do his best to turn the circumstances against Mr. Seacombe's election. That gentleman and Lord T—— knew well enough that the Crimsworths were an unscrupulous and determined race; they knew also that they had influence in the borough of X——; and, making a virtue of necessity, they consented to defray the expenses of my education. I was sent to Eton, where I remained ten years, during which space of time Edward and I never met. He, when he grew up, entered into trade, and pursued his calling with such diligence, ability, and success, that now, in his thirtieth year, he was fast making a fortune. Of this I was apprised by the occasional short letters I received from him some three or four times a year, which said letters never concluded without some expression of determined enmity against the house of Seacombe, and some reproach to me for living, as he said, on the bounty of that house. At first, while still in boyhood, I could not understand why, as I had no parents, I should not be indebted to my uncles Tynedale and Seacombe for my education; but as I grew up, and heard by degrees of the persevering hostility, the hatred till death evinced by them against my father—of the sufferings of my mother — of all the wrongs, in short, of our house, then did I conceive shame of the dependence in which I lived, and form a resolution no more to take bread from hands which had refused to minister to the necessities of my dying mother. It was by these feelings I was influenced when I refused the Rectory of Seacombe, and the union with one of my patrician cousins.

"An irreparable breach thus being effected between my uncles and myself, I wrote to Edward, told him what had occurred, and informed him of my intention to follow his steps and be a tradesman. I asked, moreover, if he could give me employment. His answer expressed no approbation of my conduct, but he said I might come down to ——shire if I liked, and he would 'see what could be done in the way of furnishing me with work.' I repressed all—even *mental* comment on his note, packed my trunk and carpet-bag, and started for the North directly.

"After two days' traveling (rail-roads were not then in existence) I arrived, one wet October afternoon, in the town of X——. I had always understood that Edward lived in this town, but on inquiry I found that it was only Mr. Crimsworth's mill and warehouse which were situated in the smoky atmosphere of Bigben Close; his *residence* lay four miles out, in the country.

"It was late in the evening when I alighted at the gates of the habitation designated to me as my brother's. As I advanced up the avenue, I could see through the shades of twilight, and the dark, gloomy mists which deepened those shades, that the house was large, and the grounds surrounding it sufficiently spacious. I paused a moment on the lawn in front, and, leaning my back against a tall tree which rose in the centre, I gazed with interest on the exterior of Crimsworth Hall.

"'Edward is rich,' thought I to myself. 'I believed him to be doing well, but I did not know he was master of a mansion like this.' Cutting short all marveling, speculation, conjecture, &c., I advanced to the front door and rang. A man-servant opened it—I announced myself—he relieved me of my wet cloak and carpet-bag, and ushered me into a room furnished as a library, where there was a bright fire, and candles burning on the table. He informed me that his master had not yet returned from X—— market, but that he would certainly be at home in the course of half an hour.

"Being left to myself, I took the stuffed easy-chair, covered with red morocco, which stood by the fireside, and while my eyes watched the flames dart from the glowing coals, and the cinders fall at intervals on the hearth, my mind busied itself in conjectures concerning the meeting about to take place. Amid much that was doubtful in the subject of these conjectures, there was one thing tolerably certain: I was in no danger of encountering severe disappointment; from this, the moderation of my expectations guaranteed me. I anticipated no overflowings of fraternal tenderness; Edward's letters had always been such as to prevent the engendering or harboring of delusions of this sort. Still, as I sat awaiting his arrival, I felt eager—very eager—I can not tell you why; my hand, so utterly a stranger to the grasp of a kindred hand, clenched itself to repress the tremor with which impatience would fain have shaken it.

"I thought of my uncles; and as I was engaged in wondering whether Edward's indifference would equal the cold disdain I had always experienced from them, I heard the avenue gates open; wheels approached the house; Mr. Crimsworth was arrived; and after the lapse of some minutes, and a brief dialogue between himself and his servant in the hall, his tread drew near the library door: that tread alone announced the master of the house.

"I still retained some confused recollection of Edward as he was ten years ago—a tall, wiry, raw youth; now, as I rose from my seat and turned toward the library door, I saw a fine-looking and powerful man, light-complexioned, well-made, and of athletic proportions. The first glance made me aware of an air of promptitude and sharpness, shown as well in his movements as in his port, his eye, and the general expression of his face. He greeted me with brevity, and, in the moment of shaking hands, scanned me from head to foot. He took his seat in the morocco-covered armchair, and motioned me to another seat.

"'I expected you would have called at the counting-house in the Close,' said he; and his voice, I noticed, had an abrupt accent, probably habitual to him.

He spoke, also, with a guttural Northern tone, which sounded harsh in my ears, accustomed to the silvery utterance of the South.

" ' The landlord of the inn, where the coach stopped, directed me here,' said I. 'I doubted at first the accuracy of his information, not being aware that you had such a residence as this.'

" ' Oh, it is all right,' he replied, 'only I was kept half an hour behind time, waiting for you—that is all. I thought you must be coming by the eight o'clock coach.'

" I expressed regret that he had had to wait. He made no answer, but stirred the fire, as if to cover a movement of impatience; then he scanned me again.

" I felt an inward satisfaction that I had not, in the first moment of meeting, betrayed any warmth—any enthusiasm; that I had saluted this man with a quiet and steady phlegm.

" ' Have you quite broken with Tynedale and Seacombe ?' he asked, hastily.

" ' I do not think I shall have any further communication with them. My refusal of their proposals will, I fancy, operate as a barrier against all future intercourse.'

" ' Why,' said he, 'I may as well remind you, at the very outset of our connection, " that no man can serve two masters." Acquaintance with Lord Tynedale will be incompatible with assistance from me.' There was a kind of gratuitous menace in his eye as he looked at me in finishing this observation.

" Feeling no disposition to reply to him, I contented myself with an inward speculation on the differences

which exist in the constitution of men's minds. I do
not know what inference Mr. Crimsworth drew from
my silence—whether he considered it a symptom of
contumacity or an evidence of my being cowed by his
peremptory manner. After a long and hard stare at
me, he rose sharply from his seat.

" 'To-morrow,' said he, 'I shall call your attention
to some other points; but now it is supper-time, and
Mrs. Crimsworth is probably waiting; will you come?'

"He strode from the room, and I followed. In
crossing the hall, I wondered what Mrs. Crimsworth
might be. 'Is she,' thought I, 'as alien to what I like
as Tynedale, Seacombe, the Misses Seacombe—as the
affectionate relative now striding before me? or is she
better than these? Shall I, in conversing with her,
feel free to show something of my real nature; or—'
Further conjectures were arrested by my entrance into
the dining-room.

"A lamp, burning under a shade of ground glass,
showed a handsome apartment, wainscoted with oak;
supper was laid on the table; by the fire-place, standing as if waiting our entrance, appeared a lady; she
was young, tall, and well shaped; her dress was handsome and fashionable: so much my first glance sufficed to ascertain. A gay salutation passed between
her and Mr. Crimsworth. She chid him, half playful-
ly, half poutingly, for being late; her voice (I always
take voices into the account in judging of character)
was lively: it indicated, I thought, good animal spirits. Mr. Crimsworth soon checked her animated scolding with a kiss—a kiss that still told of the bridegroom
(they had not yet been married a year). She took her

seat at the supper-table in first-rate spirits.   Perceiving me, she begged my pardon for not noticing me before, and then shook hands with me, as ladies do when
a flow of good-humor disposes them to be cheerful to
all, even the most indifferent of their acquaintance.   It
was now further obvious to me that she had a good
complexion, and features sufficiently marked but agreeable; her hair was red—quite red.   She and Edward
talked much, always in a way of playful contention.
She was vexed, or pretended to be vexed, that he had
that day driven a vicious horse in the gig, and made
light of her fears.   Sometimes she appealed to me.

"'Now, Mr. William, isn't it absurd in Edward to
talk so?   He says he will drive Jack, and no other
horse, and the brute has thrown him twice already.'

"She spoke with a kind of lisp, not disagreeable,
but childish.   I soon saw, also, that there was a more
than girlish—a somewhat infantine expression in her
by no means small features.   This lisp and expression
were, I have no doubt, a charm in Edward's eyes, and
would be so to those of most men, but they were not
to mine.   I sought her eye, desirous to read there the
intelligence which I could not discern in her face or
hear in her conversation; it was merry, rather small;
by turns I saw vivacity, vanity, coquetry, look out
through its irid, but I watched in vain for a glimpse
of soul.   I am no Oriental; white necks, carmine lips
and cheeks, clusters of bright curls, do not suffice for
me without that Promethean spark which will live after the roses and lilies are faded, the burnished hair
grown gray.   In sunshine, in prosperity, the flowers
are very well; but how many wet days are there in

life—November seasons of disaster, when a man's hearth and home would be cold indeed without the clear, cheering gleam of intellect!

" Having perused the fair page of Mrs. Crimsworth's face, a deep, involuntary sigh announced my disappointment. She took it as a homage to her beauty, and Edward, who was evidently proud of his rich and handsome young wife, threw on me a glance, half ridicule, half ire.

" I turned from them both, and gazing wearily round the room, I saw two pictures set in the oak paneling, one on each side the mantel-piece. Ceasing to take part in the bantering conversation that flowed on between Mr. and Mrs. Crimsworth, I bent my thoughts to the examination of these pictures. They were portraits—a lady and a gentleman, both costumed in the fashion of twenty years ago. The gentleman was in the shade. I could not see him well. The lady had the benefit of a full beam from the softly shaded lamp. I presently recognized her. I had seen this picture before, in childhood—it was my mother; that and the companion picture being the only heir-looms saved out of the sale of my father's property.

" The face, I remembered, had pleased me as a boy, but *then* I did not understand it; *now* I knew how rare that class of face is in the world, and I appreciated keenly its thoughtful yet gentle expression. The serious gray eye possessed for me a strong charm, as did certain lines in the features indicative of most true and tender feeling. I was sorry it was only a picture.

" I soon left Mr. and Mrs. Crimsworth to themselves. A servant conducted me to my bed-room. In closing

my chamber door, I shut out all intruders — you,
Charles, as well as the rest.

"Good-by for the present.

"WILLIAM CRIMSWORTH."

To this letter I never got an answer. Before my
old friend received it he had accepted a government
appointment in one of the colonies, and was already on
his way to the scene of his official labors. What has
become of him since I know not.

The leisure time I have at command, and which I
intended to employ for his private benefit, I shall now
dedicate to that of the public at large. My narrative
is not exciting, and, above all, not marvelous; but it
may interest some individuals, who, having toiled in
the same vocation as myself, will find in my experience frequent reflections of their own. The above letter will serve as introduction. I now proceed.

CHAPTER II.

A FINE October morning succeeded to the foggy
evening that had witnessed my first introduction to
Crimsworth Hall. I was early up and walking in the
large park-like meadow surrounding the house. The
autumn sun, rising over the —— shire hills, disclosed a
pleasant country; woods brown and mellow varied the
fields from which the harvest had been lately carried;
a river, gliding between the woods, caught on its surface the somewhat cold gleam of the October sun and

sky; at frequent intervals along the banks of the river, tall, cylindrical chimneys, almost like slender round towers, indicated the factories which the trees half concealed; here and there mansions, similar to Crimsworth Hall, occupied agreeable sites on the hill side; the country wore, on the whole, a cheerful, active, fertile look. Steam, trade, machinery had long banished from it all romance and seclusion. At a distance of five miles, a valley, opening between the low hills, held in its cups the great town of X——. A dense, permanent vapor brooded over this locality: there lay Edward's "concern."

I forced my eye to scrutinize this prospect, I forced my mind to dwell on it for a time, and when I found that it communicated no pleasurable emotion to my heart—that it stirred in me none of the hopes a man ought to feel when he sees laid before him the scene of his life's career, I said to myself, " William, you are a rebel against circumstances; you are a fool, and know not what you want; you have chosen trade, and you shall be a tradesman. Look!" I continued, mentally, "look at the sooty smoke in that hollow, and know that there is your post. There you can not dream, you can not speculate and theorize—there you shall out and work."

Thus self-schooled, I returned to the house. My brother was in the breakfast-room. I met him collectedly—I could not meet him cheerfully. He was standing on the rug, his back to the fire. How much did I read in the expression of his eye as my glance encountered his, when I advanced to bid him good-morning—how much that was contradictory to my na-

ture! He said "Good-morning" abruptly, and nodded, and then he snatched, rather than took, a newspaper from the table, and began to read it with the air
of a master who seizes a pretext to escape the bore of
conversing with an underling. It was well I had taken
a resolution to endure for a time, or his manner would
have gone far to render insupportable the disgust I had
just been endeavoring to subdue. I looked at him.
I measured his robust frame and powerful proportions;
I saw my own reflection in the mirror over the mantel-
piece; I amused myself with comparing the two pictures. In face I resembled him, though I was not so
handsome; my features were less regular; I had a
darker eye and a broader brow; in form I was greatly inferior—thinner, slighter, not so tall. As an animal, Edward excelled me far; should he prove as paramount in mind as in person, I must be his slave, for
I must expect from him no lion-like generosity to one
weaker than himself; his cold, avaricious eye, his
stern, forbidding manner told me he would not spare.
Had I, then, force of mind to cope with him? I did
not know; I had never been tried.

Mrs. Crimsworth's entrance diverted my thoughts
for a moment. She looked well, dressed in white, her
face and her attire shining in morning and bridal freshness. I addressed her with the degree of ease her last
night's careless gayety seemed to warrant, but she replied with coolness and restraint. Her husband had
tutored her; she was not to be too familiar with his
clerk.

As soon as breakfast was over, Mr. Crimsworth intimated to me that they were bringing the gig round

to the door, and that in five minutes he should expect
me to be ready to go down with him to X——. I
did not keep him waiting; we were soon dashing at a
rapid rate along the road. The horse he drove was
the same vicious animal about which Mrs. Crimsworth
had expressed her fears the night before. Once or
twice Jack seemed disposed to turn restive, but a vigorous and determined application of the whip from the
ruthless hand of his master soon compelled him to
submission, and Edward's dilated nostril expressed his
triumph in the result of the contest. He scarcely
spoke to me during the whole of the brief drive, only
opening his lips at intervals to damn his horse.

X—— was all stir and bustle when we entered it.
We left the clean streets where there were dwelling-
houses and shops, churches and public buildings—we
left all these, and turned down to a region of mills and
warehouses; thence we passed through two massive
gates into a great paved yard, and we were in Bigben
Close, and the mill was before us, vomiting soot from
its long chimney, and quivering through its thick brick
walls with the commotion of its iron bowels. Work-
people were passing to and fro; a wagon was being
laden with pieces. Mr. Crimsworth looked from side
to side, and seemed at one glance to comprehend all
that was going on. He alighted, and leaving his horse
and gig to the care of a man who hastened to take the
reins from his hand, he bid me follow him to the counting-house. We entered it; a very different place from
the parlors of Crimsworth Hall—a place for business,
with a bare planked floor, a safe, two high desks and
stools, and some chairs. A person was seated at one

of the desks, who took off his square cap when Mr. Crimsworth entered, and in an instant was again absorbed in his occupation of writing or calculating, I know not which.

Mr. Crimsworth, having removed his Mackintosh, sat down by the fire. I remained standing near the hearth. He said presently,

"Steighton, you may leave the room. I have some business to transact with this gentleman. Come back when you hear the bell."

The individual at the desk rose and departed, closing the door as he went out. Mr. Crimsworth stirred the fire, then folded his arms, and sat a moment thinking, his lips compressed, his brow knit. I had nothing to do but to watch him. How well his features were cut! what a handsome man he was! Whence, then, came that air of contraction—that narrow and hard aspect on his forehead, in all his lineaments?

Turning to me, he began abruptly,

"You are come down to ——shire to learn to be a tradesman?"

"Yes, I am."

"Have you made up your mind on the point? Let me know that at once."

"Yes."

"Well, I am not bound to help you, but I have a place here vacant, if you are qualified for it. I will take you on trial. What can you do? Do you know any thing besides that useless trash of college learning—Greek, Latin, and so forth?"

"I have studied mathematics."

"Stuff! I dare say you have."

"I can read and write French and German."

"Hum!" He reflected a moment, then opening a drawer in a desk near him, took out a letter and gave it to me.

"Can you read that?" he asked.

It was a German commercial letter. I translated it. I could not tell whether he was gratified or not: his countenance remained fixed.

"It is well," he said, after a pause, "that you are acquainted with something useful, something that may enable you to earn your board and lodging. Since you know French and German, I will take you as second clerk to manage the foreign correspondence of the house. I shall give you a good salary—£90 a year— and now," he continued, raising his voice, "hear once for all what I have to say about our relationship, and all that sort of humbug. I must have no nonsense on that point; it would never suit me. I shall excuse you nothing on the plea of being my brother. If I find you stupid, negligent, dissipated, idle, or possessed of any faults detrimental to the interests of the house, I shall dismiss you as I would any other clerk. Ninety pounds a year are good wages, and I expect to have the full value of my money out of you; remember, too, that things are on a practical footing in my establishment—business-like habits, feelings, and ideas suit me best. Do you understand?"

"Partly," I replied. "I suppose you mean that I am to do my work for my wages; not to expect favor from you, and not to depend on you for any help but what I earn? That suits me exactly, and on these terms I will consent to be your clerk."

I turned on my heel and walked to the window. This time I did not consult his face to learn his opinion. What it was I do not know, nor did I then care. After a silence of some minutes he recommenced:

" You perhaps expect to be accommodated with apartments at Crimsworth Hall, and to go and come with me in the gig. I wish you, however, to be aware that such an arrangement would be quite inconvenient to me. I like to have the seat in my gig at liberty for any gentleman whom for business reasons I may wish to take down for a night or so. You will seek out lodgings in X——."

Quitting the window, I walked back to the hearth.

" Of course I shall seek out lodgings in X——," I answered. " It would not suit me either to lodge at Crimsworth Hall."

My tone was quiet; I always speak quietly. Yet Mr. Crimsworth's blue eye became incensed. He took his revenge rather oddly. Turning to me, he said bluntly,

" You are poor enough, I suppose; how do you expect to live till your quarter's salary becomes due?"

" I shall get on," said I.

" How do you expect to live?" he repeated, in a louder voice.

" As I can, Mr. Crimsworth."

" Get into debt at your peril, that's all," he answered. " For aught I know, you may have extravagant aristocratic habits; if you have, drop them; I tolerate nothing of the sort here, and I will never give you a shilling extra, whatever liabilities you may incur—mind that."

" Yes, Mr. Crimsworth, you will find I have a good memory."

I said no more. I did not think the time was come for such parley. I had an instinctive feeling that it would be folly to let one's temper effervesce often with such a man as Edward. I said to myself, " I will place my cup under this continual dropping; it shall stand there still and steady; when full, it will run over of itself—meantime patience. Two things are certain: I am capable of performing the work Mr. Crimsworth has set me; I can earn my wages conscientiously, and those wages are sufficient to enable me to live. As to the fact of my brother assuming toward me the bearing of a proud, harsh master, the fault is his, not mine; and shall his injustice, his bad feeling, turn me at once aside from the path I have chosen? No; at least, ere I deviate, I will advance far enough to see whither my career tends. As yet I am only pressing in at the entrance—a strait gate enough; it ought to have a good terminus." While I thus reasoned, Mr. Crimsworth rang a bell; his first clerk, the individual dismissed previously to our conference, re-entered.

" Mr. Steighton," said he, " show Mr. William the letters from Voss, Brothers, and give him English copies of the answers : he will translate them."

Mr. Steighton, a man of about thirty-five, with a face at once sly and heavy, hastened to execute this order. He laid the letters on the desk, and I was soon seated at it, and engaged in rendering the English answers into German. A sentiment of keen pleasure accompanied this first effort to earn my own living—a

sentiment neither poisoned nor weakened by the pre
ence of the taskmaster, who stood and watched me f(
some time as I wrote.   I thought he was trying
read my character, but I felt as secure against h
scrutiny as if I had had on a casque with the vis(
down—or. rather I showed him my countenance wil
the confidence that one would show an unlearned m(
a letter written in Greek.   He might see lines ar
trace characters, but he could make nothing of then
my nature was not his nature, and its signs were
him like the words of an unknown tongue.   Ere loı
he .turned away abruptly, as if baffled, and 'left tl
counting-house.   He returned to it but twice in tl
course of that day; each time he mixed and swallow(
a glass. of brandy and water, the materials for makiı
which he extracted from a cupboard on one side (
the fire-place.   Having glanced at my translations-
he could read both French and German—he went oı
again in silence.

CHAPTER III.

I SERVED Edward as his second clerk faithfull
punctually, diligently.   What was given me to do
had the power and the determination to do well.   M
Crimsworth watched sharply for defects, but fouı
none; he set Timothy Steighton, his favorite aı
head man, to watch also.   Tim was baffled; I was
exact as himself, and quicker.   Mr. Crimsworth ma(
inquiries as to how I lived—whether I got into det

No, my accounts with my landlady were always straight. I had hired small lodgings, which I contrived to pay for out of a slender fund, the accumulated savings of my Eton pocket-money; for, as it had ever been abhorrent to my nature to ask pecuniary assistance, I had early acquired habits of self-denying economy, husbanding my monthly allowance with anxious care, in order to obviate the danger of being forced, in some moment of future exigency, to beg additional aid. I remember many called me miser at the time, and I used to couple the reproach with this consolation—better to be misunderstood now than repulsed hereafter. At this day I had my reward; I had had it before, when, on parting with my irritated uncles, one of them threw down on the table before me a £5 note, which I was able to leave there, saying that my traveling expenses were already provided for. Mr. Crimsworth employed Tim to find out whether my landlady had any complaint to make on the score of my morals. She answered that she believed I was a very religious man, and asked Tim, in her turn, if he thought I had any intention of going into the Church some day; for, she said, she had had young curates to lodge in her house who were nothing equal to me for steadiness and quietness. Tim was "a religious man" himself; indeed, he was "a joined Methodist," which did not (be it understood) prevent him from being at the same time an ingrained rascal, and he came away much posed at hearing this account of my piety. Having imparted it to Mr. Crimsworth, that gentleman, who himself frequented no place of worship, and owned no God but Mammon, turned the information

into a weapon of attack against the equability of r
temper.   He commenced a series of covert sneers,
which I did not at first perceive the drift, till my lar
lady happened to relate the conversation she had h
with Mr. Steighton ; this enlightened me ; afterwar
came to the counting-house prepared, and managed
receive the mill-owner's blasphemous sarcasms, wb
next leveled at me, on a buckler of impenetrable inc
ference.   Ere long he tired of wasting his ammuniti
on a statue, but he did not throw away the shafts
he only kept them quiet in his quiver.

Once during my clerkship I had an invitation
Crimsworth Hall : it was on the occasion of a la:
party given in honor of the master's birthday. :
had always been accustomed to invite his clerks
similar anniversaries, and could not well pass me ov
I was, however, kept in the background.   Mrs. Crir
worth, elegantly dressed in satin and lace, bloom
in youth and health, vouchsafed me no more not
than was expressed by a distant move.   Crimswor
of course, never spoke to me.   I was introduced
none of the band of young ladies, who, enveloped
silvery clouds of white gauze and muslin, sat in ar
against me on the opposite of a long and large roo
in fact, I was fairly isolated, and could but conte
plate the shining ones from afar, and, when weary
such a dazzling scene, turn for a change to the cons
eration of the carpet pattern.   Mr. Crimsworth, sta
ing on the rug, his elbow supported by the mar
mantel-piece, and about him a group of very pre
girls, with whom he conversed gayly—Mr. Crimswoi
thus placed, glanced at me.   I looked weary, solita

kept down like some desolate tutor or governess. He
was satisfied.

Dancing began. I should have liked well enough
to be introduced to some pleasing and intelligent girl,
and to have freedom and opportunity to show that I
could both feel and communicate the pleasure of social
intercourse—that I was not, in short, a block, or a
piece of furniture, but an acting, thinking, sentient
man. Many smiling faces and graceful figures glided
past me, but the smiles were lavished on other eyes,
the figures sustained by other hands than mine. I
turned away tantalized, left the dancers, and wandered
into the oak-paneled dining-room. No fibre of sympathy united me to any living thing in this house. I
looked for and found my mother's picture. I took a
wax taper from a stand, and held it up. I gazed long,
earnestly; my heart grew to the image. My mother,
I perceived, had bequeathed to me much of her features and countenance—her forehead, her eyes, her
complexion. No regular beauty pleases egotistical
human beings so much as a softened and refined like-
ness of themselves; for this reason, fathers regard
with complacency the lineaments of their daughters'
faces, where frequently their own similitude is found
flatteringly associated with softness of hue and delicacy of outline. I was just wondering how that picture, to me so interesting, would strike an impartial
spectator, when a voice close behind me pronounced
the words,

"Humph! there's some sense in that face."

I turned. At my elbow stood a tall man, young,
though probably five or six years older than I—in

other respects of an appearance the opposite to com
monplace; though just now, as I am not disposed t
paint his portrait in detail, the reader must be conter
with the silhouette I have just thrown off; it was a
I myself saw of him for the moment: I did not in
vestigate the color of his eyebrows, nor of his eye
either; I saw his stature, and the outline of his shape
I saw, too, his fastidious *retroussé* nose: these obse:
vations, few in number and general in character (th
last excepted), sufficed, for they enabled me to recog
nize him.

"Good-evening, Mr. Hunsden," muttered I, with
bow, and then, like a shy noodle as I was, I bega
moving away—and why? Simply because Mr. Hun
den was a manufacturer and a mill-owner, and I wa
only a clerk, and my instinct propelled me from m
superior. I had frequently seen Hunsden in Bigbe
Close, where he came almost weekly to transact bus
ness with Mr. Crimsworth, but I had never spoken 1
him, nor he to me, and I owed him a sort of involun
tary grudge, because he had more than once been th
tacit witness of insults offered by Edward to me.
had the conviction that he could only regard me as
poor-spirited slave, wherefore I now went about 1
shun his presence and eschew his conversation.

"Where are you going?" asked he, as I edged o:
sideways. I had already noticed that Mr. Hunsde
indulged in abrupt forms of speech, and I perversel
said to myself,

"He thinks he may speak as he likes to a poo
clerk; but my mood is not perhaps so supple as I
deems it, and his rough freedom pleases me not at all.

I made some slight reply, rather indifferent than
courteous, and continued to move away. He coolly
planted himself in my path.

"Stay here a while," said he: "it is so hot in the
dancing-room; besides, you don't dance; you have
not had a partner to-night."

He was right; and as he spoke, neither his look,
tone, nor manner displeased me; my *amour-propre*
was propitiated; he had not addressed me out of con-
descension, but because, having repaired to the cool
dining-room for refreshment, he now wanted some one
to talk to by way of temporary amusement. I hate
to be condescended to, but I like well enough to oblige:
I staid.

"That is a good picture," he continued, recurring
to the portrait.

"Do you consider the face pretty?" I asked.

"Pretty! no: how can it be pretty with sunk eyes
and hollow cheeks? But it is peculiar; it seems to
think. You could have a talk with that woman, if
she were alive, on other subjects than dress, visiting,
and compliments."

I agreed with him, but did not say so. He went on:—

"Not that I admire a head of that sort; it wants
character and force; there's too much of the sen-si-tive
(so he articulated it, curling his lip at the same time)
in that mouth; besides, there is Aristocrat written on
the brow and defined in the figure; I hate your aris-
tocrats."

"You think, then, Mr. Hunsden, that patrician descent may be read in a distinctive cast of form and
features?"

B 2

"Patrician descent be hanged! Who doubts tl
your lordlings may have their 'distinctive cast of fo
and features' as much as we ——shire tradesmen ha
ours? But which is the best? Not theirs, assured
As to their women, it is a little different: they cul
vate beauty from childhood upward, and may by c;
and training attain to a certain degree of excellence
that point, just like the Oriental odalisques. Yet ev
this superiority is doubtful. ˌCompare the figure
that frame with Mrs. Edward Crimsworth—which
the finer animal?"

I replied quietly, "Compare yourself and Mr. I
ward Crimsworth, Mr. Hunsden."

"Oh, Crimsworth is better filled up than I am
know; besides, he has a straight nose, arched e·
brows, and all that; but these advantages—if they ;
advantages—he did not inherit from his mother, 1
patrician, but from his father, old Crimsworth, wl
my father says, was as veritable a ——shire blue-d˙
as ever put indigo into a vat, yet, withal, the hai
somest man in the three Ridings. · It is you, Willia
who are the aristocrat of your family, and you are 1
as fine a fellow as your plebeian brother by a lc
chalk."

There was something in Mr. Hunsden's point-bla
mode of speech which rather pleased me than oth
wise, because it set me at my ease. I continued 1
conversation with a degree of interest.

"How do you happen to know that I am Mr. Crin
worth's brother? I thought you and every body e
looked upon me only in the light of a poor clerk."

"Well, and so we do; and what are you but a pc

clerk ? You do Crimsworth's work, and he gives you wages—shabby wages they are, too."

I was silent. Hunsden's language now bordered on the impertinent; still, his manner did not offend me in the least—it only piqued my curiosity. I wanted him to go on, which he did in a little while.

" This world is an absurd one," said he.

" Why so, Mr. Hunsden ?"

" I wonder you should ask: you are yourself a strong proof of the absurdity I allude to."

I was determined he should explain himself of his own accord, without my pressing him so to do, so I resumed my silence.

" Is it your intention to become a tradesman ?" he inquired, presently.

" It was my serious intention three months ago."

" Humph! the more fool you—you look like a trades-man ! What a practical business-like face you have !"

" My face is as the Lord made it, Mr. Hunsden."

" The Lord never made either your face or head for X——. What good can your bumps of ideality, com-parison, self-esteem, conscientiousness, do you here ? But if you like Bigben Close, stay there ; it's your own affair, not mine."

" Perhaps I have no choice."

" Well, I care naught about it; it will make little difference to me what you do or where you go; but I'm cool now: I want to dance again ; and I see such a fine girl sitting in the corner of the sofa there by her mamma—see if I don't get her for a partner in a jiffy ! There's Waddy—Sam Waddy making up to her ; won't I cut him out ?"

And Mr. Hunsden strode away. I watched h
through the open folding-doors. He outstripped W:
dy, applied for the hand of the fine girl, and led]
off triumphant. She was a tall, well-made, full-for
ed, dashingly-dressed young woman, much in the st:
of Mrs. E. Crimsworth. Hunsden whirled her throu
the waltz with spirit. He kept at her side during 1
remainder of the evening, and I read in her animat
and gratified countenance that he succeeded in maki
himself perfectly agreeable. The mamma too (a st(
person in a turban—Mrs. Lupton by name) looked w
pleased; prophetic visions probably flattered her
ward eye. The Hunsdens were of an old stem; a
scornful as Yorke (such was my late interlocutc
name) professed to be of the advantages of birth, in :
secret heart he well knew and fully appreciated 1
distinction his ancient, if not high lineage conferred
him in a mushroom place like X——, concerning wh(
inhabitants it was proverbially said that not one ir
thousand knew his own grandfather. Moreover, 1
Hunsdens, once rich, were still independent; and
port affirmed that Yorke bade fair, by his success
business, to restore to pristine prosperity the partia
decayed fortunes of his house. These circumstan(
considered, Mrs. Lupton's broad face might well w(
a smile of complacency as she contemplated the h
of Hunsden Wood occupied in paying assiduous co1
to her darling Sarah Martha. I, however, whose (
servations, being less anxious, were likely to be m(
accurate, soon saw that the grounds for maternal s€
congratulation were slight indeed; the gentleman ɛ
peared to me much more desirous of making than si

ceptible of receiving an impression. I know not what it was in Mr. Hunsden that, as I watched him (I had nothing better to do), suggested to me, every now and then, the idea of a foreigner. In form and features he might be pronounced English, though even there one caught a dash of something Gallic; but he had no English shyness. He had learned somewhere, somehow, the art of setting himself quite at his ease, and of allowing no insular timidity to intervene as a barrier between him and his convenience or pleasure. Refinement he did not affect, yet vulgar he could not be called; he was not odd—no quiz; yet he resembled no one else I had ever seen before. His general bearing intimated complete, sovereign satisfaction with himself; yet, at times, an indescribable shade passed like an eclipse over his countenance, and seemed to me like the sign of a sudden and strong inward doubt of himself, his words and actions—an energetic discontent at his life or his social position, his future prospects or his mental attainments, I know not which; perhaps, after all, it might only be a bilious caprice.

CHAPTER IV.

No man likes to acknowledge that he has made a mistake in the choice of his profession, and every man worthy of the name will row long against wind and tide before he allows himself to cry out "I am baffled," and submits to be floated passively back to land. From the first week of my residence in X—— I felt

my occupation irksome.   The thing itself—the work
of copying and translating business letters—was a dry
and tedious task enough, but had that been all, I should
long have borne with the nuisance.   I am not of an
impatient nature, and influenced by the double desire
of getting my living and justifying to myself and others the resolution I had taken to become a tradesman,
I should have endured in silence the rust and cramp
of my best faculties ; I should not have whispered,
even inwardly, that I longed for liberty ; I should have
pent in every sigh by which my heart might have ventured to intimate its distress under the closeness, smoke,
monotony, and joyless tumult of Bigben Close, and its
panting desire for freer and fresher scenes; I should
have set up the image of Duty, the fetish of Pererver-
ance, in my small bed-room at Mrs. King's lodgings,
and they two should have been my household gods,
from which my darling, my cherished-in-secret, Imagination, the tender and the mighty, should never,
either by softness or strength, have severed me.   But
this was not all ; the antipathy which had sprung up
between myself and my employer striking deeper root
and spreading denser shade daily, excluded me from
every glimpse of the sunshine of life, and I began to
feel like a plant growing in humid darkness out of the
slimy walls of a well.

Antipathy is the only word which can express the
feeling Edward Crimsworth had for me—a feeling in
a great measure involuntary, and which was liable to
be excited by every, the most trifling movement, look,
or word of mine.   My Southern accent annoyed him ;
the degree of education evinced in my language irri-

tated him; my punctuality, industry, and accuracy
fixed his dislike, and gave it the high flavor and poignant relish 'of envy; he feared that I too should one
day make a successful tradesman. Had I been in any
thing inferior to him, he would not have hated me so
thoroughly; but I knew all that he knew, and, what
was worse, he suspected that I kept the padlock of silence on mental wealth in which he was no sharer. If
he could have once placed me in a ridiculous or morti-
fying position, he would have forgiven me much, but I
was guarded by three faculties—Caution, Tact, Observation; and prowling and prying as was Edward's
malignity, it could never baffle the lynx-eyes of these,
my natural sentinels. Day by day did his malice
watch my tact, hoping it would sleep, and prepared to
steal snake-like on its slumber; but tact, if it be genuine, never sleeps.

I had received my first quarter's wages and was returning to my lodgings, possessed heart and soul with
the pleasant feeling that the master who had paid me
grudged every penny of that hard-earned pittance—(I
had long ceased to regard Mr. Crimsworth as my brother: he was a hard, grinding master; he wished to be
an inexorable tyrant—that was all). Thoughts, not
varied but strong, occupied my mind; two voices spoke
within me; again and again they uttered the same
monotonous phrases. One said, "William, your life
is intolerable." The other, "What can you do to al-
ter it?" I walked fast, for it was a cold, frosty night
in January. As I approached my lodgings, I turned
from a general view of my affairs to the particular speculation as to whether my fire would be out. Look-

ing toward the window of my sitting-room, I saw no cheering red gleam.

"That slut of a servant has neglected it as usual," said I. "I shall see nothing but pale ashes if I go in. It is a fine starlight night—I will walk a little farther."

It *was* a fine night, and the streets were dry and even clean for X——; there was a crescent curve of moonlight to be seen by the parish church tower, and hundreds of stars.shone keenly bright in all quarters of the sky.

Unconsciously I steered my course toward the country. I had got into Grove Street, and began to feel the pleasure of seeing dim trees at the extremity, round a suburban house, when a person leaning over the iron gate of one of the small gardens which front the neat dwelling-houses in this street addressed me as I was hurrying with quick stride past.

"What the deuce is the hurry? Just so must Lot have left Sodom when he expected fire to pour down upon it out of burning brass clouds."

I stopped short and looked toward the speaker. · I smelt the fragrance, and saw the red spark of a cigar; the dusk outline of a man, too, bent toward me over the wicket.

"You see I am meditating in the field at eventide," continued this shade. "God knows it's cool work, especially as, instead of Rebecca on a camel's hump, with bracelets on her arms and a ring in her nose, Fate sends me only a counting-house clerk in a gray tweed wrapper."

The voice was familiar to me; its second utterance enabled me to seize the speaker's identity.

" Mr. Hunsden—good-evening."

" Good-evening, indeed! Yes, but you would have passed me without recognition if I had not been so civil as to speak first."

" I did not know you."

" A famous excuse! You ought to have known me; I knew you, though you were going ahead like a steam-engine. Are the police after you?"

" It wouldn't be worth their while; I'm not of consequence enough to attract them."

" Alas! poor shepherd. Alack and well-a-day! What a theme for regret, and how down in the mouth you must be, judging from the sound of your voice! But, since you're not running from the police, from whom are you running—the devil?"

" On the contrary, I am going post to him."

" That is well; you're just in luck. This is Tuesday evening; there are scores of market gigs and carts returning to Dinneford to-night, and he, or some of his, have a seat in all regularly; so, if you'll step in and sit half an hour in my bachelor's parlor, you will catch him as he passes without much trouble. I think, though, you'd better let him alone to-night, he'll have so many customers to serve; Tuesday is his busy day in X—— and Dinneford. Come in, at all events."

He swung the wicket open as he spoke.

" Do you really wish me to go in?" I asked.

" As you please—I'm alone; your company for an hour or two would be agreeable to me; but, if you don't choose to favor me so far, I'll not press the point. I hate to bore any one."

It suited me to accept the invitation as it suited

Hunsden to give it. I passed through the gate, and followed him to the front door, which he opened; thence we traversed a passage and entered his parlor; the door being shut, he pointed me to an arm-chair by the hearth. I sat down, and glanced round me.

It was a comfortable room, at once snug and handsome; the bright grate was filled with a genuine ——shire fire, red, clear, and generous—no penurious south of England embers happed in the corner of a grate. On the table a shaded lamp diffused around a soft, pleasant, and equal light; the furniture was almost luxurious for a young bachelor, comprising a couch and two very easy chairs; book-shelves filled the recesses on each side of the mantel-piece: they were well-furnished, and arranged with perfect order. The neatness of the room suited my taste; I hate irregular and slovenly habits. From what I saw, I concluded that Hunsden's ideas on that point corresponded with my own. While he removed from the centre-table to the sideboard a few pamphlets and periodicals, I ran my eye along the shelves of the book-case nearest me. French and German works predominated, the old French dramatists, sundry modern authors, Thiers, Villemain, Paul de Kock, George Sand, Eugene Sue; in German, Goëthe, Schiller, Zschokke, Jean Paul Richter; in English there were works on Political Economy. I examined no further, for Mr. Hunsden himself recalled my attention.

"You shall have something," said he, "for you ought to feel disposed for refreshment after walking nobody knows how far on such a Canadian night as this; but it shall not be brandy and water, and it shall not be a bottle of port, nor ditto of sherry. I keep no such poison. I have Rhein wein for my own drinking, and you may choose between that and coffee."

Here again Hunsden suited me. If there was one generally received practice I abhorred more than another, it was the habitual imbibing of spirits and strong wines. I had, however, no fancy for his acid German nectar, but I liked coffee, so I responded,

" Give me some coffee, Mr. Hunsden."

I perceived my answer pleased him. He had doubtless expected to see a chilling effect produced by his steady announcement that he would give me neither wine nor spirits. He just shot one searching glance at my face to ascertain whether my cordiality was genuine or a mere feint of politeness. I smiled, because I quite understood him ; and, while I honored his conscientious firmness, I was amused at his mistrust. He seemed satisfied, rang the bell, and ordered coffee, which was presently brought ; for himself, a bunch of grapes and half a pint of something sour sufficed. My coffee was excellent. I told him so, and expressed the shuddering pity with which his anchorite fare inspired me. He did not answer, and I scarcely think heard my remark. At that moment one of those momentary eclipses I before alluded to had come over his face, extinguishing his smile, and replacing, by an abstracted and alienated look, the customarily shrewd, bantering glance of his eye. I employed the interval of silence in a rapid scrutiny of his physiognomy. I had never observed him closely before, and, as my sight is very short, I had gathered only a vague, general idea of his appearance. I was surprised now, on

examination, to perceive how small and even feminine were his lineaments.   His tall figure, long and
dark locks, his voice and general bearing, had impressed me with the notion of something powerful and massive.   Not at all; my own features were cast in a
harsher and squarer mould than his.   I discerned that
there would be contrasts between his inward and outward man; contentions too; for I suspected his soul
had more of will and ambition than his body had of
fibre and muscle.   Perhaps in these incompatibilities
of the "physique" with the "morale" lay the secret
of that fitful gloom; he *would* but *could* not, and the
athletic mind scowled scorn on its more fragile companion.   As to his good looks, I should have liked to
have a woman's opinion on that subject : it seemed to
me that his face might produce the same effect on a
lady that a very piquant and interesting, though
scarcely pretty female face would on a man.   I have
mentioned his dark locks: they were brushed sideways above a white and sufficiently expansive forehead; his cheek had a rather hectic freshness; his
features might have done well on canvas, but indiffer-
ently in marble : they were plastic; character had set
a stamp upon each; expression recast them at her
pleasure, and strange metamorphoses she wrought,
giving him now the mien of a morose bull, and anon
that of an arch and mischievous girl; more frequently
the two semblances were blent, and a queer, composite
countenance they made.

Starting from his silent fit, he began :

"William, what a fool you are to live in those dismal lodgings of Mrs. King's, when you might take

ooms here in Grove Street, and have a garden like
ne." ·

" I should be too far from the mill."

" What of that ? It would do you good to walk
here and back two or three times a day; besides, are
rou such a fossil that you never wish to see a flower
ir a green leaf ?"

" I am no fossil."

" What are you, then ? You sit at that desk in
Jrimsworth's counting-house day by day and week by
veek, scraping with a pen on paper just like an au-
omaton; you never get up; you never say you are
ired; you never ask for a holiday; you never take
hange or relaxation; you give way to no excess of
n evening; you neither keep wild company, nor in-
lulge in strong drink."

" Do you, Mr. Hunsden ?"

" Don't think to pose me with short questions.
Tour case and mine are diametrically different, and it
s nonsense to draw a parallel. I say that when a
nan endures patiently what ought to be unendurable,
le is a fossil."

" Whence do you acquire the knowledge of my pa-
ience ?"

" Why, man, do you suppose you are a mystery ?
The other night you seemed surprised at my knowing
o what family you belonged; now you find subject
or wonderment in my calling you patient. What do
you think I do with my eyes and ears ? I've been in
your counting-house more than once when Crimsworth
las treated you like a dog; called for a book, for instance, and when you gave him the wrong one, or what

he chose to consider the wrong one, flung it back almost in your face; desired you to shut or open the
door as if you had been his flunkey; to say nothing
of your position at the party about a month ago, where
you had neither place nor partner, but hovered about
like a poor, shabby hanger-on; and how patient you
were under each and all of these circumstances!"

"Well, Mr. Hunsden, what then?"

"I can hardly tell you what then. The conclusion
to be drawn as to your character depends upon the
nature of the motives which guide your conduct. If
you are patient because you expect to make something
eventually out of Crimsworth, notwithstanding his tyranny, or perhaps by means of it, you are what the
world calls an interested and mercenary, but may be a
very wise fellow; if you are patient because you think
it a duty to meet insult with submission, you are an
essential sap, and in no shape the man for my money;
if you are patient because your nature is phlegmatic,
flat, inexcitable, and that you can not get up to the
pitch of resistance, why, God made you to be crushed; and lie down, by all means, and lie flat, and let
Juggernaut ride well over you."

Mr. Hunsden's eloquence was not, it will be perceived, of the smooth and oily order. As he spoke, he
pleased me ill. I seemed to recognize in him one of
those characters who, sensitive enough themselves, are
selfishly relentless toward the sensitiveness of others.
Moreover, though he was neither like Crimsworth nor
Lord Tynedale, yet he was acrid, and, I suspected,
overbearing in his way: there was a tone of despotism in the urgency of the very reproaches by which he

imed at goading the oppressed into rebellion against
he oppressor. Looking at him still more fixedly than
I had yet done, I saw written in his eye and mien a
esolution to arrogate to himself a freedom so unlimit-
d that it might often trench on the just liberty of his
neighbors. I rapidly ran over these thoughts, and
hen I laughed a low and involuntary laugh, moved
hereto by a slight inward revelation of the inconsist-
ncy of man. It was as I thought. Hunsden had
xpected me to take with calm his incorrect and of-
ensive surmises, his bitter and haughty taunts, and
himself was chafed by a laugh scarce louder than a
whisper.

His brow darkened, his thin nostril dilated a little.

"Yes," he began, "I told you that you were an
aristocrat, and who but an aristocrat would laugh such
a laugh as that, and look such a look? A laugh frigid-
y jeering; a look lazily mutinous; gentlemanlike
irony, patrician resentment. What a nobleman you
would have made, William Crimsworth! You are cut
out for one; pity Fortune has balked Nature! Look at
the features, figure, even to the hands—distinction all
over—ugly distinction! Now, if you'd only an estate,
and a mansion, and a park, and a title, how you could
play the exclusive, maintain the rights of your class,
train your tenantry in habits of respect to the peerage,
oppose at every step the advancing power of the people, support your rotten order, and be ready, for its
sake, to wade knee-deep in churls' blood! As it is,
you've no power; you can do nothing; you're wreck-
ed and stranded on the shores of commerce; forced
into collision with practical men, with whom you can
not cope, for *you'll never be a trademsan*."

The first part of Hunsden's speech moved me not
at all, or, if it did, it was only to wonder at the per-
version into which prejudice had twisted his judgment
of my character; the concluding sentence, however,
not only moved, but shook me; the blow it gave was
a severe one, because Truth wielded the weapon. If I
smiled now, it was only in disdain of myself.

Hunsden saw his advantage; he followed it up.

"You'll make nothing by trade," continued he;
"nothing more than the crust of dry bread and the
draught of fair water on which you now live. Your
only chance of getting a competency lies in marrying
a rich widow, or running away with an heiress."

"I leave such shifts to be put in practice by those
who devise them," said I, rising.

"And even that is hopeless," he went on, coolly.
"What widow would have you? much less, what heiress? You're not bold and venturesome enough for
the one, nor handsome and fascinating enough for the
other. You think, perhaps, you look intelligent and
polished. Carry your intellect and refinement to market, and tell me in a private note what price is bid for
them."

Mr. Hunsden had taken his tone for the night; the
string he struck was out of tune; he would finger no
other. Averse to discord, of which I had enough every day and all day long, I concluded, at last, that silence and solitude were preferable to jarring converse.
I bade him good-night.

"What! are you going, lad? Well, good-night;
you'll find the door." And he sat still in front of the
fire, while I left the room and the house. I had got

a good way on my return to my lodgings before I found out that I was walking very fast and breathing very hard, and that my nails were almost stuck into the palms of my clenched hands, and that my teeth were set fast. On making this discovery, I relaxed both my pace, fists, and jaws, but I could not so soon cause the regrets rushing rapidly through my mind to slacken their tide. Why did I make myself a tradesman? Why did I enter Hunsden's house this evening? Why, at dawn to-morrow, must I repair to Crimsworth's mill? All that night did I ask myself these questions, and all that night fiercely demanded of my soul an answer. I got no sleep; my head burned, my feet froze; at last the factory bells rang, and I sprang from my bed with other slaves.

CHAPTER V.

THERE is a climax to every thing—to every state of feeling as well as to every position in life. I turned this truism over in my mind as, in the frosty dawn of a January morning, I hurried down the steep and now icy street which descended from Mrs. King's to the Close. The factory work-people had preceded me by nearly an hour, and the mill was all lighted up and in full operation when I reached it. I repaired to my post in the counting-house as usual; the fire there, but just lit, as yet only smoked; Steighton was not yet arrived. I shut the door and sat down at the desk; my hands, recently washed in half-frozen water, were

C

still numb; I could not write till they had regained vitality, so I went on thinking, and still the theme of my thoughts was "the climax." Self-dissatisfaction troubled exceedingly the current of my meditations.

"Come, William Crimsworth," said my conscience, or whatever it is that within ourselves takes ourselves to task, "come, get a clear notion of what you would have or what you would not have. You talk of a climax; pray has your endurance reached its climax? It is not four months old. What a fine, resolute fellow you imagined yourself to be when you told Tynedale you would tread in your father's steps, and a pretty treading you are likely to make of it! How well you like X——! Just at this moment, how redolent of pleasant associations are its streets, its shops, its warehouses, its factories! How the prospect of this day cheers you! Letter-copying till noon, solitary dinner at your lodgings, letter-copying till evening, solitude; for you neither find pleasure in Brown's, nor Smith's, nor Nicholls's, nor Eccle's company; and as to Hunsden, you fancied there was pleasure to be derived from his society—he! he! how did you like the taste of him you had last night? was it sweet? Yet he is a talented, an original-minded man, and even he does not like you; your self-respect defies you to like him; he has always seen you to disadvantage; he always will see you to disadvantage; your positions are unequal, and, were they on the same level, your minds could not assimilate; never hope, then, to gather the honey of friendship out of that thorn-guarded plant. Hollo, Crimsworth! where are your thoughts tending? You leave the recollection of Hunsden as a

ee would a rock, as a bird a desert; and your aspira-
ons spread eager wings toward a land of visions
where, now in advancing daylight—in X—— daylight
—you dare to dream of congeniality, repose, union.
Those three you will never meet in this world; they
re angels. The souls of just men made perfect may
ncounter them in heaven, but your soul will never be
1ade perfect. Eight o'clock strikes! your hands are
hawed; get to work."

"Work? why should I work?" said I, sullenly: "I
an not please though I toil like a slave." "Work,
rork!" reiterated the inward voice. "I may work, it
rill do no good," I growled; but, nevertheless, I drew
ut a packet of letters and commenced my task—task
hankless and bitter as that of the Israelite crawling
ver the sun-baked fields of Egypt in search of straw
nd stubble wherewith to accomplish his tale of
ricks.

About ten o'clock I heard Mr. Crimsworth's gig
urn into the yard, and in a minute or two he entered
he counting-house. It was his custom to glance his
ye at Steighton and myself, to hang up his Mackin-
osh, stand a minute with his back to the fire, and then
ralk out. To-day he did not deviate from his usual
1abits; the only difference was that when he looked
t me, his brow, instead of being merely hard, was
urly; his eye, instead of being cold, was fierce. He
tudied me a minute or two longer than usual, but
rent out in silence.

Twelve o'clock arrived; the bell rang for a suspen-
ion of labor; the work-people went off to their din-
1ers; Steighton, too, departed, desiring me to lock the

counting-house door, and take the key with me. I
was tying up a bundle of papers, and putting them in
their place, preparatory to closing my desk, when
Crimsworth reappeared at the door, and, entering,
closed it behind him.

"You'll stay here a minute," said he, in a deep
brutal voice, while his nostrils distended and his eye
shot a spark of sinister fire.

Alone with Edward, I remembered our relationship,
and, remembering that, forgot the difference of position. I put away deference and careful forms of speech;
I answered with simple brevity.

"It is time to go home," I said, turning the key in
my desk.

"You'll stay here," he reiterated. "And take your
hand off that key. Leave it in the lock."

"Why?" asked I. "What cause is there for
changing my usual plans?"

"Do as I order," was the answer, "and no questions. You are my servant; obey me. What have
you been about?" He was going on in the same
breath, when an abrupt pause announced that rage
had for the moment got the better of articulation.

"You may look, if you wish to know," I replied.
"There is the open desk; there are the papers."

"Confound your insolence. What have you been
about?"

"Your work, and have done it well."

"Hypocrite and twaddler! smooth-faced, sniveling
greasehorn!" (this last term is, I believe, purely
——shire, and alludes to the horn of black, rancid
whale-oil usually to be seen suspended to cart-wheels

" Come, Edward Crimsworth, enough of this. It is
time you and I wound up accounts. I have now
given your service three months' trial, and I find it
the most nauseous slavery under the sun. Seek another clerk. I stay no longer."

" What! do you dare to give me notice? Stop at
least for your wages." He took down the heavy gig
whip hanging beside his Mackintosh.

I permitted myself to laugh with a degree of scorn
I took no pains to temper or hide. His fury boiled
up, and when he had sworn half a dozen vulgar, im-
pious oaths, without, however, venturing to lift the
whip, he continued:

" I've found you out and know you thoroughly, you
mean, whining lickspittle. What have you been saying all over X—— about me? Answer me that."

" You? I have neither inclination nor temptation
to talk about you."

" You lie. It is your practice to talk about me;
it is your constant habit to make public complaint of
the treatment you receive at my hands. You have
gone and told it far and near that I give you low
wages and knock you about like a dog. I wish you
were a dog; I'd set to this minute, and never stir from
the spot till I'd cut every strip of flesh from your
bones with this whip."

He flourished his tool. The end of the lash just
touched my forehead. A warm, excited thrill ran
through my veins, my blood seemed to give a bound,
and then raced fast and hot along its channels. I
got up nimbly, came round to where he stood, and
faced him.

" Down with your whip," said I, "and explain this instant what you mean."

" Sirrah, to whom are you speaking ?"

" To you. There is no one else present, I think. You say I have been calumniating you—complaining of your low wages and bad treatment. Give your grounds for these assertions."

Crimsworth had no dignity, and when I sternly demanded an explanation, he gave one in a loud, scolding voice.

"Grounds! you shall have them; and turn to the light, that I may see your brazen face blush black when you hear yourself proved to be a liar and a hypocrite. At a public meeting in the Town-hall yesterday I had the pleasure of hearing myself insulted by the speaker opposed to me in the question under discussion by allusions to my private affairs; by cant about monsters without natural affection, family despots, and such trash; and when I rose to answer, I was met by a shout from the filthy mob, where the mention of your name enabled me at once to detect the quarter in which this base attack had originated. When I looked round, I saw that treacherous villain, Hunsden, acting as fugleman. I detected you in close conversation with Hunsden at my house a month ago, and I know you were at Hunsden's rooms last night. Deny it if you dare."

" Oh, I shall not deny it. And if Hunsden hounded on the people to hiss you, he did quite right. You deserve popular execration; for a worse man, a harder master, a more brutal brother than you are has seldom existed."

"Sirrah! sirrah!" reiterated Crimsworth; and, to complete his apostrophe, he cracked the whip straight over my head.

A minute sufficed to wrest it from him, break it in two pieces, and throw it under the grate. He made a headlong rush at me, which I evaded, and said,

"Touch me, and I'll have you up before the nearest magistrate."

Men like Crimsworth, if firmly and calmly resisted, always abate something of their exorbitant insolence. He had no mind to be brought before a magistrate, and I suppose he saw I meant what I said. After an odd and long stare at me, at once bull-like and amazed, he seemed to bethink himself that, after all, his money gave him sufficient authority over a beggar like me, and that he had in his hands a surer and more dignified mode of revenge than the somewhat hazardous one of personal chastisement.

"Take your hat," said he—"take what belongs to you, and go out at that door. Get away to your parish, you pauper; beg, steal, starve, get transported, do what you like; but, at your peril, venture again into my sight. If ever I hear of your setting foot on an inch of ground belonging to me, I'll hire a man to cane you."

"It is not likely you'll have the chance. Once off your premises, what temptation can I have to return to them? I leave a prison, I leave a tyrant; I leave what is worse than the worst that can lie before me, so no fear of my coming back."

"Go, or I'll make you," exclaimed Crimsworth.

I walked deliberately to my desk, took out such of its contents as were my own property, put them in my pocket, locked the desk, and placed the key on the top.

"What are you abstracting from that desk?" demanded the mill-owner. "Leave all behind in its place, or I'll send for a policeman to search you."

"Look sharp about it, then," said I, and I took down my hat, drew on my gloves, and walked leisurely out of the counting-house—walked out of it to enter it no more.

I recollect that when the mill-bell rang the dinner-hour, before Mr. Crimsworth entered, and the scene above related took place, I had had rather a sharp appetite, and had been waiting somewhat impatiently to hear the signal of feeding-time. I forgot it now, however; the images of potatoes and roast mutton were effaced from my mind by the stir and tumult which the transaction of the last half hour had there excited. I only thought of walking, that the action of my muscles might harmonize with the action of my nerves; and walk I did, fast and far. How could I do otherwise? A load was lifted off my heart; I felt light and liberated. I had got away from Bigben Close without a breach of resolution—without injury to my self-respect. I had not forced circumstances—circumstances had freed me. Life was again open to me; no longer was its horizon limited by the high black wall surrounding Crimsworth's mill. Two hours elapsed before my sensations had so far subsided as to leave me calm enough to remark for what wider and clearer boundaries I had exchanged that sooty girdle. When I did look up, lo! straight before me lay Grovetown, a village of villas about five miles out of

X——. The short winter day, as I perceived from the far-declined sun, was already approaching its close; a chill frost-mist was rising from the river on which X—— stands, and along whose banks the road I had taken lay; it dimmed the earth, but did not obscure the clear, icy blue of the January sky. There was a great stillness near and far; the time of the day favored tranquillity, as the people were all employed within doors, the hour of evening release from the factories not being yet arrived; a sound of full-flowing water alone pervaded the air, for the river was deep and abundant, swelled by the melting of a late snow. I stood a while, leaning over a wall, and, looking down at the current, I watched the rapid rush of its waves. I desired memory to take a clear and permanent impression of the scene, and treasure it for future years. Grovetown church clock struck four. Looking up, I beheld the last of that day's sun glinting red through the leafless boughs of some very old oak trees surrounding the church: its light colored and characterized the picture as I wished. I paused yet a moment till the sweet, slow sound of the bell had quite died out of the air; then, ear, eye, and feeling satisfied, I quitted the wall, and once more turned my face toward X——.

CHAPTER VI.

I RE-ENTERED the town a hungry man; the dinner I had forgotten recurred seductively to my recollection; and it was with a quick step and sharp appetite I as-

C 2

cended the narrow street leading to my lodgings. It
was dark when I opened the front door and walked
into the house. I wondered how my fire would be:
the night was cold, and I shuddered at the prospect of
a grate full of sparkless cinders. To my joyful surprise, I found, on entering my sitting-room, a good fire
and a clean hearth. I had hardly noticed this phe-
nomenon, when I became aware of another subject for
wonderment : the chair I usually occupied near the
hearth was already filled ; a person sat there with his
arms folded on his chest, and his legs stretched out on
the rug. Short-sighted as I am, doubtful as was the
gleam of the firelight, a moment's examination enabled
me to recognize in this person my acquaintance, Mr.
Hunsden. I could not, of course, be much pleased to
see him, considering the manner in which I had parted
from him the night before, and as I walked to the
hearth, stirred the fire, and said coolly, "Good-evening," my demeanor evinced as little cordiality as I
felt; yet I wondered in my own mind what had brought
him there, and I wondered, also, what motives had induced him to interfere so actively between me and Edward. It was to him, it appeared, that I owed my
welcome dismissal; still, I could not bring myself to
ask him questions, to show any eagerness of curiosity ;
if he chose to explain, he might, but the explanation
should be a perfectly voluntary one on his part ; I
thought he was entering upon it.

"You owe me a debt of gratitude," were his first
words.

"Do I?" said I; "I hope it is not a large one, for
I am much too poor to charge myself with heavy liabilities of any kind."

" Then declare yourself bankrupt at once, for this liability is a ton weight at least. When I came in I found your fire out, and I had it lit again, and made that sulky drab of a servant stay and blow at it with the bellows till it had burned up properly; now say ' Thank you.'"

" Not till I have had something to eat; I can thank nobody while I am so famished."

I rang the bell, and ordered tea and some cold meat.

"Cold meat!" exclaimed Hunsden, as the servant closed the door; "what a glutton you are, man! Meat with tea! you'll die of eating too much."

" No, Mr. Hunsden, I shall not." I felt a necessity for contradicting him. I was irritated with hunger, and irritated at seeing him there, and irritated at the continued roughness of his manner.

" It is overeating that makes you so ill tempered," said he.

" How do you know?" I demanded. "It is like you to give a pragmatical opinion without being acquainted with any of the circumstances of the case. I have had no dinner."

What I said was petulant and snappish enough, and Hunsden only replied by looking in my face and laughing.

"Poor thing!" he whined, after a pause. " It has had no dinner, has it? What! I suppose its master would not let it come home. Did Crimsworth order you to fast by way of punishment, William?"

" No, Mr. Hunsden." Fortunately, at this sulky juncture, tea was brought in, and I fell to upon some bread and butter and cold beef directly. Having clear-

ed a plateful, I became so far humanized as to intimate
to Mr. Hunsden "that he need not sit there staring,
but might come to the table and do as I did, if he
liked."

"But I don't like in the least," said he, and there-
with he summoned the servant by a fresh pull of the
bell-rope, and intimated a desire to have a glass of
toast and water.   "And some more coal," he added;
"Mr. Crimsworth shall keep a good fire while I stay."

His orders being executed, he wheeled his chair
round to the table so as to be opposite me.

"Well," he proceeded, "you are out of work, I suppose?"

"Yes," said I; and not disposed to show the satisfaction I felt on this point, I, yielding to the whim of
the moment, took up the subject as though I considered myself aggrieved rather than benefited by what
had been done.   "Yes—thanks to you, I am.   Crimsworth turned me off at a minute's notice, owing to
some interference of yours at a public meeting, I understand."

"Ah!   What! he mentioned that?   He observed
me signaling the lads, did he?   What had he to say
about his friend Hunsden—any thing sweet?"

"He called you a treacherous villain."

"Oh, he hardly knows me yet.   I'm one of those
shy people who don't come out all at once, and he is
only just beginning to make my acquaintance; but
he'll find I've some good qualities — excellent ones.
The Hunsdens were always unrivaled 'at tracking a
rascal; a downright, dishonorable villain is their natural prey; they could not keep off him wherever they

met him. You used the word pragmatical just now: that word is the property of our family; it has been applied to us from generation to generation; we have fine noses for abuses; we scent a scoundrel a mile off; we are reformers born—radical reformers; and it was impossible for me to live in the same town with Crims-worth, to come into weekly contact with him, to wit-ness some of his conduct to you (for whom personally I care nothing; I only consider the brutal injustice with which he violated your natural claim to equality) —I say it was impossible for me to be thus situated, and not feel the angel or the demon of my race at work within me. I followed my instinct, opposed a tyrant, and broke a chain."

. Now this speech interested me much, both because it brought out Hunsden's character, and because it ex-plained his motives; it interested me so much that I forgot to reply to it, and sat silent, pondering over a throng of ideas it had suggested.

"Are you grateful to me?" he asked, presently.

In fact I was grateful, or almost so, and I believe I half liked him at the moment, notwithstanding his proviso that what he had done was not out of regard for me. But human nature is perverse. Impossible to answer his blunt question in the affirmative, so I disclaimed all tendency to gratitude, and advised him, if he expected any reward for his championship, to look for it in a better world, as he was not likely to meet with it here. In reply, he termed me "a dry-hearted aristocratic scamp," whereupon I again charged him with having taken the bread out of my mouth.

"Your bread was dirty, man," cried Hunsden—

"dirty and unwholesome. It came through the hands of a tyrant; for I tell you Crimsworth is a tyrant—a tyrant to his work-people, a tyrant to his clerks, and will some day be a tyrant to his wife."

"Nonsense; bread is bread, and a salary is a salary. I've lost mine, and through your means."

"There's sense in what you say, after all," rejoined Hunsden. "I must say I am rather agreeably surprised to hear you make so practical an observation as that last. I had imagined now, from my previous observation of your character, that the sentimental delight you would have taken in your newly regained liberty would, for a while at least, have effaced all ideas of forethought and prudence. I think better of you for looking steadily to the needful."

"Looking steadily to the needful! How can I do otherwise? . I must live, and to live I must have what you call 'the needful,' which I can only get by working. I repeat it, you have taken my work from me."

"What do you mean to do?" pursued Hunsden, coolly. "You have influential relations; I suppose they'll soon provide you with another place."

"Influential relations? Who? I should like to know their names."

"The Seacombes."

"Stuff! I have cut them."

Hunsden looked at me incredulously.

"I have," said I, "and that definitively."

"You must mean they have cut you, William.

"As you please. They offered me their patronage on condition of my entering the Church; I declined both the terms and the recompense; I withdrew from

my cold uncles, and preferred throwing myself into my
elder brother's arms, from whose affectionate embrace
I am now torn by the cruel intermeddling of a stranger—of yourself, in short."

I could not repress a half smile as I said this; a
similar demi-manifestation of feeling appeared at the
same moment on Hunsden's lips.

"Oh, I see!" said he, looking into my eyes, and it
was evident he *did* see right down into my heart.
Having sat a minute or two with his chin resting on
his hand, diligently occupied in the continued perusal
of my countenance, he went on:

"Seriously, have you then nothing to expect from
the Seacombes?"

"Yes, rejection and repulsion. Why do you ask
me twice? How can hands stained with the ink of a
counting-house, soiled with the grease of a wool-ware-
house, ever again be permitted to come into contact
with aristocratic palms?"

"There would be a difficulty, no doubt; still, you
are such a complete Seacombe in appearance, feature,
language, almost manner, I wonder they should dis-
own you."

"They have disowned me, so talk no more about it."

"Do you regret it, William?"

"No."

"Why not, lad?"

"Because they are not people with whom I could
ever have had any sympathy."

"I say you are one of them."

"That merely proves that you know nothing at all
about it. I am my mother's son, but not my uncle's
nephew."

" Still, one of your uncles is a lord, though rather an obscure and not a very wealthy one, and the other a right honorable: you should consider worldly interest."

" Nonsense, Mr. Hunsden. You know, or may know that, even had I desired to be submissive to my uncles, I could not have stooped with a good enough grace ever to have won their favor. I should have sacrificed my own comfort, and not have gained their patronage in return."

" Very likely; so you calculated your wisest plan was to follow your own devices at once?"

" Exactly. I must follow my own devices—I must till the day of my death, because I can neither comprehend, adopt, nor work out those of other people."

Hunsden yawned. "Well," said he, "in all this I see but one thing clearly—that is, that the whole affair is no business of mine." He stretched himself and again yawned. "I wonder what time it is," he went on; "I have an appointment for seven o'clock."

" Three quarters past six by my watch."

" Well, then I'll go." He got up. "You'll not meddle with trade again?" said he, leaning his elbow on the mantel-piece.

" No, I think not."

" You would be a fool if you did. Probably, after all, you'll think better of your uncles' proposal and go into the Church?"

" A singular regeneration must take place in my whole inner and outer man before I do that. A good clergyman is one of the best of men."

" Indeed! Do you think so?" interrupted Hunsden, scoffingly.

"I do, and no mistake. But I have not the peculiar points which go to make a good clergyman, and, rather than adopt a profession for which I have no vocation, I would endure extremities of hardship from poverty."

"You're. a mighty difficult customer to suit. You won't be a tradesman or a parson; you can't be a lawyer, or a doctor, or a gentleman, because ·you've no money. I'd recommend you to travel."

"What, without money?"

"You must travel in search of money, man. You can speak French—with a vile English accent, no doubt—still you can speak it. Go on to the Continent, and see what will turn up for you there."

"God knows, I should like to go," exclaimed I, with involuntary ardor.

"Go; what the deuce hinders you? You may get to Brussels, for instance, for five or six pounds, if you know how to manage with economy."

"Necessity would teach me if I didn't.'

"Go, then, and let your wits make a way for you when you get there. I know Brussels almost as well as I know X——, and I am sure it would suit such a one as you better than London."

"But occupation, Mr. Hunsden—I must go where occupation is to be had; and how could I get recommendation, or introduction, or employment at Brussels?"

"There speaks the organ of caution. You hate to advance a step before you know every inch of the way. You haven't a sheet of paper, and a pen and ink?"

"I hope so;" and I produced writing materials with

alacrity, for I guessed what he was going to do. He sat down, wrote a few lines, folded, sealed, and addressed a letter, and held it out to me.

"There, Prudence, there's a pioneer to hew down the first rough difficulties of your path. I know well enough, lad, you are not one of those who will run their neck into a noose without seeing how they are to get it out again, and you're right there. A reckless man is my aversion, and nothing should ever persuade me to meddle with the concerns of such a one. Those who are reckless for themselves are generally ten times more so for their friends."

"This is a letter of introduction, I suppose?" said I, taking the epistle.

"Yes. With that in your pocket you will run no risk of finding yourself in a state of absolute destitution, which, I know, you will regard as a degradation; so should I, for that matter. The person to whom you will present it generally has two or three respectable places depending upon his recommendation."

"That will just suit me," said I.

"Well, and where's your gratitude?" demanded Mr. Hunsden; "don't you know how to say 'Thank you?'"

"I've fifteen pounds and a watch, which my godmother, whom I never saw, gave me eighteen years ago," was my rather irrelevant answer; and I further avowed myself a happy man, and professed that I did not envy any being in Christendom.

"And your gratitude?"

"I shall be off presently, Mr. Hunsden—to-morrow, if all be well. I'll not stay a day longer in X—— than I am obliged."

"Very good; but it will be decent to make due acknowledgment for the assistance you have received; be quick. It is just going to strike seven; I'm waiting to be thanked."

"Just stand out of the way, will you, Mr. Hunsden? I want a key there is on the corner of the mantel-piece. I'll pack my portmanteau before I go to bed."

The house clock struck seven.

"The lad is a heathen," said Hunsden; and, taking his hat from a sideboard, he left the room, laughing to himself. I had half an inclination to follow him. I really intended to leave X—— the next morning, and should certainly not have another opportunity of bidding him good-by. The front door banged to.

"Let him go," said I; "we shall meet again some day."

CHAPTER VII.

READER, perhaps you were never in Belgium? Haply you don't know the physiognomy of the country? You have not its lineaments defined upon your memory as I have them on mine?

Three—nay, four pictures line the four-walled cell where are stored for me the records of the past. First, Eton. All in that picture is in far perspective, receding, diminutive, but freshly colored, green, dewy, with a spring sky, piled with glittering yet showery clouds; for my childhood was not all sunshine; it had its overcast, its cold, its stormy hours. Second, X——, huge, dingy; the canvas cracked and smoked; a yellow sky, sooty clouds; no sun, no azure; the verdure of the suburbs blighted and sullied—a very dreary scene.

Third, Belgium; and I will pause before this landscape. · As to the fourth, a curtain covers it, which I may hereafter withdraw, or may not, as suits my convenience or capacity. At any rate, for the present it must hang undisturbed. Belgium! name unromantic and unpoetic, yet name that whenever uttered has in my ear a sound, in my heart an echo, such as no other assemblage of syllables, however sweet or classic, can produce. Belgium! I repeat the word now as I sit alone near midnight. It stirs my world of the past like a summons to resurrection; the graves unclose, the dead are raised; thoughts, feelings, memories that slept, are seen by me ascending from the clods—haloed the most of them—but while I gaze on their vapory forms, and strive to ascertain definitely their outline, the sound which wakened them dies, and they sink, each and all, like a light wreath of mist, absorbed in the mould, recalled to urns, resealed in monuments. Farewell, luminous phantoms!

This is Belgium, reader. Look! don't call the picture a flat or a dull one: it was neither flat nor dull to me when I first beheld it. When I left Ostend, on a mild February morning, and found myself on the road to Brussels, nothing could look vapid to me. My sense of enjoyment possessed an edge whetted to the finest, untouched, keen, exquisite. I was young; I had good health; pleasure and I had never met; no indulgence of hers had enervated or sated one faculty

of my nature. Liberty I clasped in my arms for the
first time, and the influence of her smile and embrace
revived my life like the sun and the west wind. Yes,
at that epoch I felt like a morning traveler who doubts
not that from the hill he is ascending he shall behold
a glorious sunrise. What if the track be strait, steep,
and stony? he sees it not; his eyes are fixed on that
summit, flushed already, flushed and gilded, and, having gained it, he is certain of the scene beyond. He
knows that the sun will face him, that his chariot is
even now coming over the eastern horizon, and that
the herald breeze he feels on his cheek is opening for
the god's career a clear, vast path of azure, amid clouds
soft as pearl and warm as flame. Difficulty and toil
were to be my lot, but sustained by energy, drawn on
by hopes as bright as vague, I deemed such a lot no
hardship. I mounted now the hill, in the shade; there
were pebbles, inequalities, briers in my path, but my
eyes were fixed on the crimson peak above; my imagination was with the refulgent firmament beyond, and
I thought nothing of the stones turning under my feet,
or of the thorns scratching my face and hands.

I gazed often, and always with delight, from the
window of the diligence (these, be it remembered, were
not the days of trains and rail-roads). Well, and what
did I see? I will tell you faithfully. Green, reedy
swamps; fields, fertile but flat, cultivated in patches
that made them look like magnified kitchen-gardens;
belts of cut trees, formal as pollard willows, skirting
the horizon; narrow canals, gliding slow by the road
side; painted Flemish farm-houses; some very dirty
hovels; a gray, dead sky; wet road, wet fields, wet

house-tops: not a beautiful, scarcely a picturesque
object met my eye along the whole route; yet to me
all was beautiful, all was more than picturesque.   It
continued fair so long as daylight lasted, though the
moisture of many preceding damp days had sodden the
whole country.   As it grew dark, however, the rain recommenced, and it was through streaming and starless
darkness my eye caught the first gleam of the lights
of Brussels.   I saw little of the city but its lights that
night.   Having alighted from the diligence, a fiacre
conveyed me to the Hotel de ———, where I had been
advised by a fellow-traveler to put up.   Having eaten
a traveler's supper, I retired to bed, and slept a traveler's sleep.

Next morning I awoke from prolonged and sound
repose with the impression that I was yet in X———,
and, perceiving it to be broad daylight, I started up,
imagining that I had overslept myself, and should be
behind time at the counting-house.   The momentary
and painful sense of restraint vanished before the revived and reviving consciousness of freedom, as, throwing back the white curtains of my bed, I looked forth
into a wide, lofty foreign chamber.   How different
from the small and dingy, though not uncomfortable
apartment I had occupied for a night or two at a respectable inn in London, while waiting for the sailing
of the packet!   Yet far be it from me to profane the
memory of that little dingy room.   It, too, is dear to
my soul, for there, as I lay in quiet and darkness, I
first heard the great bell of St. Paul's telling London
it was midnight, and well do I recall the deep, deliberate tones, so full charged with colossal phlegm and

force. From the small, narrow window of that room
I first saw *the* dome, looming through a London mist.
I suppose the sensations stirred by those first sounds,
first sights, are felt but once; treasure them, Memory;
seal them in urns, and keep them in safe niches. Well,
I rose. Travelers talk of the apartments in foreign
dwellings being bare and uncomfortable; I thought
my chamber looked stately and cheerful : it had such
large windows—*croisées* that opened like doors, with
such broad, clear panes of glass ; such a great looking-
glass stood on my dressing-table; such a fine mirror
glittered over the mantel-piece ; the painted floor looked so clean and glossy. When I had dressed and
was descending the stairs, the broad marble steps almost awed me, and so did the lofty hall into which
they conducted. On the first landing I met a Flemish housemaid. She had wooden shoes, a short red
petticoat, a printed cotton bed-gown, her face was
broad, her physiognomy eminently stupid. When I
spoke to her in French, she answered me in Flemish,
with an air the reverse of civil, yet I thought her
charming; if she was not pretty or polite, she was, I
conceived, very picturesque. She reminded me of the
female figures in certain Dutch paintings I had seen
in other years at Seacombe Hall.

I repaired to the public room ; that, too, was very
large and very lofty, and warmed by a stove ; the floor
was black, and most of the furniture was black; yet I
never experienced a freer sense of exhilaration than
when I sat down at a very long black table (covered,
however, in part by a white cloth), and, having ordered breakfast, began to pour out my coffee from a little

black coffee-pot. The stove might be dismal-looking
to some eyes, not to mine, but it was indisputably
very warm, and there were two gentlemen seated by
it talking in French; impossible to follow their rapid
utterance, or comprehend much of the purport of what
they said; yet French, in the mouths of Frenchmen
or Belgians (I was not then sensible of the horrors of
the Belgian accent), was as music to my ears. One
of these gentlemen presently discerned me to be an
Englishman—no doubt from the fashion in which I
addressed the waiter; for I would persist in speaking
French in my execrable south of England style, though
the man understood English. The gentleman, after
looking toward me once or twice, politely accosted me
in very good English. I remember I wished to God
that I could speak French as well; his fluency and
correct pronunciation impressed me for the first time
with a due notion of the cosmopolitan character of the
capital I was in; it was my first experience of that
skill in living languages I afterward found to be so
general in Brussels.

I lingered over my breakfast as long as I could.
While it was there on the table, and while that stranger continued talking to me, I was a free, independent
traveler; but at last the things were removed, the two
gentlemen left the room; suddenly the illusion ceased,
reality and business came back. I, a bondsman just
released from the yoke, freed for one week from twen-
ty-one years of constraint, must, of necessity, resume
the fetters of dependency. Hardly had I tasted the
delight of being without a master when duty issued
her stern mandate: "Go forth and seek another serv-

ice." I never linger over a painful and necessary task; I never take pleasure before business; it is not in my nature to do so; impossible to enjoy a leisurely walk over the city, though I perceived the morning was very fine, until I had first presented Mr. Hunsden's letter of introduction, and got fairly on to the track of a new situation. Wrenching my mind from liberty and delight, I seized my hat, and forced my reluctant body out of the Hotel de ——— into the foreign street.

It was a fine day, but I would not look at the blue sky or at the stately houses round me. My mind was bent on one thing, finding out " Mr. Brown, Numero —, Rue Royale," for so my letter was addressed. By dint of inquiry I succeeded. I stood at last at the desired door, knocked, asked for Mr. Brown, and was admitted.

Being shown into a small breakfast-room, I found myself in the presence of an elderly gentleman—very grave, business-like, and respectable-looking. I presented Mr. Hunsden's letter; he received me very civilly. After a little desultory conversation, he asked me if there was any thing in which his advice or experience could be of use. I said "Yes," and then proceeded to tell him that I was not a gentleman of fortune, traveling for pleasure, but an ex-counting-house clerk, who wanted employment of some kind, and that immediately too. He replied that, as a friend of Mr. Hunsden's, he would be willing to assist me as well as he could. After some meditation, he named a place in a mercantile house at Liege, and another in a bookseller's shop at Louvain.

D

"Clerk and shopman!" murmured I to myself.
"No." I shook my head. I had tried the high stool;
I hated it; I believed there were other occupations
that would suit me better; besides, I did not wish to
leave Brussels.

"I know of no place in Brussels," answered Mr.
Brown, "unless, indeed, you were disposed to turn
your attention to teaching. I am acquainted with the
director of a large establishment who is in want of a
professor of English and Latin."

I thought two minutes; then I seized the idea eagerly.

"The very thing, sir," said I.

"But," asked he, "do you understand French well
enough to teach Belgian boys English?"

Fortunately, I could answer this question in the affirmative. Having studied French under a Frenchman, I could speak the language intelligibly, though
not fluently. I could also read it well, and write it
decently.

"Then," pursued Mr. Brown, "I think I can promise you the place, for Monsieur Pelet will not refuse a
professor recommended by me; but come here again
at five o'clock this afternoon, and I will introduce you
to him."

The word "professor" struck me. "I am not a
professor," said I.

"Oh," returned Mr. Brown, "professor here in Belgium means a teacher, that is all."

My conscience thus quieted, I thanked Mr. Brown,
and for the present withdrew. This time I stepped
out into the street with a relieved heart; the task I had

imposed on myself for that day was executed. I might
now take some hours of holiday. I felt free to look
up. For the first time I remarked the sparkling clearness of the air, the deep blue of the sky, the gay, clean
aspect of the whitewashed or painted houses; I saw
what a fine street was the Rue Royale, and, walking
leisurely along its broad pavement, I continued to survey its stately hotels, till the palisades, the gates, and
trees of the park appearing in sight, offered to my eye
a new attraction. I remember, before entering the
park, I stood a while to contemplate the statue of General Belliard, and then advanced to the top of the great
staircase just beyond, and looked down into a narrow
back street, which I afterward learned was called the
Rue d'Isabelle. I well recollect that my eye rested
on the green door of a rather large house opposite,
where on a brass plate was inscribed "Pensionnat de-
Demoiselles." Pensionnat! the word excited an uneasy sensation in my mind; it seemed to speak of restraint. Some of the demoiselles, externats no doubt,
were at that moment issuing from the door. I looked
for a pretty face among them, but their close little
French bonnets hid their features; in a moment they
were gone.

I had traversed a good deal of Brussels before five
o'clock arrived, but punctually as that hour struck I
was again in the Rue Royale. Readmitted to Mr.
Brown's breakfast-room, I found him, as before, seated
at the table, and he was not alone—a gentleman stood
by the hearth. Two words of introduction designated
him as my future master. "M. Pelet, Mr. Crimsworth
—Mr. Crimsworth, M. Pelet." A bow on each side

finished the ceremony. I don't know what sort of a
bow I made; an ordinary one, I suppose, for I was in
a tranquil, commonplace frame of mind; I felt none
of the agitation which had troubled my first interview
with Edward Crimsworth. M. Pelet's bow was extremely polite, yet not theatrical, scarcely French; he
and I were presently seated opposite to each other. In
a pleasing voice, low, and, out of consideration to my
foreign ears, very distinct and deliberate, M. Pelet intimated that he had just been receiving from "le respectable M. Brown" an account of my attainments
and character, which relieved him from all scruple as
to the propriety of engaging me as professor of English
and Latin in his establishment; nevertheless, for form's
sake, he would put a few questions to test my powers.
He did, and expressed in flattering terms his satisfaction at my answers. The subject of salary next came
on: it was fixed at one thousand francs per annum,
besides board and lodging. "And, in addition," suggested M. Pelet, "as there will be some hours in each
day during which your services will not be required in
my establishment, you may, in time, obtain employment in other seminaries, and thus turn your vacant
moments to profitable account."

I thought this very kind, and, indeed, I found afterward that the terms on which M. Pelet had engaged
me were really liberal for Brussels, instruction being
cheap there on account of the number of teachers. It
was further arranged that I should be installed in my
new post the very next day, after which M. Pelet and
I parted.

Well, and what was he like? and what were my

impressions concerning him? He was a man of about
forty years of age, of middle size, and rather emaciated
figure; his face was pale, his cheeks were sunk, and,
his eyes hollow; his features were pleasing and regular; they had a French turn (for M. Pelet was no
Fleming, but a Frenchman both by birth and parent-
age), yet the degree of harshness inseparable from Gallic lineaments was, in his case, softened by a mild blue
eye, and a melancholy, almost suffering expression of
countenance; his physiognomy was "fine et spiritu-
elle." I use two French words because they define
better than any English terms the species of intelligence with which his features were imbued. He was
altogether an interesting and prepossessing personage.
I wondered only at the utter absence of all the ordinary characteristics of his profession, and almost feared he could not be stern and resolute enough for a
schoolmaster. Externally at least M. Pelet presented
an absolute contrast to my late master, Edward Crimsworth.

Influenced by the impression I had received of his
gentleness, I was a good deal surprised when, on arriving the next day at my new employer's house, and
being admitted to a first view of what was to be the
sphere of my future labors, namely, the large, lofty, and
well-lighted school-rooms, I beheld a numerous assemblage of pupils, boys of course, whose collective appearance showed all the signs of a full, flourishing, and
well-disciplined seminary. As I traversed the classes
in company with M. Pelet, a profound silence reigned
on all sides, and if by chance a murmur or a whisper
arose, one glance from the pensive eye of this most

gentle pedagogue stilled it instantly. It was astonishing, I thought, how so mild a check could prove so
effectual. When I had perambulated the length and
breadth of the classes, M. Pelet turned and said to me,

"Would you object to taking the boys as they are,
and testing their proficiency in English?"

The proposal was unexpected. I had thought I
should have been allowed at least a day to prepare;
but it is a bad omen to commence any career by hesitation, so I just stepped to the professor's desk near
which we stood, and faced the circle of my pupils. I
took a moment to collect my thoughts, and likewise
to frame in French the sentence by which I proposed
to open business. I made it as short as possible:

"Messieurs, prenez vos livres de lecture."

"Anglais ou Français, Monsieur?" demanded a thick
set, moon-faced young Flamand in a blouse. The
answer was fortunately easy:

"Anglais."

I determined to give myself as little trouble as possible in this lesson. It would not do yet to trust my
unpracticed tongue with the delivery of explanations;
my accent and idiom would be too open to the criticisms of the young gentlemen before me, relative to
whom I felt already it would be necessary at once to
take up an advantageous position, and I proceeded to
employ means accordingly.

"Commencez," cried I, when they had all produced
their books. The moon-faced youth (by name Jules
Vanderkelkov, as I afterward learned) took the first
sentence. The "livre de lecture" was the "Vicar of
Wakefield," much used in foreign schools because it

is supposed to contain prime samples of conversational English; it might, however, have been a Runic scroll for any resemblance the words, as enunciated by Jules, bore to the language in ordinary use among the natives of Great Britain. My God, how he did snuffle, snort, and wheeze! All he said was said in his throat and nose, for it is thus the Flamands speak; but I heard him to the end of his paragraph without proffering a word of correction, whereat he looked vastly self-complacent, convinced, no doubt, that he had acquitted himself like a real born and bred "Anglais." In the same unmoved silence I listened to a dozen in rotation, and when the twelfth had concluded with splutter, hiss, and mumble, I solemnly laid down the book.

"Arrêtez," said I. There was a pause, during which I regarded them all with a steady and somewhat stern gaze: a dog, if stared at hard enough and long enough, will show symptoms of embarrassment, and so at length did my bench of Belgians. Perceiving that some of the faces before me were beginning to look sullen, and others ashamed, I slowly joined my hands, and ejaculated in a deep "voix de poitrine,"

"Comme c'est affreux."

They looked at each other, pouted, colored, swung their heels; they were not pleased, I saw, but they were impressed, and in the way I wished them to be. Having thus taken them down a peg in their self-conceit, the next step was to raise myself in their estimation; not a very easy thing, considering that I hardly dared to speak for fear of betraying my own deficiencies.

"Ecoutez, Messieurs," said I; and I endeavored to

throw into my accents the compassionate tone of a superior being, who, touched by the extremity of the helplessness which at first only excited his scorn, deigns at length to bestow aid. I then began at the very beginning of the "Vicar of Wakefield," and read, in a slow, distinct voice, some twenty pages, they all the while sitting mute and listening with fixed attention. By the time I had done nearly an hour had elapsed. I then rose and said,

"C'est assez pour aujourd'hui, Messieurs; demain nous recommençerons, et j'espère que tout ira bien."

With this oracular sentence I bowed, and, in company with M. Pelet, quitted the school-room.

"C'est bien! c'est très bien!" said my principal as we entered his parlor. "Je vois que Monsieur a de l'adresse; cela me plait, car, dans l'instruction, l'adresse fait tout autant que le savoir."

From the parlor M. Pelet conducted me to my apartment, my "chambre," as Monsieur said with a certain air of complacency. It was a very small room, with an excessively small bed, but M. Pelet gave me to understand that I was to occupy it quite alone, which was, of course, a great comfort. Yet, though so limited in dimensions, it had two windows. Light not being taxed in Belgium, the people never grudge its admission into their houses; just here, however, this observation is not very *apropos*, for one of these windows was boarded up; the open window looked into the boys' playground. I glanced at the other, as wondering what aspect it would present if disencumbered of the boards. M. Pelet read, I suppose, the expression of my eye; he explained:

"La fenêtre fermée donne sur un jardin appartenant à un pensionnat de demoiselles," said he, "et les convenances exigent—enfin, vous comprenez—n'est-ce pas, Monsieur ?"

—"Oui, oui," was my reply, and I looked, of course, quite satisfied ; but when M. Pelet had retired and closed the door after him, the first thing I did was 'to scrutinize closely the nailed boards, hoping to find some chink or crevice which I might enlarge, and so get a peep at the consecrated ground. My researches were vain, for the boards were well joined and strongly nailed. It is astonishing how disappointed I felt. I thought it would have been so pleasant to have looked out upon a garden planted with flowers and trees ; so amusing to have watched the demoiselles at their play —to have studied female character in a variety of phases, myself the while sheltered from view by a modest muslin curtain ; whereas, owing doubtless to the absurd scruples of some old duenna of a directress, I had now only the option of looking at a bare graveled court, with an enormous "pas de géant" in the middle, and the monotonous walls and windows of a boy's school-house round. Not only then, but many a time after, especially in moments of weariness and low spirits, did I look with dissatisfied eyes on that most tantalizing board, longing to tear it away and get a glimpse of the green region which I imagined to lie beyond. I knew a tree grew close up to the window, for, though there were as yet no leaves to rustle, I often heard at night the tapping of branches against the panes. In the daytime, when I listened attentively, I could hear, even through the boards, the

D 2

voices of the demoiselles in their hours of recreation,
and, to speak the honest truth, my sentimental reflections were occasionally a trifle disarranged by the not
quite silvery, in fact, the too often brazen sounds
which, rising from the unseen paradise below, penetrated clamorously into my solitude.   Not to mince
matters, it really seemed to me a doubtful case whether the lungs of Mdlle. Reuter's girls or those of M.
Pelet's boys were the strongest; and when it came to
shrieking, the girls indisputably beat the boys hollow.
I forgot to say, by-the-by, that Reuter was the name
of the old lady who had had my window boarded up.
I say old, for such I, of course, concluded her to be,
judging from her cautious, chaperon-like proceedings;
besides, nobody ever spoke of her as young.   I remember I was very much amused when I first heard
her Christian name; it was Zoraïde—Mademoiselle
Zoraïde Reuter.   But the Continental nations do allow themselves vagaries in the choice of names, such
as we sober English never run into.   I think, indeed,
we have too limited a list to choose from.

Meantime my path was gradually growing smooth
before me.   I in a few weeks conquered the teasing
difficulties inseparable from the commencement of almost every career.   Ere long I had acquired as much
facility in speaking French as set me at my ease with
my pupils, and as I had encountered them on a right
footing at the very beginning, and continued tenacious-
ly to retain the advantage I had early gained, they
never attempted mutiny, which circumstance all who
are in any degree acquainted with the ongoings of
Belgian schools, and who know the relation in which

professors and pupils too frequently stand toward each other in those establishments, will consider an important and uncommon one. Before concluding this chapter I will say a word on the system I pursued with regard to my classes : my experience may possibly be of use to others.

It did not require very keen observation to detect the character of the youth of Brabant, but it needed a certain degree of tact to adopt one's measures to their capacity. Their intellectual faculties were generally weak, their animal propensities strong; thus there was at once an impotence and a kind of inert force in their natures ; they were dull, but they were also singularly stubborn, heavy as lead, and, like lead, most difficult to move. Such being the case, it would have been truly absurd to exact from them much in the way of mental exertion. Having short memories, dense intelligence, feeble reflective powers, they recoiled with repugnance from any occupation that demanded close study or deep thought. Had the abhorred effort been extorted from them by injudicious and arbitrary measures on the part of the professor, they would have resisted as obstinately, as clamorously as desperate swine ; and, though not brave singly, they were relentless acting *en masse.*

I understood that, before my arrival in M. Pelet's establishment, the combined insubordination of the pupils had effected the dismissal of more than one English master. It was necessary, then, to exact only the most moderate application from natures so little qualified to apply ; to assist, in every practicable way, understandings so opaque and contracted ; to be ever

gentle, considerate, yielding even, to a certain point,
with dispositions so irrationally perverse; but, having
reached that culminating point of indulgence, you must
fix your foot, plant it, root it in rock—become immu-
table as the towers of Ste. Gudule; for a step—but
half a step further, and you would plunge headlong
into the gulf of imbecility; there lodged, you would
speedily receive proofs of Flemish gratitude and mag-
nanimity in showers of Brabant saliva and handfuls
of Low-Country mud. You might smooth to the ut-
most the path of learning, remove every pebble from
the track; but then you must finally insist with decision on the pupil taking your arm, and allowing himself to be led quietly along the prepared road. When
I had brought down my lesson to the lowest level of
my dullest pupil's capacity—when I had shown myself the mildest, the most tolerant of masters, a word
of impertinence, a movement of disobedience, changed
me at once into a despot. I offered then but one alternative—submission and acknowledgment of error,
or ignominious expulsion. This system answered,
and my influence, by degrees, became established on
a firm basis. "The boy is father to the man," it is
said, and so I often thought when I looked at my
boys and remembered the political history of their ancestors. Pelet's school was merely an epitome of the
Belgian nation.

CHAPTER VIII.

AND Pelet himself—how did I continue to like him ? Oh, extremely well. Nothing could be more smooth, gentlemanlike, and even friendly than his demeanor to me. I had to endure from him neither cold neglect, irritating interference, nor pretentious assumption of superiority. I fear, however, two poor, hard-worked Belgian ushers in the establishment could not have said as much: to them the director's manner was invariably dry, stern, and cool. I believe he perceived once or twice that I was a little shocked at the difference he made between them and me, and accounted for it by saying, with a quiet, sarcastic smile,

"Ce ne sont que des Flamands—allez."

And then he took his cigar gently from his lips, and spat on the painted floor of the room in which we were sitting. Flamands certainly they were, and both had the true Flamand physiognomy, where intellectual inferiority is marked in lines none can mistake ; still they were men, and, in the main, honest men ; and I could not see why their being aboriginals of the flat, dull soil should serve as a pretext for treating them with perpetual severity and contempt. This idea of injustice somewhat poisoned the pleasure I might otherwise have derived from Pelet's soft, affable manner to myself. Certainly it was agreeable, when the day's work was over, to find in one's employer an in-

telligent and cheerful companion ; and if he was sometimes a little sarcastic and sometimes a little too insinuating, and if I did discover that his mildness was
more a matter of appearance than of reality—if I did
occasionally suspect the existence of flint or steel under an external covering of velvet, still we are none of
us perfect; and weary as I was of the atmosphere of
brutality and insolence in which I had constantly lived
at X——, I had no inclination now, on casting anchor
in calmer regions, to institute at once a prying search
after defects that were scrupulously withdrawn and
carefully veiled from my view.   I was willing to take
Pelet for what he seemed—to believe him benevolent
and friendly until some untoward event should prove
him otherwise.   He was not married, and I soon perceived he had all a Frenchman's, all a Parisian's notions about matrimony and women.   I suspected a
degree of laxity in his code of morals, there was something so cold and *blasé* in his tone whenever he alluded
to what he called " le beau sexe ;" but he was too gentlemanlike to intrude topics I did not invite, and as he
was really intelligent and really fond of intellectual
subjects of discourse, he and I always found enough
to talk about without seeking themes in the mire.   I
hated his fashion of mentioning love; I abhorred, from
my soul, mere licentiousness.   He felt the difference
of our notions, and, by mutual consent, we kept off
ground debatable.

Pelet's house was kept and his kitchen managed by
his mother, a real old Frenchwoman.   She had been
handsome—at least she told me so, and I strove to
believe her; she was now ugly, as only Continental

old women can be; perhaps, though, her style of dress
made her look uglier than she really was. In-doors
she would go about without cap, her gray hair strange-
ly disheveled; then, when at home, she seldom wore
a gown—only a shabby cotton camisole; shoes, too,
were strangers to her feet, and in lieu of them she
sported roomy slippers, trodden down at the heels.
On the other hand, whenever it was her pleasure to
appear abroad, as on Sundays and fête-days, she would
put on some very brilliant-colored dress, usually of
thin texture, a silk bonnet with a wreath of flowers,
and a very fine shawl. She was not, in the main, an
ill-natured old woman, but an incessant and most in-
discreet talker. She kept chiefly in and about the
kitchen, and seemed rather to avoid her son's august presence; of him, indeed, she evidently stood in
awe. When he reproved her, his reproofs were bitter and unsparing; but he seldom gave himself that
trouble.

Madame Pelet had her own society, her own circle
of chosen visitors, whom, however, I seldom saw, as
she generally entertained them in what she called her
"cabinet," a small den of a place adjoining the kitch-
en, and descending into it by one or two steps. On
these steps, by-the-by, I have not unfrequently seen
Madame Pelet seated with a trencher on her knee, engaged in the threefold employment of eating her dinner, gossiping with her favorite servant, the housemaid, and scolding her antagonist, the cook. She never dined, and seldom, indeed, took any meal with her
son; and as to showing her face at the boys' table,
that was quite out of the question. These details will

sound very odd in English ears, but Belgium is not England, and its ways are not our ways.

Madame Pelet's habits of life, then, being taken into consideration, I was a good deal surprised when, one Thursday evening (Thursday was always a half-holiday), as I was sitting all alone in my apartment, correcting a huge pile of English and Latin exercises, a servant tapped at the door, and, on its being opened, presented Madame Pelet's compliments, and she would be happy to see me to take my " goûter" (a meal which answers to our English " tea") with her in the dining-room.

" Plait-il?" said I; for I thought I must have misunderstood, the message and invitation were so unusual. The same words were repeated. I accepted, of course; and as I descended the stairs, I wondered what whim had entered the old lady's brain. Her son was out—gone to pass the evening at the salle of the Grande Harmonic or some other club of which he was a member. Just as I laid my hand on the handle of the dining-room door, a queer idea glanced across my mind.

" Surely she's not going to make love to me," said I. " I've heard of old French women doing odd things in that line; and the goûter? They generally begin such affairs with eating and drinking, I believe."

There was a fearful dismay in this suggestion of my excited imagination, and if I had allowed myself time to dwell upon it, I should no doubt have cut there and then, rushed back to my chamber, and bolted myself in; but whenever a danger or a horror is veiled with uncertainty, the primary wish of the mind is to

scertain first the naked truth, reserving the expedient
f flight for the moment when its dread anticipation
hall be realized. I turned the door-handle, and in
n instant had crossed the fatal threshold, closed the
oor behind me, and stood in the presence of Madame
Pelet.

Gracious heavens! the first view of her seemed to
confirm my worst apprehensions. There she sat, dress-
d out in a light green muslin gown; on her head a
ace cap, with flourishing red roses in the frill. Her
able was carefully spread : there were fruit, cakes, and
coffee, with a bottle of something, I did not know what.
Already the cold sweat started on my brow; already
I glanced back over my shoulder at the closed door,
when, to my unspeakable relief, my eye, wandering
wildly in the direction of the stove, rested upon a second figure, seated in a large fauteuil beside it. This
was a woman too, and, moreover, an old woman, and
is fat and as rubicund as Madame Pelet was meagre
and yellow. Her attire was likewise very fine, and
spring flowers of different hues circled in a bright
wreath the crown of her violet-colored velvet bonnet.

I had only time to make these general observations
when Madame Pelet, coming forward with what she
ntended should be a graceful and elastic step, thus
accosted me :

"Monsieur is indeed most obliging to quit his books,
his studies, at the request of an insignificant person
ike me. Will Monsieur complete his kindness by al-
owing me to present him to my dear friend Madame
Reuter, who resides in the neighboring house—the
young ladies' school?"

"Ah!" thought I, "I knew she was old," and I bowed and took my seat. Madame Reuter placed herself at the table opposite to me.

"How do you like Belgium, Monsieur?" asked she, in an accent of the broadest Bruxellois. I could now well distinguish the difference between the fine and pure utterance of M. Pelet, for instance, and the guttural enunciation of the Flamands. I answered politely, and then wondered how so coarse and clumsy an old woman as the one before me should be at the head of a ladies' seminary which I had always heard spoken of in terms of high commendation. In truth, there was something to wonder at. Madame Reuter looked more like a joyous, free-living old Flemish fermière, or even a maîtresse d'auberge, than a staid, grave, rigid directrice de pensionnat. In general, the Continental, or at least the Belgian old women, permit themselves a license of manners, speech, and aspect such as our venerable granddames would recoil from as absolutely disreputable, and Madame Reuter's jolly face bore evidence that she was no exception to the rule of her country; there was a twinkle and leer in her left eye; her right she kept habitually half shut, which I thought very odd indeed. After several vain attempts to comprehend the motives of these two droll old creatures for inviting me to join them at their goûter, I at last fairly gave it up, and, resigning myself to inevitable mystification, sat and looked first at one, then at the other, taking care meantime to do justice to the confitures, cakes, and coffee with which they amply supplied me. They too ate, and that with no delicate appetite; and having demolished a large porɔn of the solids, they proposed a "petit verre." I ɔclined; not so Mesdames Pelet and Reuter; each ɪxed herself what I thought rather a stiff tumbler of ɪnch, and placing it on a stand near the stove, they ·ew up their chairs to that convenience, and invited ɛ to do the same. I obeyed, and, being seated fairly ɔtween them, was thus addressed first by Madame ɛlet, then by Madame Reuter.

" We will now speak of business," said Madame ɛlet, and she went on to make an elaborate speech, hich, being interpreted, was to the effect that she had ɪked for the pleasure of my company that evening in ·der to give her friend Madame Reuter an opportuni- · of broaching an important proposal which might ɪrn out greatly to my advantage.

"Pourvu que vous soyez sage," said Madame Reu- ɪ, " et à vrai dire, vous en avez bien l'air. Take one ·op of the punch (or ponche, as she pronounced it); ɪs an agreeable and wholesome beverage after a full ɛal."

I bowed, but again declined it. She went on:

" I feel," said she, after a solemn sip, " I feel pro- undly the importance of the commission with which ɪy dear daughter has intrusted me, for you are aware, [onsieur, that it is my daughter who directs the estab- ɪshment in the next house."

" Ah! I thought it was yourself, Madame," though, ɪdeed, at that moment I recollected that it was called [ademoiselle, not Madame Reuter's pensionnat.

" I! oh no. I manage the house and look after ɪe servants, as my friend Madame Pelet does for Mon- ɛur her son—nothing more. Ah! you thought I ɪve lessons in class, did you?"

And she laughed loud and long, as though the idea tickled her fancy amazingly.

"Madame is in the wrong to laugh," I observed; "if she does not give lessons, I am sure it is not because she can not," and I whipped out a white pocket-handkerchief, and wafted it, with a French grace, past my nose, bowing at the same time.

"Quel charmant jeune homme," murmured Madame Pelet, in a low voice. Madame Reuter, being less sentimental, as she was Flamand and not French, only laughed again.

"You are a dangerous person, I fear," said she; "if you can forge compliments at that rate, Zoraïde will positively be afraid of you; but if you are good, I will keep your secret, and not tell her how well you can flatter. Now listen what sort of a proposal she makes to you. She has heard that you are an excellent professor, and as she wishes to get the very best masters for her school (car Zoraïde fait tout comme une reine, c'est une véritable maîtresse-femme), she has commissioned me to step over this afternoon, and sound Madame Pelet as to the possibility of engaging you. Zoraïde is a wary general; she never advances without first examining well her ground. I don't think she would be pleased if she knew I had already disclosed her intentions to you. She did not order me to go so far, but I thought there would be no harm in letting you into the secret, and Madame Pelet was of the same opinion. Take care, however, you don't betray either of us to Zoraïde—to my daughter, I mean; she is so discreet and circumspect herself, she can not understand that one should find a pleasure in gossiping a little— ;

" C'est absolument comme mon fils," cried Madame
.let.

"All the world is so changed since our girlhood,"
joined the other: "young people have such old heads
w. But to return, Monsieur. Madame Pelet will
antion the subject of your giving lessons in my daugh-
t's establishment to her son, and he will speak to you;
d then, to-morrow, you will step over to our house,
d ask to see my daughter, and you will introduce
e subject as if the first intimation of it had reached
u from M. Pelet himself; and be sure you never
antion my name, for I would not displease Zoraïde
ι any account."

" Bien! bien!" interrupted I, for all this chatter and
rcumlocution began to bore me very much ; " I will
nsult M. Pelet, and the thing shall be settled as you
;sire. Good - evening, mesdames ; I am infinitely
)liged to you."

" Comment! vous vous en allez déjà ?" exclaimed
.adame Pelet.

" Prenez encore quelquechose, Monsieur ; une pom-
e cuite, des biscuits, encore une tasse de café ?"

" Merci, merci, Madame—au revoir." And I back-
l at last out of the apartment.

Having regained my own room, I set myself to turn
/er in my mind the incident of the evening. It
emed a queer affair altogether, and queerly managed ;
ie two old women had made quite a little intricate
ess of it; still I found that the uppermost feeling in
y mind on the subject was one of satisfaction. In
ie first place, it would be a change to give lessons in
other seminary, and then to teach young ladies would

be an occupation so interesting—to be admitted at all into a ladies' boarding-school would be an incident so new in my life.   Besides, thought I, as I glanced at the boarded window, "I shall now at last see the mysterious garden; I shall gaze both on the angels and their Eden."

CHAPTER IX.

M. PELET could not, of course, object to the proposal made by Mdlle. Reuter, permission to accept such additional employment, should it offer, having formed an article of the terms on which he had engaged me.   It was therefore arranged in the course of next day that I should be at liberty to give lessons in Mdlle. Reuter's establishment four afternoons in every week.

When evening came I prepared to step over in order to seek a conference with Mademoiselle herself on the subject; I had not had time to pay the visit before, having been all day closely occupied in class.   I remember very well that, before quitting my chamber, I held a brief debate with myself as to whether I should change my ordinary attire for something smarter.   At last I concluded it would be a waste of labor. "Doubtless," thought I, "she is some stiff old maid; for, though the daughter of Madame Reuter, she may well number upward of forty winters; besides, if it were otherwise, if she be both young and pretty, I am not handsome, and no dressing can make me so, therefore I'll go as I am."   And off I started, cursorily glanc-

g sideways as I passed the toilet-table, surmounted
r a looking-glass; a thin irregular face I saw, with
ınk, dark eyes under a large, square forehead, com-
exion destitute of bloom or attraction—something
)ung but not youthful, no object to win a lady's love,
) butt for the shafts of Cupid.

I was soon at the entrance of the Pensionnat; in a
oment I had pulled the bell; in another moment the
)or was opened, and within appeared a passage paved
ternately with black and white marble; the walls
ere painted in imitation of marble also; and at the
r end opened a glass door, through which I saw
ırubs and a grass-plat, looking pleasant in the sun-
ıine of the mild spring evening, for it was now the
iddle of April.

This, then, was my first glimpse of *the* garden; but
had not time to look long; the portress, after having
ıswered in the affirmative my question as to whether
ɜr mistress was at home, opened the folding-doors
: a room to the left, and having ushered me in, closed
ıem behind me. I found myself in a salon with a
ɜry well painted, highly varnished floor; chairs and
)fas covered with white draperies, a green porcelain
;ove, walls hung with pictures in gilt frames, a gilt
ɜndule, and other ornaments on the mantel-piece, a
.rge lustre pendent from the centre of the ceiling,
iirrors, consoles, muslin curtains, and a handsome
ɜntre-table, completed the inventory of furniture. All
)oked extremely clean and glittering, but the general
ffect would have been somewhat chilling had not a
ɜcond large pair of folding-doors, standing wide open,
nd disclosing another and smaller salon, more snugly

furnished, offered some relief to the eye. This room was carpeted, and therein was a piano, a couch, a chif-fonnière—above all, it contained a lofty window with a crimson curtain, which, being undrawn, afforded another glimpse of the garden, through the large, clear panes, round which some leaves of ivy, some tendrils of vine were trained.

"Monsieur Creemsvort, n'est ce pas?" said a voice behind me; and, starting involuntarily, I turned. I had been so taken up with the contemplation of the pretty little salon that I had not noticed the entrance of a person into the larger room. It was, however, Mdlle. Reuter who now addressed me, and stood close beside me; and when I had bowed with instantaneously recovered *sang froid*—for I am not easily embarrassed—I commenced the conversation by remarking on the pleasant aspect of her little cabinet, and the advantage she had over M. Pelet in possessing a garden.

"Yes," she said, "she often thought so;" and added, "It is my garden, Monsieur, which makes me retain this house, otherwise I should probably have removed to larger and more commodious premises long since; but you see I could not take my garden with me, and I could scarcely find one so large and pleasant any where else in town."

I approved her judgment.

"But you have not seen it yet," said she, rising; "come to the window and take a better view." I followed her. She opened the sash, and, leaning out, I saw in full the inclosed demesne which had hitherto been to me an unknown region. It was a long, not

:ry broad strip of cultured ground, with an alley bor-
:red by enormous old fruit-trees down the middle;
iere was a sort of lawn, a parterre of rose-trees, some
>wer-borders, and, on the far side, a thickly-planted
ipse of lilacs, laburnums, and acacias. It looked
.easant to me—very pleasant, so long a time had
apsed since I had seen a garden of any sort. But
was not only on Mdlle. Reuter's garden that my
'es dwelt; when I had taken a view of her well-
immed beds and budding shrubberies, I allowed my
ance to come back to herself, nor did I hastily with-
:aw it.

I had thought to see a tall, meagre, yellow, convent-
il image in black, with a close white cap, bandaged
ider the chin like a nun's head-gear, whereas there
ood by me a little and roundly-formed woman, who
ight, indeed, be older than I, but was still young.
he could not, I thought, be more than six or seven-
id-twenty; she was as fair as a fair Englishwoman;
ie had no cap; her hair was nut-brown, and she wore
in curls. Pretty her features were not, nor very
)ft, nor very regular, but neither were they in any
:gree plain, and I already saw cause to deem them
cpressive. What was their predominant cast? Was
sagacity? sense? Yes, I thought so; but I could
:arcely as yet be sure. I discovered, however, that
iere was a certain serenity of eye and freshness of
)mplexion most pleasing to behold. The color on her
ieek was like the bloom on a good apple, which is as
)und at the core as it is red on the rind.

Mdlle. Reuter and I entered upon business. She
iid she was not absolutely certain of the wisdom of

E

the step she was about to take, because I was so young,
and parents might possibly object to a professor like
me for their daughters. "But it is often well to act
on one's own judgment," said she, "and to lead parents
rather than be led by them. The fitness of a professor
is not a matter of age; and from what I have heard,
and from what I observe myself, I would much rather
trust you than M. Ledru, the music-master, who is a
married man of near fifty."

I remarked that I hoped she would find me worthy
of her good opinion; that, if I knew myself, I was incapable of betraying any confidence reposed in me.
"Du reste," said she; "the surveillance will be strictly attended to." And then she proceeded to discuss
the subject of terms. She was very cautious—quite
on her guard. She did not absolutely bargain, but
she warily sounded me to find out what my expectations might be; and when she could not get me to
name a sum, she reasoned and reasoned with a fluent
yet quiet circumlocution of speech, and at last nailed
me down to five hundred francs per annum—not too
much, but I agreed. Before the negotiation was completed it began to grow a little dusk. I did not hasten
it, for I liked well enough to sit and hear her talk. I
was amused with the sort of business talent she dis-
played. Edward could not have shown himself more
practical, though he might have evinced more coarseness and urgency; and then she had so many reasons,
so many explanations; and, after all, she succeeded in
proving herself quite disinterested and even liberal. At
last she concluded. She could say no more, because,
as I acquiesced in all things, there was no further

ground for the exercise of her parts of speech. I was obliged to rise. I would rather have sat a little longer. What had I to return to but my small, empty room? And my eyes had a pleasure in looking at Mdlle. Reuter, especially now, when the twilight softened her features a little, and, in the doubtful dusk, I could fancy her forehead as open as it was really elevated, her mouth touched with turns of sweetness as well as defined in lines of sense. When I rose to go I held out my hand on purpose, though I knew it was contrary to the etiquette of foreign habits. She smiled and said,

"Ah! c'est comme tous les Anglais;" but gave me her hand very kindly.

"It is the privilege of my country, Mademoiselle," said I; "and, remember, I shall always claim it."

She laughed a little, quite good-naturedly, and with the sort of tranquillity obvious in all she did—a tranquillity which soothed and suited me singularly; at least I thought so that evening. Brussels seemed a very pleasant place to me when I got out again into the street, and it appeared as if some cheerful, eventful, upward-tending career were even then opening to me on that self-same mild, still April night. So impressionable a being is man, or at least such a man as I was in those days.

CHAPTER X.

NEXT day the morning hours seemed to pass very slowly at M. Pelet's. I wanted the afternoon to come, that I might go again to the neighboring pensionnat and give my first lesson within its precincts, for pleasant they appeared to me. At noon the hour of recreation arrived; at one o'clock we had lunch; this got on the time, and at last Ste. Gudule's deep bell, tolling slowly two, marked the moment for which I had been waiting.

At the foot of the narrow back stairs that descended from my room I met M. Pelet.

"Comme vous avez l'air rayonnant," said he. "Je ne vous ai jamais vu aussi gai que s'est-il donc passé?"

"Apparemment que j'aime les changements," replied I.

"Ah! je comprends—c'st cela—soyez sage seulement. Vous êtes bien jeune—trop jeune pour le rôle que vous allez jouer; il faut prendre garde—savez-vous?"

"Mais quel danger y a-t-il?"

"Je ne'en sais rien—ne vous laissez pas aller à de vives impressions—voilà tout."

I laughed; a sentiment of exquisite pleasure played over my nerves at the thought that "vives impressions" were likely to be created; it was the deadness, the sameness of life's daily ongoings that had hitherto

been my bane; my blouse-clad élèves in the boy's seminary never stirred in me any "vives impressions," except it might be occasionally some of anger. I broke
from M. Pelet, and as I strode down the passage he
followed me with one of his laughs—a very French,
rakish, mocking sound.

Again I stood at the neighboring door, and soon was
readmitted into the cheerful passage, with its clear,
dove-color imitation marble walls. I followed the
portress, and descending a step and making a turn, I
found myself in a sort of corridor; a side-door opened;
Mdlle. Reuter's little figure, as graceful as it was
plump, appeared. I could now see her dress in full
daylight: a neat, simple mousseline-de-laine gown fitted her compact round shape to perfection; delicate
little collar and manchettes of lace, trim Parisian bro-
dequins showed her neck, wrists, and feet to complete
advantage; but how grave was her face as she came
suddenly upon me! Solicitude and business were in
her eye—on her forehead; she looked almost stern.
Her "bon jour, Monsieur," was quite polite, but so
orderly, so commonplace, it spread directly a cool,
damp towel over my "vives impressions." The servant turned back when her mistress appeared, and I
walked slowly along the corridor, side by side with
Mdlle. Reuter.

"Monsieur will give a lesson in the first class to-
day," said she. "Dictation or reading will perhaps
be the best thing to begin with, for those are the easi-
est forms of communicating instruction in a foreign
language; and, at the first, a master naturally feels a
little unsettled."

She was quite right, as I had found from experience; it only remained for me to acquiesce. We proceeded now in silence. The corridor terminated in a hall, large, lofty, and square; a glass door on one side showed within a long, narrow refectory, with tables, an armoire, and two lamps: it was empty; large glass doors, in front, opened on the play-ground and garden; a broad staircase ascended spirally on the opposite side; the remaining wall showed a pair of great folding-doors, now closed, and admitting, doubtless, to the classes.

Mdlle. Reuter turned her eye laterally on me, to ascertain probably whether I was collected enough to be ushered into her sanctum sanctorum. I suppose she judged me to be in a tolerable state of self-government, for she opened the door, and I followed her through. A rustling sound of uprising greeted our entrance. Without looking to the right or left, I walked straight up the lane between two sets of benches and desks, and took possession of the empty chair and isolated desk raised on an estrade of one step high, so as to command one division, the other division being under the surveillance of a maîtresse similarly elevated. At the back of the estrade, and attached to a movable partition dividing this school-room from another beyond, was a large tableau of wood, painted black and varnished; a thick crayon of white chalk lay on my desk for the convenience of elucidating any grammatical or verbal obscurity which might occur in my lessons by writing it upon the tableau; a wet sponge appeared beside the chalk to enable me to efface the marks when they had served the purpose intended.

I carefully and deliberately made these observations before allowing myself to take one glance at the benches before me. Having handled the crayon, looked back at the tableau, fingered the sponge in order to ascertain that it was in a right state of moisture, I found myself cool enough to admit of looking calmly up and gazing deliberately round me.

And first I observed that Mdlle. Reuter had already glided away: she was nowhere visible; a maîtresse or teacher, the one who occupied the corresponding estrade to my own, alone remained to keep guard over me. She was a little in the shade, and, with my short sight, I could only see that she was of a thin, bony figure, and rather tallowy complexion, and that her attitude, as she sat, partook equally of listlessness and affectation. More obvious, more prominent, shone on by the full light of the large window, were the occupants of the benches just before me, of whom some were girls of fourteen, fifteen, sixteen, some young women from eighteen (as it appeared to me) up to twenty; the most modest attire, the simplest fashion of wearing the hair, were apparent in all, and good features, ruddy, blooming complexions, large and brilliant eyes, forms full, even to solidity, seemed to abound. I did not bear the first view like a stoic. I was dazzled; my eyes fell, and in a voice somewhat too low I murmured,

"Prenez vos cahiers de dictée, Mesdemoiselles."

Not so had I bid the boys at Pelet's take their reading-books. A rustle followed, and an opening of desks. Behind the lifted lids which momentarily screened the heads bent down to search for exercise-books I heard tittering and whispers.

"Eulalie, je suis prête à pâmer de rire," observed one.

"Comme il a rougi en parlant!"

"Oui, c'est un véritable blanc-bec."

"Tais-toi, Hortense—il nous écoute."

And now the lids sank and the heads reappeared. I had marked three, the whisperers, and I did not scruple to take a very steady look at them as they emerged from their temporary eclipse. It is astonishing what ease and courage their little phrases of flippancy had given me. The idea by which I had been awed was that the youthful beings before me, with their dark, nun-like robes and softly braided hair, were a kind of half-angels. The light titter, the giddy whisper, had already, in some measure, relieved my mind of that fond and oppressive fancy.

The three I allude to were just in front, within half a yard of my estrade, and were among the most womanly-looking present. Their names I knew afterward, and may as well mention now; they were Eulalie, Hortense, Caroline. Eulalie was tall and very finely shaped. She was fair, and her features were those of a Low-Country Madonna. Many a "figure de vierge" have I seen in Dutch pictures exactly resembling hers. There were no angles in her shape or in her face; all was curve and roundness: neither thought, sentiment, nor passion disturbed by line or flush the equality of her pale, clear skin; her noble bust heaved with her regular breathing, her eyes moved a little: by these evidences of life alone could I have distinguished her from some large, handsome figure moulded in wax.

Hortense was of middle size and stout; her form

was ungraceful; her face striking—more alive and brilliant than Eulalie's; her hair was dark brown, her complexion richly colored; there were frolic and mischief in her eye: consistency and good sense she might possess, but none of her features betokened those qualities.

Caroline was little, though evidently full grown; raven-black hair, very dark eyes, absolutely regular features, with a colorless olive complexion, clear as to the face and sallow about the neck, formed in her that assemblage of points whose union many persons regard as the perfection of beauty. How, with the tintless pallor of her skin and the classic straightness of her lineaments, she managed to look sensual, I don't know. I think her lips and eyes contrived the affair between them, and the result left no uncertainty on the beholder's mind. She was sensual now, and in ten years' time she would be coarse—promise plain was written in her face of much future folly.

If I looked at these girls with little scruple, they looked at me with still less. Eulalie raised her unmoved eye to mine, and seemed to expect, passively but securely, an impromptu tribute to her majestic charms. Hortense regarded me boldly and giggled at the same time, while she said with an air of impudent freedom,

"Dictez-nous quelquechose de facile pour commencer, Monsieur."

Caroline shook her loose ringlets of abundant but somewhat coarse hair over her rolling black eyes. Parting her lips, as full as those of a hot-blooded Maroon, she showed her well-set teeth sparkling between

E 2

them, and treated me at the same time to a smile "de sa façon." Beautiful as Pauline Borghese, she looked at the moment scarcely purer than Lucrèce de Borgia. Caroline was of noble family. I heard her lady-mother's character afterward, and then I ceased to wonder at the precocious accomplishments of the daughter. These three, I at once saw, deemed themselves the queens of the school, and conceived that by their splendor they threw all the rest into the shade. In less than five minutes they had thus revealed to me their characters, and in less than five minutes I had buckled on a breastplate of steely indifference, and let down a visor of impassible austerity.

"Take your pens and commence writing," said I, in as dry and trite a voice as if I had been addressing only Jules Vanderkelkov and Co.

The dictée now commenced. My three belles interrupted me perpetually with little silly questions and uncalled-for remarks, to some of which I made no answer, and to others replied very quietly and briefly.

"Comment dit-on point et virgule en Anglais, Monsieur?"

"Semicolon, Mademoiselle."

"Semi-collong? Ah comme c'est drôle!" (giggle.)

"J'ai une si mauvaise plume—impossible d'écrire."

"Mais, Monsieur—je ne sais pas suivre—vous allez si vîte."

"Je n'ai rien compris, moi."

Here a general murmur arose, and the teacher, opening her lips for the first time, ejaculated,

"Silence, Mesdemoiselles."

No silence followed; on the contrary, the three ladies in front began to talk more loudly.

"C'est si difficile, l'Anglais."

"Je déteste la dictée."

"Quel ennui d'écrire quelquechose que l'on ne comprend pas."

Some of those behind laughed; a degree of confusion began to pervade the class; it was necessary to take prompt measures.

"Donnez-moi votre cahier," said I to Eulalie, in an abrupt tone; and, bending over, I took it before she had time to give it.

Et vous, Mademoiselle—donnez-moi le vôtre," continued I, more mildly, addressing a little pale, plain-looking girl who sat in the first row of the other division, and whom I had remarked as being at once the ugliest and the most attentive in the room. She rose up, walked over to me, and delivered her book with a grave, modest courtesy. I glanced over the two dictations: Eulalie's was slurred, blotted, and full of silly mistakes: Sylvie's (such was the name of the ugly little girl) was clearly written: it contained no error against sense, and but few faults of orthography. I coolly read aloud both exercises, marking the faults; then I looked at Eulalie:

"C'est honteux," said I, and I deliberately tore her dictation in four parts, and presented her with the fragments. I returned Sylvie her book with a smile, saying,

"C'est bien—je suis content de vous."

Sylvie looked calmly pleased, Eulalie swelled like an incensed turkey; but the mutiny was quelled; the conceited coquetry and futile flirtation of the first bench were exchanged for a taciturn sullenness, much more convenient to me, and the rest of my lesson passed without interruption.

A bell clanging out in the yard announced the moment for the cessation of school labors. I heard our own bell at the same time, and that of a certain public college immediately after. Order dissolved instantly. Up started every pupil. I hastened to seize my hat, bow to the maîtresse, and quit the room before the tide of externats should pour from the inner class, where I knew near a hundred were prisoned, and whose rising tumult I already heard.

I had scarcely crossed the hall and gained the corridor when Mdlle. Reuter came again upon me.

"Step in here a moment," said she, and she held open the door of the side-room from whence she had issued on my arrival: it was a *salle-a-manger*, as appeared from the beaufet and the armoire vitrée, filled with glass and china, which formed part of its furniture. Ere she had closed the door on me and herself, the corridor was already filled with day-pupils, tearing down their cloaks, bonnets, and cabas from the wooden pegs on which they were suspended. The shrill voice of a maîtresse was heard at intervals vainly endeavoring to enforce some sort of order; vainly, I say: discipline there was none in these rough ranks, and yet this was considered one of the best-conducted schools in Brussels.

"Well, you have given your first lesson," began Mdlle. Reuter in the most calm, equable voice, as though quite unconscious of the chaos from which we were separated only by a single wall.

"Were you satisfied with your pupils, or did any circumstance in their conduct give you cause for complaint? Conceal nothing from me; repose in me entire confidence."

Happily, I felt in myself complete power to manage my pupils without aid; the enchantment, the golden haze which had dazzled my perspicuity at first, had been a good deal dissipated. I can not say I was chagrined or downcast by the contrast which the reality of a pensionnat de demoiselles presented to my vague ideal of the same community; I was only enlightened and amused; consequently, I felt in no disposition to complain to Mdlle. Reuter, and I received her considerate invitation to confidence with a smile.

"A thousand thanks, Mademoiselle; all has gone very smoothly."

She looked more than doubtful.

"Et les trois demoiselles du premier banc?" said she.

"Ah! tout va au mieux," was my answer, and Mdlle. Reuter ceased to question me; but her eye—not large, not brilliant, not melting or kindling, but astute, penetrating, practical, showed she was even with me; it let out a momentary gleam, which said plainly, "Be as close as you like, I am not dependent on your candor; what you would conceal I already know."

By a transition so quiet as to be scarcely perceptible, the directress's manner changed; the anxious, business air passed from her face, and she began chatting about the weather and the town, and asking in neighborly wise after M. and Madame Pelet. I answered all her little questions. She prolonged her

talk; I went on following its many little windings.
She sat so long, said so much, varied so often the topics of discourse, that it was not difficult to perceive she
had a particular aim in thus detaining me.   Her mere
words could have afforded no clew to this aim, but her
countenance aided.   While her lips uttered only affable
commonplaces, her eyes reverted continually to my
face.   Her glances were not given in full, but out of
the corners, so quietly, so stealthily, yet I think I lost
not one.   I watched her as keenly as she watched me.
I perceived soon that she was feeling after my real character; she was searching for salient points, and weak
points, and eccentric points; she was applying now
this test, now that, hoping in the end to find some
chink, some niche, where she could put in her little
firm foot and stand upon my neck—mistress of my nature.   Do not mistake me, reader, it was no amorous
influence she wished to gain ; at that time it was only
the power of the politician to which she aspired.   I
was now installed as a professor in her establishment,
and she wanted to know where her mind was superior
to mine—by what feeling or opinion she could lead
me.

I enjoyed the game much, and did not hasten its
conclusion.   Sometimes I gave her hopes, beginning a
sentence rather weakly, when her shrewd eye would
light up: she thought she had me.   Having led her a
little way, I delighted to turn round and finish with
sound, hard sense, whereat her countenance would fall.
At last a servant entered to announce dinner.   The
conflict being thus necessarily terminated, we parted
without having gained any advantage on either side:

Mdlle. Reuter had not even given me an opportunity of attacking her with feeling, and I had managed to baffle her little schemes of craft. It was a regular drawn battle. I again held out my hand when I left the room ; she gave me hers ; it was a small and white hand, but how cool! I met her eye, too, in full, obliging her to give me a straightforward look. This last test went against me : it left her as it found her —moderate, temperate, tranquil ; me it disappointed.

"I am growing wiser," thought I, as I walked back to M. Pelet's. "Look at this little woman ; is she like the women of novelists and romancers ? To read of female character as depicted in Poetry and Fiction, one would think it was made up of sentiment, either for good or bad. Here is a specimen, and a most sensible and respectable specimen too, whose staple ingredient is abstract reason. No Talleyrand was ever more passionless than Zoraïde Reuter." So I thought then ; I found afterward that blunt susceptibilities are very consistent with strong propensities.

CHAPTER XI.

I HAD indeed had a very long talk with the crafty little politician, and on regaining my quarters I found that dinner was half over. To be late at meals was against a standing rule of the establishment, and, had it been one of the Flemish ushers who thus entered after the removal of the soup and the commencement of the first course, M. Pelet would probably have

greeted him with a public rebuke, and would certainly have mulcted him both of soup and fish ; as it was,
that polite though partial gentleman only shook his
head, and as I took my place, unrolled my napkin,
and said my heretical grace to myself, he civilly dis-
patched a servant to the kitchen to bring me a plate
of "purée aux carrottes" (for this was a maigre-day),
and before sending away the first course reserved for
me a portion of the stock-fish of which it consisted.
Dinner being over, the boys rushed out for their evening play ; Kint and Vandam (the two ushers) of course
followed them.   Poor fellows ! if they had not looked
so very heavy, so very soulless, so very indifferent to
all things in heaven above or in the earth beneath, I
could have pitied them greatly for the obligation they
were under to trail after those rough lads every where
and at all times ; even as it was, I felt disposed to
scout myself as a privileged prig when I turned to ascend to my chamber, sure to find there, if not enjoyment, at least liberty ; but this evening (as had often
happened before) I was to be still further distinguished.

"Eh bien mauvais sujet," said the voice of M. Pelet behind me as I set my foot on the first step of the
stair.   "Où allez-vous ?   Venez à la salle-à manger,
que je vous gronde un peu."

"I beg pardon, Monsieur," said I, as I followed
him to his private sitting-room, "for having returned
so late ; it was not my fault."

"That is just what I want to know," rejoined M.
Pelet, as he ushered me into the comfortable parlor
with a good wood fire, for the stove had now been re-

moved for the season. Having rung the bell, he ordered "coffee for two," and presently he and I were seated, almost in English comfort, one on each side of the hearth, a little round table between us with a coffee-pot, a sugar-basin, and two large white china cups. While M. Pelet employed himself in choosing a cigar from a box, my thoughts reverted to the two outcast ushers, whose voices I could hear even now crying hoarsely for order in the play-ground.

"C'est une grande responsabilité, que la surveillance," observed I.

"Plait-il?" dit M. Pelet.

I remarked that I thought Messieurs Vandam and Kint must sometimes be a little fatigued with their labors.

"Des bêtes de somme—des bêtes de somme," murmured scornfully the director. Meantime I offered him his cup of coffee.

"Servez-vous, mon garçon," said he, blandly, when I had put a couple of huge lumps of Continental sugar into his cup. "And now tell me why you staid so long at Mdlle. Reuter's. I know that lessons conclude, in her establishment as in mine, at four o'clock, and when you returned it was past five."

"Mademoiselle wished to speak with me, Monsieur."

"Indeed! on what subject? if one may ask."

"Mademoiselle talked about nothing, Monsieur."

"A fertile topic. And did she discourse thereon in the school-room, before the pupils?"

"No; like you, Monsieur, she asked me to walk into her parlor."

"And Madame Reuter—the old duenna—my mother's gossip, was there, of course."

"No, Monsieur; I had the honor of being quite alone with Mademoiselle."

"C'est joli—cela," observed M. Pelet; and he smiled and looked into the fire.

"Honi soit qui mal y pense," murmured I, significantly.

"Je connais un peu ma petite voisine—voyez-vous."

"In that case, Monsieur will be able to aid me in finding out what was Mademoiselle's reason for making me sit before her sofa one mortal hour, listening to the most copious and fluent dissertation on the merest frivolities."

"She was sounding your character."

"I thought so, Monsieur."

"Did she find out your weak point?"

"What is my weak point?"

"Why, the sentimental. Any woman, sinking her shaft deep enough, will at last reach a fathomless spring of sensibility in thy breast, Crimsworth."

I felt the blood stir about my heart and rise warm to my cheek.

. "Some women might, Monsieur."

"Is Mdlle. Reuter of the number? Come, speak frankly, mon fils; elle est encore jeune, plus agée que toi peutêtre, mais juste assez pour unir la tendresse d'une petite maman à l'amour d'une épouse dévouée; n'est-ce pas que cela t'irait supérieurement?"

"No, Monsieur; I should like my wife to be my wife, and not half my mother."

" She is, then, a little too old for you ?"

" No, Monsieur, not a day too old, if she suited me in other things."

" In what does she not suit you, William ? She is personally agreeable, is she not ?"

" Very; her hair and complexion are just what I admire, and her turn of form, though quite Belgian, is full of grace."

" Bravo! and her face—her features—how do you like them ?"

" A little harsh, especially her mouth."

" Ah! yes, her mouth," said M. Pelet, and he chuckled inwardly. " There is character about her mouth—firmness—but she has a very pleasant smile; don't you think so ?"

" Rather crafty."

" True; but that expression of craft is owing to her eyebrows. Have you remarked her eyebrows ?"

I answered that I had not.

" You have not seen her looking down, then?" said he.

" No."

" It is a treat, notwithstanding. Observe her when she has some knitting, or some other woman's work in hand, and sits the image of peace, calmly intent on her needles and her silk, some discussion meantime going on around her, in the course of which peculiarities of character are being developed, or important interests canvassed. She takes no part in it; her humble, feminine mind is wholly with her knitting; none of her features move; she neither presumes to smile approval nor frown disapprobation; her little hands assiduously ply their unpretending task; if she can only get this purse finished, or this bonnet-grec completed, it is enough for her. If gentlemen approach her chair, a deeper quiescence, a meeker modesty settles on her features, and clothes her general mien; observe then her eyebrows, et dîtes-moi s'il n'y a pas du chat dans l'un et du renard dans l'autre."

" I will take careful notice the first opportunity," said I.

" And then," continued M. Pelet, "the eyelid will flicker, the light-colored lashes be lifted a second, and a blue eye, glancing out from under the screen, will take its brief, sly, searching survey, and retreat again."

I smiled, and so did Pelet; and, after a few minutes' silence, I asked,

" Will she ever marry, do you think ?"

" Marry ! Will birds pair ? Of course it is both her intention and resolution to marry when she finds a suitable match, and no one is better aware than herself of the sort of impression she is capable of producing; no one likes better to captivate in a quiet way. I am mistaken if she will not yet leave the print of her stealing steps on thy heart, Crimsworth."

" Of her steps ? Confound it, no! My heart is not a plank to be walked on."

" But the soft touch of a patte de velours will do it no harm."

" She offers me no patte de velours; she is all form and reserve with me."

" That to begin with ; let respect be the foundation, affection the first floor, love the superstructure; Mdlle. Reuter is a skillful architect."

"And interest, M. Pelet—interest. Will not Mademoiselle consider that point?"

"Yes, yes, no doubt; it will be the cement between every stone. And now we have discussed the directress, what of the pupils? N'y-a-t-il pas de belles études parmi ces jeunes têtes?"

"Studies of character? Yes; curious ones, at least, I imagine; but one can not divine much from a first interview."

"Ah! you affect discretion; but tell me now, were you not a little abashed before those blooming young creatures?"

"At first, yes; but I rallied and got through with all due sang froid."

"I don't believe you."

"It is true, notwithstanding. At first I thought them angels, but they did not leave me long under that delusion; three of the eldest and handsomest undertook the task of setting me right, and they managed so cleverly that in five minutes I knew *them*, at least, for what they were—three arrant coquettes."

"Je les connais," exclaimed M. Pelet. "Elles sont toujours au premier rang à l'eglise et à la promenade; une blonde superbe, une jolie espiègle, une belle brune."

"Exactly."

"Lovely creatures, all of them—heads for artists! what a group they would make, taken together! Eulalie (I know their names), with her smooth braided hair, and calm ivory brow; Hortense, with her rich chestnut locks so luxuriantly knotted, plaited, twisted, as if she did not know how to dispose of all their abundance, with her vermilion lips, damask cheek, and roguish, laughing eye; and Caroline de Blémont! Ah! there is beauty—beauty in perfection. What a cloud of sable curls about the face of a houri! What fascinating lips! What glorious black eyes! Your Byron would have worshiped her; and you—you cold, frigid islander—you played the austere, the insensible in the presence of an Aphrodite so exquisite?"

I might have laughed at the director's enthusiasm had I believed it real, but there was something in his tone which indicated got-up raptures. I felt he was only affecting fervor in order to put me off my guard, to induce me to come out in return, so I scarcely even smiled. He went on:

"Confess, William, do not the mere good looks of Zoraïde Reuter appear dowdyish and commonplace compared with the splendid charms of some of her pupils?"

The question discomposed me; but I now felt plainly that my principal was endeavoring (for reasons best known to himself—at that time I could not fathom them) to excite ideas and wishes in my mind alien to what was right and honorable. The iniquity of the instigation proved its antidote; and when he further added,

"Each of those three beautiful girls will have a handsome fortune; and with a little address, a gentlemanlike, intelligent young fellow like you might make himself master of the hand, heart, and purse of any one of the trio."

I replied by a look and an interrogative "Monsieur?" which startled him.

He laughed a forced laugh, affirmed that he had only been joking, and demanded whether I could possibly have thought him in earnest. Just then the bell rang; the play-hour was over; it was an evening on which M. Pelet was accustomed to read passages from the drama and the belles-lettres to his pupils. He did not wait for my answer, but, rising, left the room, humming as he went some gay strain of Béranger's.

CHAPTER XII.

DAILY, as I continued my attendance at the seminary of Mdlle. Reuter, did I find fresh occasions to compare the ideal with the real. What had I known of female character previously to my arrival at Brussels? Precious little. And what was my notion of it? Something vague, slight, gauzy, glittering; now, when I came in contact with it, I found it to be a palpable substance enough; very hard too sometimes, and often heavy; there was metal in it, both lead and iron.

Let the idealists, the dreamers about earthly angels and human flowers, just look here while I open my portfolio and show them a sketch or two, penciled after nature. I took these sketches in the second-class school-room of Mdlle. Reuter's establishment, where about a hundred specimens of the genus "jeune fille" collected together offered a fertile variety of subject. A miscellaneous assortment they were, differing both in caste and country. As I sat on my estrade and

glanced over the long range of desks, I had under my
eye French, English, Belgians, Austrians, and Prus-
sians. The majority belonged to the class bourgeois;
but there were many comtesses—there were the daughters of two generals and of several colonels, captains,
and government employés: these ladies sat side by
side with young females destined to be demoiselles de
magasins, and with some Flamandes, genuine aborig-
inés of the country. In dress all were nearly similar,
and in manners there was small difference; exceptions
there were to the general rule, but the majority gave
the tone to the establishment, and that tone was rough,
boisterous, marked by a point-blank disregard of all
forbearance toward each other or their teachers; an
eager pursuit by each individual of her own interest
and convenience, and a coarse indifference to the interest and convenience of every one else. Most of
them could lie with audacity when it appeared advantageous to do so. All understood the art of speaking
fair when a point was to be gained, and could with
consummate skill and at a moment's notice turn the
cold shoulder the instant civility ceased to be profitable. Very little open quarreling ever took place among
them, but backbiting and tale-bearing were universal.
Close friendships were forbidden by the rules of the
school, and no one girl seemed to cultivate more regard for another than was just necessary to secure a
companion when solitude would have been irksome.
They were each and all supposed to have been reared
in utter unconsciousness of vice. The precautions
used to keep them ignorant, if not innocent, were innumerable. How was it, then, that scarcely one of

those girls having attained the age of fourteen could
look a man in the face with modesty and propriety?
An air of bold, impudent flirtation, or a loose, silly
leer, was sure to answer the most ordinary glance from
a masculine eye. I know nothing of the arcana of the
Roman Catholic religion, and I am not a bigot in matters of theology, but I suspect the root of this precocious impurity, so obvious, so general in Popish countries, is to be found in the discipline, if not the doc-
trines of the Church of Rome. I record what I have
seen: these girls belonged to what are called the respectable ranks of society; they had all been carefully
brought up, yet was the mass of them mentally depraved. So much for the general view; now for one
or two selected specimens.

The first picture is a full-length of Aurelia Koslow,
a German fräulein, or rather a half-breed between German and Russian. She is eighteen years of age, and
has been sent to Brussels to finish her education.
She is of middle size, stiffly made, body long, legs
short, bust much developed but not compactly moulded, waist disproportionately compressed by an inhu-
manly braced corset, dress carefully arranged, large
feet tortured into small bottines, head small, hair
smoothed, braided, oiled, and gummed to perfection;
very low forehead, very diminutive and vindictive gray
eyes, somewhat Tartar features, rather flat nose, rather high cheek-bones, yet the ensemble not positively
ugly; tolerably good complexion. So much for person. As to mind, deeply ignorant and ill-informed;
incapable of writing or speaking correctly even German, her native tongue; a dunce in French, and her

F

attempts at learning English a mere farce, yet she has been at school twelve years; but as she invariably gets her exercises, of every description, done by a fellow-pupil, and reads her lessons off a book concealed in her lap, it is not wonderful that her progress has been so snail-like. I do not know what Aurelia's daily habits of life are, because I have not the opportunity of observing her at all times; but from what I see of the state of her desk, books, and papers, I should say she is slovenly and even dirty. Her outward dress, as I have said, is well attended to, but in passing behind her bench I have remarked that her neck is gray for want of washing, and her hair, so glossy with gum and grease, is not such as one feels tempted to pass the hand over, much less to run the fingers through. Aurelia's conduct in class, at least when I am present, is something extraordinary, considered as an index of girlish innocence. The moment I enter the room she nudges her next neighbor and indulges in a half-suppressed laugh. As I take my seat on the estrade she fixes her eye on me. She seems resolved to attract, and, if possible, monopolize my notice: to this end she launches at me all sorts of looks, languishing, provoking, leering, laughing. As I am found quite proof against this sort of artillery—for we scorn what, unasked, is lavishly offered—she has recourse to the expedient of making noises; sometimes she sighs, sometimes groans, sometimes utters inarticulate sounds for which language has no name. If, in walking up the school-room, I pass near her, she puts out her foot that it may touch mine; if I do not happen to observe the manœuvre, and my boot comes in contact with her brodequin, she affects to fall into convulsions of suppressed laughter; if I notice the snare and avoid it, she expresses her mortification in sullen muttering, where I hear myself abused in bad French, pronounced with an intolerable low German accent.

Not far from Mdlle. Koslow sits another young lady, by name Adèle Dronsart: this is a Belgian, rather low of stature, in form heavy, with broad waist, short neck and limbs, good red and white complexion, features well chiseled and regular, well-cut eyes of a clear brown color, light brown hair, good teeth, age not much above fifteen, but as full grown as a stout young Englishwoman of twenty. This portrait gives the idea of a somewhat dumpy but good-looking damsel, does it not? Well, when I looked along the row of young heads, my eye generally stopped at this of Adèle's; her gaze was ever waiting for mine, and it frequently succeeded in arresting it. She was an unnatural-looking being—so young, fresh, blooming, yet so Gorgon-like. Suspicion, sullen ill temper were on her forehead, vicious propensities in her eye, envy and panther-like deceit about her mouth. In general she sat very still; her massive shape looked as if it could not bend much, nor did her large head—so broad at the base, so narrow toward the top—seem made to turn readily on her short neck. She had but two varieties of expression; the prevalent one a forbidding, dissatisfied scowl, varied sometimes by a most pernicious and perfidious smile. She was shunned by her fellow-pupils; for, bad as many of them were, few were as bad as she.

Aurelia and Adèle were in the first division of the second class; the second division was headed by a

pensionnaire named Juanna Trista. This girl was of
mixed Belgian and Spanish origin. Her Flemish mother was dead; her Catalonian father was a merchant,
residing in the —— Isles, where Juanna had been
born, and' whence she was sent to Europe to be edu-
cated. I wonder that any one, looking at that girl's
head and countenance, would have received her under
their roof. She had precisely the same shape of skull
as Pope Alexander the Sixth. Her organs of benevolence, veneration, conscientiousness, adhesiveness,
were singularly small; those of self-esteem, firmness,
destructiveness, combativeness, preposterously large.
Her head sloped up in the pent-house shape, was contracted about the forehead, and prominent behind. She
had rather good, though large and marked features.
Her temperament was fibrous and bilious, her complexion pale and dark, hair and eyes black, form an-
gular and rigid, but proportionate; age fifteen.

Juanna was not very thin, but she had a gaunt visage, and her "regard" was fierce and hungry. Narrow as was her brow, it presented space enough for
the legible graving of two words, Mutiny and Hate.
In some one of her other lineaments—I think the eye
—cowardice had also its distinct cipher. Mdlle. Trista
thought fit to trouble my first lessons with a coarse,
work-day sort of turbulence. She made noises with
her mouth like a horse, she ejected her saliva, she uttered brutal expressions; behind and below her were
seated a band of very vulgar, inferior-looking Flamandes, including two or three examples of that deformity
of person and imbecility of intellect whose frequency
in the Low Countries would seem to furnish proof that

the climate is such as to induce degeneracy of the human mind and body; these, I soon found, were completely under her influence, and with their aid she got up and sustained a swinish tumult, which I was constrained at last to quell by ordering her and two of her tools to rise from their seats, and, having kept them standing five minutes, turning them bodily out of the school-room; the accomplices into a large place adjoining called the grand salle, the principal into a cabinet, of which I closed the door and pocketed the key. This judgment I executed in the presence of Mdlle. Reuter, who looked much aghast at beholding so decided a proceeding—the most severe that had ever been ventured on in her establishment. Her look of affright I answered with one of composure, and finally with a smile, which perhaps flattered and certainly soothed her. Juanna Trista remained in Europe long enough to repay, by malevolence and ingratitude, all who had ever done her a good turn, and she then went to join her father in the —— Isles, exulting in the thought that she should there have slaves, whom, as she said, she could kick and strike at will.

These three pictures are from the life. I possess others, as marked and as little agreeable, but I will spare my reader the exhibition of them.

Doubtless it will be thought that I ought now, by way of contrast, to show something charming; some gentle virgin head circled with a halo; some sweet personification of innocence, clasping the dove of peace to her bosom. No, I saw nothing of the sort, and therefore can not portray it. The pupil in the school possessing the happiest disposition was a young girl

from the country, Louise Path. She was sufficiently
benevolent and obliging, but not well taught nor well
mannered; moreover, the plague-spot of dissimulation
was in her also; honor and principle were unknown to
her—she had scarcely heard their names. The least
exceptionable pupil was the poor little Sylvie I have
mentioned once before. Sylvie was gentle in manners,
intelligent in mind; she was even sincere, as far as her
religion would permit her to be so, but her physical
organization was defective. Weak health stunted her
growth and chilled her spirits, and then, destined as
she was for the cloister, her whole soul was warped
to a conventual bias, and in the tame, trained subjection of her manner, one read that she had already prepared herself for her future course of life by giving up
her independence of thought and action into the hands
of some despotic confessor. She permitted herself no
original opinion, no preference of companion or employment; in every-thing she was guided by another.
With a pale, passive, automaton air, she went about
all day long doing what she was bid; never what she
liked, or what, from innate conviction, she thought it
right to do. The poor little future religieuse had been
early taught to make the dictates of her own reason
and conscience quite subordinate to the will of her
spiritual director. She was the model pupil of Mdlle.
Reuter's establishment; pale, blighted image, where
life lingered feebly, but whence the soul had been con-
jured by Romish wizard-craft.

A few English pupils there were in this school, and
these might be divided into two classes. 1st. The
Continental English—the daughters chiefly of broken

adventurers whom debt or dishonor had driven from their own country. These poor girls had never known the advantages of settled homes, decorous example, or honest Protestant education. Resident a few months now in one Catholic school, now in another, as their parents wandered from land to land—from France to Germany, from Germany to Belgium—they had picked up some scanty instruction, many bad habits, losing every notion even of the first elements of religion and morals, and acquiring an imbecile indifference to every sentiment that can elevate humanity; they were distinguishable by an habitual look of sullen dejection, the result of crushed self-respect and constant browbeating from their Popish fellow-pupils, who hated them as English, and scorned them as heretics.

The second class were British English. Of these I did not encounter half a dozen during the whole time of my attendance at the seminary. Their characteristics were clean but careless dress, ill-arranged hair (compared with the tight and trim foreigners), erect carriage, flexible figures, white and taper hands, features more irregular, but also more intellectual than those of the Belgians, grave and modest countenances, a general air of native propriety and decency; by this last circumstance alone I could at a glance distinguish the daughter of Albion and nursling of Protestantism from the foster-child of Rome, the *protégé* of Jesuitry. Proud, too, was the aspect of these British girls. At once envied and ridiculed by their Continental associates, they warded off insult with austere civility, and met hate with mute disdain; they eschewed company-keeping, and in the midst of numbers seemed to dwell isolated.

The teachers presiding over this mixed multitude were three in number, all French—their names Mdlles. Zéphyrine, Pélagie, and Suzette. The two last were commonplace personages enough; their look was ordinary, their manner was ordinary, their temper was ordinary, their thoughts, feelings, and views were all ordinary; were I to write a chapter on the subject, I could not elucidate further. Zéphyrine was somewhat more distinguished in appearance and deportment than Pélagie and Suzette, but in character a genuine Parisian coquette, perfidious, mercenary, and dry-hearted. A fourth maîtresse I sometimes saw, who seemed to come daily to teach needlework, or netting, or lace-mending, or some such flimsy art, but of her I never had more than a passing glimpse, as she sat in the carré, with her frames and some dozen of the elder pupils about her, consequently I had no opportunity of studying her character, or even of observing her person much; the latter, I remarked, had a very girlish air for a maîtresse, otherwise it was not striking; of character I should think she possessed but little, as her pupils seemed constantly "en revolte" against her authority. She did not reside in the house; her name, I think, was Mdlle. Henri.

Amid this assemblage of all that was insignificant and defective, much that was vicious and repulsive (by that last epithet many would have described the two or three stiff, silent, decently-behaved, ill-dressed British girls), the sensible, sagacious, affable directress shone like a steady star over a marsh full of Jack-o'-lanterns. Profoundly aware of her superiority, she derived an inward bliss from that consciousness which

sustained her under all the care and responsibility inseparable from her position; it kept her temper calm,
her brow smooth, her manner tranquil.   She liked—
as who would not?—on entering the school-room, to
feel that her sole presence sufficed to diffuse that order
and quiet which all the remonstrances, and even com-
mands of her underlings frequently failed to enforce;
she liked to stand in comparison, or rather contrast, with
those who surrounded her, and to know that in personal as well as mental advantages she bore away the
undisputed palm of preference—(the three teachers
were all plain).   Her pupils she managed with such
indulgence and address, taking always on herself the
office of recompenser and eulogist, and abandoning to
her subalterns every invidious task of blame and punishment, that they all regarded her with deference, if
not with affection.   Her teachers did not love her, but
they submitted bacause they were her inferiors in every thing.   The various masters who attended her
school were each and all in some way or other under
her influence : over one she had acquired power by her
skillful management of his bad temper; over another
by little attentions to his petty caprices; a third she
had subdued by flattery ; a fourth—a timid man—
she kept in awe by a sort of austere decision of mien ;
me she still watched, still tried by the most ingenious
tests.   She roved round me, baffled, yet persevering ;
I believe she thought I was like a smooth and bare
precipice, which offered neither jutting stone, nor tree-
root, nor tuft of grass to aid the climber.   Now she
flattered with exquisite tact, now she moralized, now
she tried how far I was accessible to mercenary mo-

F 2

tives; then she disported on the brink of affectation, knowing that some men are won by weakness; anon she talked excellent sense, aware that others have the folly to admire judgment. I found it at once pleasant and easy to evade all these efforts. It was sweet, when she thought me nearly won, to turn round and to smile in her very eyes, half scornfully, and then to witness her scarcely veiled though mute mortification. —Still she persevered, and at last, I am bound to confess it, her finger, essaying, proving every atom of the casket, touched its secret spring, and for a moment the lid sprung open. She laid her hand on the jewel within. Whether she stole and broke it, or whether the lid shut again with a snap on her fingers, read on, and you shall know.

It happened that I came one day to give a lesson when I was indisposed. I had a bad cold and a cough; two hours' incessant talking left me very hoarse and tired. As I quitted the school-room, and was passing along the corridor, I met Mdlle. Reuter. She remarked, with an anxious air, that I looked very pale and tired. "Yes," I said, "I was fatigued;" and then, with increased interest, she rejoined, "You shall not go away till you have had some refreshment." She persuaded me to step into the parlor, and was very kind and gentle while I staid. The next day she was kinder still. She came herself into the class to see that the windows were closed, and that there was no draught; she exhorted me with friendly earnestness not to over-exert myself; when I went away, she gave me her hand unasked, and I could not but mark, by a respectful and gentle pressure, that I was sensible of the favor, and grateful for it. My modest demonstration kindled a little merry smile on her countenance; I thought her almost charming. •During the remainder of the evening my mind was full of impatience for the afternoon of the next day to arrive, that I might see her again.

I was not disappointed, for she sat in the class during the whole of my subsequent lesson, and often looked at me almost with affection. At four o'clock she accompanied me out of the school-room, asking with solicitude after my health, then scolding me sweetly because I spoke too loud and gave myself too much trouble. I stopped at the glass door which led into the garden to hear her lecture to the end; the door was open; it was a very fine day, and while I listened to the soothing reprimand, I looked at the sunshine and the flowers, and felt very happy. The day-scholars began to pour from the school-rooms into the passage.

"Will you go into the garden a minute or two," asked she, "till they are gone?"

I descended the steps without answering, but looked back as much as to say,

"You will come with me?"

In another minute I and the directress were walk-.ing side by side down the alley bordered with fruit-trees, whose white blossoms were then in full blow, as well as their tender green leaves. The sky was blue, the air still, the May afternoon was full of brightness and fragrance. Released from the stifling class, surrounded with flowers and foliage, with a pleasing, smiling, affable woman at my side, how did I feel? Why,

very enviably. It seemed as if the romantic visions
my imagination had suggested of this garden, while it
was yet hidden from me by the jealous boards, were
more than realized; and when a turn in the alley shut
out the view of the house, and some tall shrubs excluded M. Pelet's mansion, and screened us momentarily from the other houses, rising amphitheatre-like
round this green spot, I gave my arm to Mdlle. Reuter, and led her to a garden chair nestled under some
lilacs near. She sat down; I took my place at her
side. She went on talking to me with that ease which
communicates ease, and, as I listened, a revelation
dawned in my mind that I was on the brink of falling
in love. The dinner-bell rang, both at her house and
M. Pelet's; we were obliged to part; I detained her a
moment as she was moving away.

"I want something," said I.

"What?" asked Zoraïde, naïvely.

"Only a flower."

"Gather it, then—or two, or twenty, if you like."

"No, one will do, but you must gather it, and give
it to me."

"What a caprice!" she exclaimed; but she raised
herself on her tip-toes, and, plucking a beautiful branch
of lilac, offered it to me with grace. I took it and
went away, satisfied for the present, and hopeful for
the future.

Certainly that May day was a lovely one, and it
closed in a moonlight night of summer warmth and
serenity. I remember this well; for, having sat up
late that evening, correcting devoirs, and feeling weary
and a little oppressed with the closeness of my small

room, I opened the often-mentioned boarded window, whose boards, however, I had persuaded old Madame Pelet to have removed since I had filled the post of professor in the pensionnat de demoiselles, as from that time it was no longer "inconvenient" for me to over- look my own pupils at their sports. I sat down in the window-seat, rested my arm on the sill, and leaned out. Above me was the clear-obscure of a cloudless night sky; splendid moonlight subdued the tremulous sparkle of the stars; below lay the garden, varied with silvery lustre and deep shade, and all fresh with dew; a grateful perfume exhaled from the closed blossoms of the fruit-trees; not a leaf stirred; the night was breezeless. My window looked directly down upon a certain walk of Mdlle. Reuter's garden, called "l'allée défendue," so named because the pupils were forbid- den to enter it on account of its proximity to the boys' school. It was here that the lilacs and laburnums grew especially thick; this was the most sheltered nook in the inclosure; its shrubs screened the garden chair where that afternoon I had sat with the young directress. I need not say that my thoughts were chiefly with her as I leaned from the lattice, and let my eye roam, now over the walks and borders of the garden, now along the many-windowed front of the house which rose white beyond the masses of foliage. I wondered in what part of the building was situated her apartment; and a single light, shining through the persiennes of one croisée, seemed to direct me to it.

"She watches late," thought I, "for it must be now near midnight. She is a fascinating little woman," I continued, in voiceless soliloquy; "her image forms a pleasant picture in memory. I know she is not what the world calls pretty: no matter; there is harmony in her aspect, and I like it; her brown hair, her blue eye, the freshness of her cheek, the whiteness of her neck, all suit my taste. Then I respect her talent; the idea of marrying a doll or a fool was always abhorrent to me. I know that a pretty doll, a fair fool, might do well enough for the honeymoon; but when passion cooled, how dreadful to find a lump of wax and wood laid in my bosom, a half idiot clasped in my arms, and to remember that I had made of this my equal—nay, my idol; to know that I must pass the rest of my dreary life with a creature incapable of understanding what I said, of appreciating what I thought, or of sympathizing with what I felt! Now Zoraïde Reuter," thought I, "has tact, 'caractère,' judgment, discretion; has she heart? What a good, simple little smile played about her lips when she gave me the branch of lilacs! I have thought her crafty, dissembling, interested sometimes, it is true; but may not much that looks like cunning and dissimulation in her conduct be only the efforts made by a bland temper to traverse quietly perplexing difficulties? And as to interest, she wishes to make her way in the world, no doubt, and who can blame her? Even if she be truly deficient in sound principle, is it not rather her misfortune than her fault? She has been brought up a Catholic. Had she been born an English woman, and reared a Protestant, might she not have added straight integrity to all her other excellencies? Supposing she were to marry an English and Protestant husband, would she not, rational, sensible as she is, quickly acknowledge the superiority of right over expediency, honesty over policy? It would be worth a man's while to try the experiment; to-morrow I will renew my observations. She knows that I watch her: how calm she is under scrutiny! it seems rather to gratify than annoy her." Here a strain of music stole in upon my monologue and suspended it: it was a bugle, very skillfully played, in the neighborhood of the park, I thought, or on the Place Royale. So sweet were the tones, so subduing their effect at that hour, in the midst of silence and under the quiet reign of moonlight, I ceased to think, that I might listen more intently. The strain retreated; its sound waxed fainter and was soon gone; my ear prepared to repose on the absolute hush of midnight once more. No. What murmur was that which, low, and yet near and approaching nearer, frustrated the expectation of total silence? It was some one conversing — yes, evidently, an audible though subdued voice spoke in the garden immediately below me. Another answered: the first voice was that of a man, the second that of a woman; and a man and a woman I saw coming slowly down the alley. Their forms were at first in shade; I could but discern a dusk outline of each, but a ray of moonlight met them at the termination of the walk, when they were under my very nose, and revealed very plainly, very unequivocally, Mdlle. Zoraïde Reuter arm in arm or hand in hand (I forget which) with my principal, confidant, and counselor, M. François Pelet. And M. Pelet was saying,

" A quand donc le jour des noces, ma bien-aimée ?"
And Mdlle. Reuter answered,

" Mais, François, tu sais bien qu'il me serait impossible de me marier avant les vacances."

" June, July, August, a whole quarter !" exclaimed the director. " How can I wait so long—I, who am ready, even now, to expire at your feet with impatience."

" Ah! if you die, the whole affair will be settled without any trouble about notaries and contracts. I shall only have to order a slight mourning dress, which will be much sooner prepared than the nuptial trousseau."

" Cruel Zoraïde, you laugh at the distress of one who loves you so devotedly as I do ; my torment is your sport ; you scruple not to stretch my soul on the rack of jealousy ; for, deny it as you will, I am certain you have cast encouraging glances on that school-boy, Crimsworth ; he has presumed to fall in love, which he dared not have done unless you had given him room to hope."

" What do you say, François ? Do you say Crimsworth is in love with me ?"

" Over head and ears."

" Has he told you so ?"

" No ; but I see it in his face : he blushes whenever your name is mentioned."

A little laugh of exulting coquetry announced Mdlle. Reuter's gratification at this piece of intelligence (which was a lie, by-the-by ; I had never been so far gone as that, after all). M. Pelet proceeded to ask what she intended to do with me, intimating pretty plainly, and

not very gallantly, that it was nonsense for her to think
of taking such a "blanc-bec" as a husband, since she
must be at least ten years older than I (was she then
thirty-two? I should not have thought it). I heard
her disclaim any intentions on the subject. The director, however, still pressed her to give a definite answer.

"François," said she, "you are jealous," and still
she laughed; then, as if suddenly recollecting that this
coquetry was not consistent with the character for
modest dignity she wished to establish, she proceeded,
in a demure voice, "Truly, my dear François, I will
not deny that this young Englishman may have made
some attempts to ingratiate himself with me, but, so far
from giving him any encouragement, I have always
treated him with as much reserve as it was possible to
combine with civility; affianced as I am to you, I
would give no man false hopes; believe me, dear
friend."

Still Pelet uttered murmurs of distrust; so I judged,
at least, from her reply.

"What folly! How could I prefer an unknown
foreigner to you? And then—not to flatter your vanity—Crimsworth could not bear comparison with you
either physically or mentally. He is not a handsome
man at all; some may call him gentleman-like and in-
telligent-looking, but, for my part—"

The rest of the sentence was lost in the distance, as
the pair, rising from the chair in which they had been
seated, moved away. I waited their return, but soon
the opening and shutting of a door informed me that
they had re-entered the house. I listened a little lon-

ger; all was perfectly still. I continued to listen for
more than an hour; at last I heard M. Pelet come in
and ascend to his chamber. Glancing once more toward the long front of the garden-house, I perceived
that its solitary light was at length extinguished; so,
for a time, was my faith in love and friendship. I
went to bed, but something feverish and fiery had got
into my veins which prevented me from sleeping much
that night.

CHAPTER XIII.

NEXT morning I rose with the dawn, and having
dressed myself, and stood half an hour, my elbow leaning on the chest of drawers, considering what means I
should adopt to restore my spirits, fagged with sleep-
lessness, to their ordinary tone—for I had no intention
of getting up a scene with M. Pelet, reproaching him
with perfidy, sending him a challenge, or performing
other gambadoes of the sort—I hit at last on the expedient of walking out in the cool of the morning to a
neighboring establishment of baths, and treating myself to a bracing plunge. The remedy produced the
desired effect. I came back at seven o'clock steadied
and invigorated, and was able to greet M. Pelet, when
he entered to breakfast, with an unchanged and tranquil countenance. Even a cordial offering of the hand
and the flattering appellation of "mon fils," pronounced
in that caressing tone with which Monsieur had, of late
days especially, been accustomed to address me, did
not elicit any external sign of the feeling which, though

subdued, still glowed at my heart. Not that I nursed
vengeance—no; but the sense of insult and treachery
lived in me like a kindling, though as yet smothered
coal. God knows I am not by nature vindictive. I
would not hurt a man because I can no longer trust or
like him; but neither my reason nor feelings are of the
vacillating order; they are not of that sand-like sort
where impressions, if soon made, are as soon effaced.
Once convinced that my friend's disposition is incompatible with my own, once assured that he is indelibly
stained with certain defects obnoxious to my principles, and I dissolve the connection. I did so with
Edward. As to Pelet, the discovery was yet new;
should I act thus with him? It was the question I
placed before my mind as I stirred my cup of coffee
with a half pistolet (we never had spoons), Pelet meantime being seated opposite, his pallid face looking as
knowing and more haggard than usual, his blue eye
turned, now sternly on his boys and ushers, and now
graciously on me.

"Circumstances must guide me," said I; and meeting Pelet's false glance and insinuating smile, I thanked heaven that I had last night opened my window
and read by the light of a full moon the true meaning
of that guileful countenance. I felt half his master,
because the reality of his nature was now known to
me; smile and flatter as he would, I saw his soul lurk
behind his smile, and heard in every one of his smooth
phrases a voice interpreting their treacherous import.

But Zoraïde Reuter—of course, her defection had
cut me to the quick? That sting must have gone too
deep for any consolations of philosophy to be available

in curing its smart? Not at all. The night fever
over, I looked about for balm to that wound also, and
found some nearer home than at Gilead. Reason was
my physician. She began by proving that the prize
I had missed was of little value. She admitted that,
physically, Zoraïde might have suited me, but affirmed that our souls were not in harmony, and that discord must have resulted from the union of her mind
with mine. She then insisted on the suppression of
all repining, and commanded me rather to rejoice that
I had escaped a snare. Her medicament did me good.
I felt its strengthening effect when I met the directress
the next day; its stringent operation on the nerves
suffered no trembling, no faltering; it enabled me to
face her with firmness, to pass her with ease. She
had held out her hand to me—that I did not choose to
see. She had greeted me with a charming smile—it
fell on my heart like light on stone. I passed on to
the estrade—she followed me. Her eye, fastened on
my face, demanded of every feature the meaning of
my changed and careless manner. " I will give her
an answer," thought I; and, meeting her gaze full, arresting, fixing her glance, I shot into her eyes from my
own a look where there was no respect, no love, no
tenderness, no gallantry; where the strictest analysis
could detect nothing but scorn, hardihood, irony. I
made her bear it, and feel it. Her steady countenance
did not change, but her color rose, and she approached
me as if fascinated. She stepped on to the estrade,
and stood close by my side. She had nothing to say.
I would not relieve her embarrassment, and negligent-
ly turned over the leaves of a book.

"I hope you feel quite recovered to-day," at last she said, in a low tone.

"And I, Mademoiselle, hope that you took no cold last night in consequence of your late walk in the garden."

Quick enough of comprehension, she understood me directly. Her face became a little blanched—a very little, but no muscle in her rather marked features moved; and, calm and self-possessed, she retired from the estrade, taking her seat quietly at a little distance, and occupying herself with netting a purse. I proceeded to give my lesson: it was a "Composition," *i. e.*, I dictated certain general questions, of which the pupils were to compose the answers from memory, access to books being forbidden. While Mdlle. Eulalie, Hortense, Caroline, &c., were pondering over the string of rather abstruse grammatical interrogatories I had propounded, I was at liberty to employ the vacant half hour in further observing the directress herself. The green silk purse was progressing fast in her hands; her eyes were bent upon it; her attitude, as she sat netting within two yards of me, was still yet guarded; in her whole person were expressed, at once, and with equal clearness, vigilance and repose—a rare union. Looking at her, I was forced, as I had often been before, to offer her good sense, her wondrous self-control, the tribute of involuntary admiration. She had felt that I had withdrawn from her my esteem; she had seen contempt and coldness in my eye, and to her, who coveted the approbation of all around her, who thirsted after universal good opinion, such discovery must have been an acute wound. I had witnessed its effect in the momentary pallor of her cheek—cheek unused to vary; yet how quickly, by dint of self-control, had she recovered her composure! With what quiet dignity she now sat, almost at my side, sustained by her sound and vigorous sense; no trembling in her somewhat lengthened though shrewd upper lip, no coward shame on her austere forehead.

"There is metal there," I said, as I gazed. "Would that there were fire also—living ardor to make the steel glow—then I could love her."

Presently I discovered that she knew I was watching her, for she stirred not, she lifted not her crafty eyelid. She had glanced down from her netting to her small foot, peeping from the soft folds of her purple merino gown; thence her eye reverted to her hand, ivory white, with a bright garnet ring on the forefinger, and a light frill of lace round the wrist; with a scarcely perceptible movement she turned her head, causing her nut-brown curls to wave gracefully. In these slight signs I read that the wish of her heart, the design of her brain, was to lure back the game she had scared. A little incident gave her the opportunity of addressing me again.

While all was silence in the class—silence but for the rustling of copy-books and the traveling of pens over their pages—a leaf of the large folding-door, opening from the hall, unclosed, admitting a pupil who, after making a hasty obeisance, ensconced herself with some appearance of trepidation, probably occasioned by her entering so late, in a vacant seat at the desk nearest the door. Being seated, she proceeded, still with an air of hurry and embarrassment, to open her cabas, to take out her books; and, while I was waiting for her to look up, in order to make out her identity—for, short-sighted as I was, I had not recognized her at her entrance—Mdlle. Reuter, leaving her chair, approached the estrade.

"Monsieur Creemsvort," said she, in a whisper— for, when the school-rooms were silent, the directress always moved with velvet tread, and spoke in the most subdued key, enforcing order and stillness fully as much by example as precept—"Monsieur Creemsvort, that young person who has just entered wishes to have the advantage of taking lessons with you in English. She is not a pupil of the house. She is, indeed, in one sense, a teacher, for she gives instruc- tion in lace-mending, and in little varieties of orna- mental needle-work. She very properly proposes to qualify herself for a higher department of education, and has asked permission to attend your lessons, in order to perfect her knowledge of English, in which language she has, I believe, already made some prog- ress; of course, it is my wish to aid her in an effort so praiseworthy; you will permit her, then, to benefit by your instruction—n'est ce pas, Monsieur?" And Mdlle. Reuter's eyes were raised to mine with a look at once naïve, benign, and beseeching.

I replied, "Of course," very laconically, almost ab- ruptly.

"Another word," she said, with softness; "Mdlle. Henri has not received a regular education; perhaps her natural talents are not of the highest order; but I can assure you of the excellence of her intentions, and even of the amiability of her disposition. Monsieur

will then, I am sure, have the goodness to be considerate with her at first, and not expose her backward-
ness, her inevitable deficiencies, before the young ladies, who, in a sense, are her pupils. Will Monsieur
Creemsvort favor me by attending to this hint?" I
nodded. She continued with subdued earnestness,

"Pardon me, Monsieur, if I venture to add that
what I have just said is of importance to the poor
girl. She already experiences great difficulty in im-
pressing these giddy young things with a due degree
of deference for her authority, and should that difficulty be increased by new discoveries of her incapaci-
ty, she might find her position in my establishment
too painful to be retained; a circumstance I should
much regret for her sake, as she can ill afford to lose
the profits of her occupation here."

Mdlle. Reuter possessed marvelous tact; but tact ·
the most exquisite, unsupported by sincerity, will
sometimes fail of its effect; thus, on this occasion, the
longer she preached about the necessity of being in-
dulgent to the governess-pupil, the more impatient I
felt as I listened. I discerned so clearly that while
her professed motive was a wish to aid the dull, though
well-meaning Mdlle. Henri, her real one was no other
than a design to impress me with an idea of her own
exalted goodness and tender considerateness; so, having again hastily nodded assent to her remarks, I ob-
viated their renewal by suddenly demanding the compositions in a sharp accent, and, stepping from the
estrade, I proceeded to collect them. As I passed the
governess-pupil, I said to her,

"You have come in too late to receive a lesson to-
day; try to be more punctual next time."

I was behind her, and could not read in her face the effect of my not very civil speech. Probably I should not have troubled myself to do so had I been full in front; but I observed that she immediately began to slip her books into her cabas again; and presently, after I had returned to the estrade, while I was arranging the mass of compositions, I heard the folding-door again open and close, and, on looking up, I perceived her place vacant. I thought to myself, "She will consider her first attempt at taking a lesson in English something of a failure;" and I wondered whether she had departed in the sulks, or whether stupidity had induced her to take my words too literally, or, finally, whether my irritable tone had wounded her feelings. The last notion I dismissed almost as soon as I had conceived it, for, not having seen any appearance of sensitiveness in any human face since my arrival in Belgium, I had begun to regard it almost as a fabulous quality. Whether her physiognomy announced it I could not tell, for her speedy exit had allowed me no time to ascertain the circumstance. I had, indeed, on two or three previous occasions, caught a passing view of her (as I believe has been mentioned before), but I had never stopped to scrutinize either her face or person, and had but the most vague idea of her general appearance. Just as I had finished rolling up the compositions, the four o'clock bell rang. With my accustomed alertness in obeying that signal, I grasped my hat and evacuated the premises.

G

CHAPTER XIV.

IF I was punctual in quitting Mdlle. Reuter's dom-
icile, I was at least equally punctual in arriving there.
I came the next day at five minutes before two, and
on reaching the school-room door, before I opened it,
I heard a rapid, gabbling sound, which warned me that
the "prière du midi" was not yet concluded. I waited the termination thereof; it would have been im-
pious to intrude my heretical presence during its progress. How the repeater of the prayer did cackle and
splutter! I never before or since heard language
enounced with such steam-engine haste. "Notre père
qui êtes au ciel" went off like a shot; then followed an
address to Marie, "vièrge céleste, reine des anges,
maison d'or, tour d'ivoire!" and then an invocation to
the saint of the day ; and then down they all sat, and
the solemn (?) rite was over; and I entered, flinging
the door wide and striding in fast, as it was my wont
to do now; for I had found that in entering with
aplomb, and mounting the estrade with emphasis, consisted the grand secret of insuring immediate silence.
The folding-doors between the two classes, opened for
the prayer, were instantly closed ; a maîtresse, work-
box in hand, took her seat at her appropriate desk;
the pupils sat still with their pens and books before
them; my three beauties in the van, now well hum-
bled by a demeanor of consistent coolness, sat erect,

with their hands folded quietly on their knees; they
had given up giggling and whispering to each other,
and no longer ventured to utter pert speeches in my
presence; they now only talked to me occasionally
with their eyes, by means of which organs they could
still, however, say very audacious and coquettish things.
Had affection, goodness, modesty, real talent, ever employed those bright orbs as interpreters, I do not think
I could have refrained from giving a kind and encouraging, perhaps an ardent reply now and then; but as
it was, I found pleasure in answering the glance of vanity with the gaze of stoicism. Youthful, fair, brilliant
as were many of my pupils, I can truly say that in me
they never saw any other bearing than such as an austere though just guardian might have observed toward
them. If any doubt the accuracy of this assertion, as in-
ferring more conscientious self-denial or Scipio-like self-
control than they feel disposed to give me credit for,
let them take into consideration the following circumstances, which, while detracting from my merit, justify
my veracity.

Know, oh incredulous reader, that a master stands
in a somewhat different relation toward a pretty, light-
headed, probably ignorant girl, to that occupied by a
partner at a ball, or a gallant on the promenade. A
professor does not meet his pupil to see her dressed in
satin and muslin, with hair perfumed and curled, neck
scarcely shaded by aerial lace, round white arms circled
with bracelets, feet dressed for the gliding dance. It
is not his business to whirl her through the waltz, to
feed her with compliments, to heighten her beauty by
the flush of gratified vanity. Neither does he encoun-

ter her on the smooth-rolled, tree-shaded boulevard, in
the green and sunny park, whither she repairs clad in
her becoming walking-dress, her scarf thrown with
grace over her shoulders, her little bonnet scarcely ·
screening her curls, the red rose under its brim adding
a new tint to the softer rose on her cheek; her face
and eyes, too, illumined with smiles, perhaps as transient as the sunshine of the gala-day, but also quite as
brilliant: it is not his office to walk by her side, to
listen to her lively chat, to carry her parasol, scarcely
larger than a broad green leaf, to lead in a ribbon her
Blenheim spaniel or Italian greyhound.   No; he finds
her in the school-room, plainly dressed, with books before her.   Owing to her education or her nature, books
are to her a nuisance, and she opens them with aversion, yet her teacher must instill into her mind the
contents of these books; that mind resists the admission of grave information; it recoils—it grows restive;
sullen tempers are shown, disfiguring frowns spoil the
symmetry of the face, sometimes coarse gestures ban-
ish grace from the deportment, while muttered expressions, redolent of native and ineradicable vulgarity,·
desecrate the sweetness of the voice.   Where the temperament is serene though the intellect be sluggish, an
unconquerable dullness opposes every effort to instruct.
Where there is cunning but not energy, dissimulation,
falsehood, a thousand schemes and tricks are put in play
to evade the necessity of application; in short, to the
tutor, female youth, female charms are like tapestry
hangings, of which the wrong side is continually turned toward him; and even when he sees the smooth,
neat, external surface, he so well knows what knots,

long stitches, and jagged ends are behind, that he has
scarce a temptation to admire too fondly the seemly
forms and bright colors exposed to general view.

Our likings are regulated by our circumstances.
The artist prefers a hilly country because it is picturesque; the engineer a flat one because it is convenient; the man of pleasure likes what he calls " a fine
woman :" she suits him; the fashionable young gentleman admires the fashionable young lady: she is of
his kind; the toil-worn, fagged, probably irritable tutor, blind almost to beauty, insensible to airs and
graces, glories chiefly in certain mental qualities: application, love of knowledge, natural capacity, docility,
truthfulness, gratefulness, are the charms that attract
his notice and win his regard. These he seeks, but
seldom meets; these, if by chance he finds, he would
fain retain forever; and, when separation deprives him
of them, he feels as if some ruthless hand had snatched from him his only ewe-lamb. Such being the case,
and the case it is, my readers will agree with me that
there was nothing either very meritorious or very marvelous in the integrity and moderation of my conduct
at Mdlle. Reuter's pensionnat de demoiselles.

My first business this afternoon consisted in reading
the list of places for the month, determined by the relative correctness of the compositions given the preceding day. The list was headed, as usual, by the
name of Sylvie, that plain, quiet little girl I have described before as being at once the best and ugliest
pupil in the establishment. The second place had
fallen to the lot of a certain Léonie Ledru, a diminutive, sharp-featured, and parchment-skinned creature

of quick wits, frail conscience, and indurated feelings;
a lawyer-like thing, of whom I used to say that, had
she been a boy, she would have made a model of an
unprincipled, clever attorney.   Then came Eulalie, the
proud beauty, the Juno of the school, whom six long
years of drilling in the simple grammar of the English
language had compelled, despite the stiff phlegm of her
intellect, to acquire a mechanical acquaintance with
most of its rules.   No smile, no trace of pleasure or
satisfaction appeared in Sylvie's nun-like and passive
face as she heard her name read first.   I always felt
saddened by the sight of that poor girl's absolute quiescence on all occasions, and it was my custom to look
at her, to address her as seldom as possible.   Her extreme docility, her assiduous perseverance, would have
recommended her warmly to my good opinion; her
modesty, her intelligence, would have induced me to
feel most kindly—most affectionately toward her, notwithstanding the almost ghastly plainness of her features, the disproportion of her form, the corpse-like lack
of animation in her countenance, had I not been aware
that every friendly word, every kindly action, would
be reported by her to her confessor, and by him mis-
interpreted and poisoned.   Once I laid my hand on her
head in token of approbation.   I thought Sylvie was
going to smile; her dim eye almost kindled; but presently she shrunk from me; I was a man and a heretic; she, poor child! a destined nun and devoted Catholic: thus a fourfold wall of separation divided her
mind from mine.   A pert smirk, and a hard glance of
triumph, was Léonie's method of testifying her gratification; Eulalie looked sullen and envious: she had

hoped to be first. Hortense and Caroline exchanged
a reckless grimace on hearing their names read out
somewhere near the bottom of the list; the brand of
mental inferiority was considered by them as no dis-
grace, their hopes for the future being based solely on
their personal attractions.

This affair arranged, the regular lesson followed.
During a brief interval, employed by the pupils in
ruling their books, my eye, ranging carelessly over the
benches, observed, for the first time, that the farthest
seat in the farthest row—a seat usually vacant—was
again filled by the new scholar, the Mdlle. Henri so
ostentatiously recommended to me by the directress.
To-day I had on my spectacles; her appearance, therefore, was clear to me at the first glance; I had not to
puzzle over it. She looked young; yet, had I been
required to name her exact age, I should have been
somewhat nonplused; the slightness of her figure
might have suited seventeen; a certain anxious and
preoccupied expression of face seemed the indication
of riper years. She was dressed, like all the rest, in
a dark stuff gown and a white collar; her features
were dissimilar to any there, not so rounded, more defined, yet scarcely regular. The shape of her head,
too, was different, the superior part more developed,
the base considerably less. I felt assured, at first
sight, that she was not a Belgian; her complexion, her
countenance, her lineaments, her figure, were all distinct from theirs, and evidently the type of another
race—of a race less gifted with fullness of flesh and
plenitude of blood; less jocund, material, unthinking.
When I first cast my eyes on her, she sat looking fix-

edly down, her chin resting on her hand, and she did
not change her attitude till I commenced the lesson.
None of the Belgian girls would have retained one position, and that a reflective one, for the same length of
time.   Yet, having intimated that her appearance was
peculiar, as being unlike that of her Flemish companions, I have little more to say respecting it.   I can
pronounce no encomiums on her beauty, for she was
not beautiful; nor offer condolence on her plainness,
for neither was she plain ; a care-worn character of
forehead, and a corresponding moulding of the mouth,
struck me with a sentiment resembling surprise, but
these traits would probably have passed unnoticed by
any less crotchety observer.

Now, reader, though I have spent a page and a half
in describing Mdlle. Henri, I know well enough that I
have left on your mind's eye no distinct picture of her;
I have not painted her complexion, nor her eyes, nor
her hair, nor even drawn the outline of her shape. You
can not tell whether her nose was aquiline or retroussé,
whether her chin was long or short, her face square or
oval; nor could I the first day, and it is not my intention to communicate to you at once a knowledge I
myself gained by little and little.

I gave a short exercise which they all wrote down.
I saw the new pupil was puzzled at first with the nov-
elty of the form and language.   Once or twice she
looked at me with a sort of painful solicitude, as not
comprehending at all what I meant; then she was not
ready when the others were ; she could not write her
phrases so fast as they did; I would not help her; I
went on relentless. She looked at me; her eye said

most plainly, "I can not follow you." I disregarded
the appeal, and, carelessly leaning back in my chair,
glancing from time to time with a *nonchalant* air out
of the window, I dictated a little faster. On looking
toward her again, I perceived her face clouded with
embarrassment, but she was still writing on most diligently. I paused a few seconds; she employed the
interval in hurriedly reperusing what she had written,
and shame and discomfiture were apparent in her countenance; she evidently found she had made great nonsense of it. In ten minutes more the dictation was
complete, and, having allowed a brief space in which
to correct it, I took their books. It was with a reluctant hand Mdlle. Henri gave up hers, but, having once
yielded it to my possession, she composed her anxious
face, as if, for the present, she had resolved to dismiss
regret, and had made up her mind to be thought un-
precedently stupid. Glancing over her exercise, I
found that several lines had been omitted, but what
was written contained very few faults. I instantly inscribed "Bon" at the bottom of the page, and returned
it to her. She smiled, at first incredulously, then as
if reassured, but did not lift her eyes. She could look
at me, it seemed, when perplexed and bewildered, but
not when gratified; I thought that scarcely fair.

G 2

CHAPTER XV.

Some time elapsed before I again gave a lesson in
the first class.   The holiday of Whitsuntide occupied three days, and on the fourth it was the turn of
the second division to receive my instructions.   As
I made the transit of the carré, I observed, as usual,
the band of sewers surrounding Mdlle. Henri; there
were only about a dozen of them, but they made as
much noise as might have sufficed for fifty; they
seemed very little under her control; three or four at
once assailed her with importunate requirements; she
looked harassed, she demanded silence, but in vain.
She saw me, and I read in her eye pain that a stranger should witness the insubordination of her pupils.
She seemed to entreat order—her prayers were useless; then I remarked that she compressed her lips and
contracted her brow; and her countenance, if I read
it correctly, said, "I have done my best; I seem to
merit blame, notwithstanding; blame me, then, who
will."   I passed on.   As I closed the school-room
door, I heard her say, suddenly and sharply, addressing one of the eldest and most turbulent of the lot,

"Amélie Müllenberg, ask me no question, and request of me no assistance for a week to come; during
that space of time I will neither speak to you nor help
you."

The words were uttered with emphasis—nay, with

vehemence, and a comparative silence followed; whether the calm was permanent, I know not; two doors now closed between me and the carré.

Next day was appropriated to the first class. On my arrival, I found the directress seated, as usual, in a chair between the two estrades, and before her was standing Mdlle. Henri in an attitude (as it seemed to me) of somewhat reluctant attention. The directress was knitting and talking at the same time. Amid the hum of a large school-room, it was easy so to speak in the ear of one person as to be heard by that person alone, and it was thus Mdlle. Reuter parleyed with her teacher. The face of the latter was a little flushed, not a little troubled; there was vexation in it, whence resulting I know not, for the directress looked very placid indeed. She could not be scolding in such gentle whispers, and with so equable a mien; no, it was presently proved that her discourse had been of the most friendly tendency, for I heard the closing words,

" C'est assez, ma bonne amie; à present je ne veux pas vous retenir davantage."

Without reply, Mdlle. Henri turned away; dissatisfaction was plainly evinced in her face, and a smile, slight and brief, but bitter, distrustful, and, I thought, scornful, curled her lip as she took her place in the class; it was a secret, involuntary smile, which lasted but a second; an air of depression succeeded, chased away presently by one of attention and interest, when I gave the word for all the pupils to take their reading-books. In general I hated the reading-lesson, it was such a torture to the ear to listen to their uncouth mouthing of my native tongue, and no effort of example or precept on my part ever seemed to effect the slightest improvement in their accent. To-day, each in her appropriate key lisped, stuttered, mumbled, and jabbered as usual; about fifteen had racked me in turn, and my auricular nerve was expecting with resignation the discords of the sixteenth, when a full though low voice read out, in clear, correct English,

"On his way to Perth, the king was met by a Highland woman, calling herself a prophetess. She stood at the side of the ferry by which he was about to travel to the north, and cried with a loud voice, 'My lord the king, if you pass this water you will never return again alive!'" (*Vide* the history of Scotland.)

I looked up in amazement; the voice was a voice of Albion; the accent was pure and silvery; it only wanted firmness and assurance to be the counterpart of what any well-educated lady in Essex or Middlesex might have enounced, yet the speaker or reader was no other than Mdlle. Henri, in whose grave, joyless face I saw no mark of consciousness that she had performed any extraordinary feat. No one else evinced surprise either. Mdlle. Reuter knitted away assiduously. I was aware, however, that at the conclusion of the paragraph she had lifted her eyelid and honored me with a glance sideways. She did not know the full excellence of the teacher's style of reading, but she perceived that her accent was not that of the others, and wanted to discover what I thought. I masked my visage with indifference, and ordered the next girl to proceed.

When the lesson was over, I took advantage of the confusion caused by breaking up to approach Mdlle.

Henri. She was standing near the window, and retired as I advanced; she thought I wanted to look out, and did not imagine that I could have any thing to say to her. I took her exercise-book out of her hand. As I turned over the leaves I addressed her:

"You have had lessons in English before?" I asked.

"No, sir."

"No! you read it well; you have been in England?"

"Oh no," with some animation.

"You have been in English families?"

Still in the answer was "No." Here my eye, resting on the fly-leaf of the book, saw written, "Frances Evans Henri."

"Your name?" I asked.

"Yes, sir."

My interrogations were cut short. I heard a little rustling behind me, and close at my back was the directress, professing to be examining the interior of a desk.

"Mademoiselle," said she, looking up and addressing the teacher, "will you have the goodness to go and stand in the corridor while the young ladies are putting on their things, and try to keep some order?"

Mdlle. Henri obeyed.

"What splendid weather!" observed the directress, cheerfully, glancing at the same time from the window. I assented, and was withdrawing. "What of your new pupil, Monsieur?" continued she, following my retreating steps. "Is she likely to make progress in English?"

"Indeed, I can hardly judge. She possesses a pretty good accent; of her real knowledge of the language I have as yet had no opportunity of forming an opinion."

"And her natural capacity, Monsieur? I have had my fears about that: can you relieve me by an assurance at least of its average power?"

"I see no reason to doubt its average power, Mademoiselle, but really I scarcely know her, and have not had time to study the calibre of her capacity. I wish you a very good afternoon."

She still pursued me. "You will observe, Monsieur, and tell me what you think; I could so much better rely on your opinion than on my own; women can not judge of these things as men can; and—excuse my pertinacity, Monsieur, but it is natural I should feel interested about this poor little girl (pauvre petite)— she has scarcely any relations; her own efforts are all she has to look to; her acquirements must be her sole fortune; her present position has once been mine, or nearly so; it is, then, but natural I should sympathize with her; and sometimes, when I see the difficulty she has in managing pupils, I feel quite chagrined. I doubt not she does her best; her intentions are excellent; but, Monsieur, she wants tact and firmness. I have talked to her on the subject, but I am not fluent, and probably did not express myself with clearness; she never appears to comprehend me. Now, would you occasionally, when you see an opportunity, slip in a word of advice to her on the subject? men have so much more influence than women have—they argue so much more logically than we do; and you, Monsieur, in particular, have so paramount a power of making

yourself obeyed; a word of advice from you could not
but do her good; even if she were sullen and head-
strong (which I hope she is not), she would scarcely
refuse to listen to you; for my own part, I can truly
say that I never attend one of your lessons without
deriving benefit from witnessing your management of
the pupils. The other masters are a constant source
of anxiety to me: they can not impress the young ladies with sentiments of respect, nor restrain the levity
natural to youth; in you, Monsieur, I feel the most absolute confidence; try, then, to put this poor child into
the way of controlling our giddy, high-spirited Braban-
toises. But, Monsieur, I would add one word more:
don't alarm her *amour propre;* beware of inflicting a
wound there. I reluctantly admit that in that particular she is blamably—some would say ridiculously—
susceptible. ·I fear I have touched this sore point in-
advertently, and she can not get over it."

During the greater part of this harangue my hand
was on the lock of the outer door; I now turned it.

"Au revoir, Mademoiselle," said I, and escaped. I
saw the directress's stock of words was yet far from
exhausted. She looked after me; she would fain have
detained me longer. Her manner toward me had been
altered ever since I had begun to treat her with hardness and indifference; she almost cringed to me on
every occasion; she consulted my countenance inces-
santly, and beset me with innumerable little officious
attentions. Servility creates despotism. This slavish
homage, instead of softening my heart, only pampered
whatever was stern and exacting in its mood. The
very circumstance of her hovering round me like a fas-

cinated bird seemed to transform me into a rigid pillar
of stone; her flatteries irritated my scorn, her blandishments confirmed my reserve.　At times I wondered
what she meant by giving herself such trouble to win
me, when the more profitable Pelet was already in her
nets, and when, too, she was aware that I possessed
her secret, for I had not scrupled to tell her as much;
but the fact is, that as it was her nature to doubt the
reality and undervalue the worth of modesty, affection,
disinterestedness—to regard these qualities as foibles
of character—so it was equally her tendency to consider pride, hardness, selfishness, as proofs of strength.
She would trample on the neck of humility, she would
kneel at the feet of disdain; she would meet tenderness with secret contempt, indifference she would woo
with ceaseless assiduities.　Benevolence, devotedness,
enthusiasm, were her antipathies; for dissimulation
and self-interest she had a preference: they were real
wisdom in her eyes; moral and physical degradation,
mental and bodily inferiority, she regarded with indulgence; they were foils capable of being turned to
good account as set-offs for her own endowments.　To
violence, injustice, tyranny, she succumbed: they
were her natural masters; she had no propensity to
hate, no impulse to resist them; the indignation their
behests awake in some hearts was unknown in hers.
From all this it resulted that the false and selfish
called her wise, the vulgar and debased termed her
charitable, the insolent and unjust dubbed her amiable, the conscientious and benevolent generally at first
accepted as valid her claim to be considered one of
themselves; but ere long the plating of pretension

wore off, the real material appeared below, and they laid her aside as a deception.

CHAPTER XVI.

In the course of another fortnight I had seen sufficient of Frances Evans Henri to enable me to form a more definite opinion of her character. I found her possessed in a somewhat remarkable degree of at least two good points, viz., perseverance and a sense of duty. I found she was really capable of applying to study, of contending with difficulties. At first I offered her the same help which I had always found it necessary to confer on the others. I began with unloosing for her each knotty point, but I soon discovered that such help was regarded by my new pupil as degrading; she recoiled from it with a certain proud impatience. Hereupon I appointed her long lessons, and left her to solve alone any perplexities they might present. She set to the task with serious ardor, and having quickly accomplished one labor, eagerly demanded more. So much for her perseverance. As to her sense of duty, it evinced itself thus: she liked to learn, but hated to teach; her progress as a pupil depended upon herself, and I saw that on herself she could calculate with certainty; her success as a teacher rested partly, perhaps chiefly, upon the will of others: it cost her a most painful effort to enter into conflict with this foreign will, to endeavor to bend it into subjection to her own; for in what regarded people in

general the action of her will was impeded by many
scruples; it was as unembarrassed as strong where her
own affairs were concerned, and to it she could at any
time subject her inclination, if that inclination went
counter to her convictions of right; yet, when called
upon to wrestle with the propensities, the habits, the
faults of others, of children especially, who are deaf to
reason, and, for the most part, insensate to persuasion,
her will sometimes almost refused to act; then came
in the sense of duty and forced the reluctant will into
operation. A wasteful expense of energy and labor
was frequently the consequence. Frances toiled for
and with her pupils like a drudge, but it was long
ere her conscientious exertions were rewarded by any
thing like docility on their part, because they saw that
they had power over her, inasmuch as by resisting
her painful attempts to convince, persuade, control—by
forcing her to the employment of coercive measures,
they could inflict upon her exquisite suffering. Human beings—human children especially, seldom deny
themselves the pleasure of exercising a power which
they are conscious of possessing, even though that
power consist only in a capacity to make others wretch-
ed; a pupil whose sensations are duller than those of
his instructor, while his nerves are tougher and his
bodily strength perhaps greater, has an immense advantage over that instructor, and he will generally use
it relentlessly, because the very young, very healthy,
very thoughtless, know neither how to sympathize nor
how to spare. Frances, I fear, suffered much; a continual weight seemed to oppress her spirits. I have
said she did not live in the house; and whether in her

own abode, wherever that might be, she wore the same preoccupied, unsmiling, sorrowfully resolved air that always shaded her features under the roof of Mdlle. Reuter, I could not tell.

One day I gave as a devoir the trite little anecdote of Alfred tending cakes in the herdsman's hut, to be related with amplifications. A singular affair most of the pupils made of it; brevity was what they had chiefly studied; the majority of the narratives were perfectly unintelligible; those of Sylvie and Léonie Ledru alone pretended to any thing like sense and connection. Eulalie, indeed, had hit upon a clever expedient for at once insuring accuracy and saving trouble; she had obtained access somehow to an abridged history of England, and had copied the anecdote out fair. I wrote on the margin of her production, "Stupid and deceitful," and then tore it down the middle.

Last in the pile of single-leaved devoirs I found one of several sheets, neatly written out and stitched together. I knew the hand, and scarcely needed the evidence of the signature, "Frances Evans Henri," to confirm my conjecture as to the writer's identity.

Night was my usual time for correcting devoirs, and my own room the usual scene of such task—task most onerous hitherto; and it seemed strange to me to feel rising within me an incipient sense of interest as I snuffed the candle and addressed myself to the perusal of the poor teacher's manuscript.

"Now," thought I, "I shall see a glimpse of what she really is; I shall get an idea of the nature and extent of her powers; not that she can be expected to express herself well in a foreign tongue, but still, if she has any mind, here will be a reflection of it."

The narrative commenced by a description of a Saxon peasant's hut, situated within the confines of a great, leafless winter forest; it represented an evening in December; flakes of snow were falling, and the herds-man foretold a heavy storm; he summoned his wife to aid him in collecting their flock, roaming far away on the pastoral banks of the Thone; he warns her that it will be late ere they return. The good woman is reluctant to quit her occupation of baking cakes for the evening meal; but, acknowledging the primary importance of securing the herds and flocks, she puts on her sheep-skin mantle, and, addressing a stranger who rests half-reclined on a bed of rushes near the hearth, bids him mind the cakes till her return.

"Take care, young man," she continues, "that you fasten the door well after us; and, above all, open to none in our absence; whatever sound you hear, stir not, and look not out. The night will soon fall; this forest is most wild and lonely; strange noises are often heard therein after sunset; wolves haunt these glades, and Danish warriors infest the country; worse things are talked of; you might chance to hear, as it were, a child cry, and, on opening the door to afford it succor, a great black bull or a shadowy goblin dog might rush over the threshold; or, more awful still, if someting flapped, as with wings against the lattice, and then a raven or a white dove flew in and settled on the hearth, such a visitor would be a sure sign of misfortune to the house; therefore heed my advice, and lift the latchet for nothing."

Her husband calls her away; both depart. The stranger, left alone, listens a while to the muffled snow-wind, the remote, swollen sound of the river, and then he speaks.

"It is Christmas eve," says he; "I mark the date; here I sit alone on a rude couch of rushes, sheltered by the thatch of a herdsman's hut; I, whose inheritance was a kingdom, owe my night's harborage to a poor serf; my throne is usurped, my crown presses the brow of an invader; I have no friends; my troops wander broken in the hills of Wales; reckless robbers spoil my country; my subjects lie prostrate, their breasts crushed by the heel of the brutal Dane. Fate, thou hast done thy worst, and now thou standest before me resting thy hand on thy blunted blade. Ay, I see thine eye confront mine, and demand why I still live—why I still hope. Pagan demon, I credit not thine omnipotence, and so can not succumb to thy power. My God, whose Son, as on this night, took on Him the form of man, and for man vouchsafed to suffer and bleed, controls thy hand, and without His behest thou canst not strike a stroke. My God is sinless, eternal, all-wise—in Him is my trust; and, though stripped and crushed by thee—though naked, desolate, void of resource, I do not despair—I can not despair; were the lance of Guthrum now wet with my blood, I should not despair. I watch, I toil, I hope, I pray; Jehovah, in his own time, will aid."

I need not continue the quotation; the whole devoir was in the same strain. There were errors of orthography, there were foreign idioms, there were

166   THE PROFESSOR.

some faults of construction, there were verbs irregular
transformed into verbs regular; it was mostly made
up, as the above example shows, of short and somewhat rude sentences, and the style stood in great need
of polish and sustained dignity; yet such as it was, I
had hitherto seen nothing like it in the course of my
professional experience.   The girl's mind had conceived a picture of the hut, of the two peasants, of the
crownless king; she had imagined the wintry forest,
she had recalled the old Saxon ghost legends, she had
appreciated Alfred's courage under calamity, she had
remembered his Christian education, and had shown
him, with the rooted confidence of those primitive
days, relying on the scriptural Jehovah for aid against
the mythological Destiny.   This she had done without a hint from me.   I had given the subject, but not
said a word about the manner of treating it.

"I will find or make an opportunity of speaking to
her," I said to myself as I rolled the devoir up; "I
will learn what she has of English in her besides the
name of Frances Evans.   She is no novice in the
language, that is evident, yet she told me she had
neither been in England, nor taken lessons in English,
nor lived in English families."

In the course of my next lesson I made a report of
the other devoirs, dealing out praise and blame in very
small retail parcels, according to my custom, for there·
was no use in blaming severely, and high encomiums
were rarely merited.   I said nothing of Mdlle. Henri's
exercise, and, spectacles on nose, I endeavored to decipher in her countenance her sentiments at the omission.   I wanted to find out whether in her existed a

consciousness of her own talents. "If she thinks she
did a clever thing in composing that devoir, she will
now look mortified," thought I. Grave as usual, almost sombre was her face ; as usual, her eyes were
fastened on the cahier open before her ; there was
something, I thought, of expectation in her attitude
as I concluded a brief review of the last devoir, and
when, casting it from me and rubbing my hands, I
bade them take their grammars, some slight change
did pass over her air and mien, as though she now relinquished a faint prospect of pleasant excitement.
She had been waiting for something to be discussed
in which she had a degree of interest ; the discussion
was not to come on, so expectation sank back, shrunk
and sad, but attention, promptly filling up the void,
repaired in a moment the transient collapse of feature ; still, I felt, rather than saw, during the whole
course of the lesson, that a hope had been wrenched
from her, and that, if she did not show distress, it was
because she would not.

At four o'clock, when the bell rang and the room
was in immediate tumult, instead of taking my hat
and starting from the estrade, I sat still a moment. I
looked at Frances ; she was putting her books into
her cabas ; having fastened the button, she raised her
head ; encountering my eye, she made a quiet, respectful obeisance, as bidding good afternoon, and was
turning to depart :

"Come here," said I, lifting my finger at the same
time. She hesitated ; she could not hear the words
amid the uproar now pervading both school-rooms ; I
repeated the sign ; she approached ; again she paused

within half a yard of the estrade, and looked shy, and still doubtful whether she had mistaken my meaning. " Step up," I said, speaking with decision. It is the only way of dealing with diffident, easily embarrassed characters, and with some slight manual aid I presently got her placed just where I wanted her to be, that is, between my desk and the window, where she was screened from the rush of the second division, and where no one could sneak behind her to listen.

"Take a seat," I said, placing a tabouret; and I made her sit down. I knew what I was doing would be considered a very strange thing, and, what was more, I did not care. Frances knew it also, and I fear, by an appearance of agitation and trembling, that she cared much. I drew from my pocket the rolled-up devoir.

"This is yours, I suppose?" said I, addressing her in English, for I now felt sure she could speak English.

"Yes," she answered, distinctly; and as I unrolled it and laid it out flat on the desk before her with my hand upon it, and a pencil in that hand, I saw her moved, and, as it were, kindled; her depression beamed as a cloud might behind which the sun is burning.

"This devoir has numerous faults," said I. "It will take you some years of careful study before you are in a condition to write English with absolute correctness. Attend; I will point out some principal defects." And I went through it carefully, noting every error, and demonstrating why they were errors, and how the words or phrases ought to have been written. In the course of this sobering process she became calm. I now went on:

"As to the substance of your devoir, Mdlle. Henri, it has surprised me. I perused it with pleasure, because I saw in it some proofs of taste and fancy. Taste and fancy are not the highest gifts of the human mind, but, such as they are, you possess them—not probably in a paramount degree, but in a degree beyond what the majority can boast. You may, then, take courage; cultivate the faculties that God and nature have bestowed on you, and do not fear in any crisis of suffering, under any pressure of injustice, to derive free and full consolation from the consciousness of their strength and rarity."

"Strength and rarity!" I repeated to myself; "ay, the words are probably true," for on looking up I saw the sun had dissevered its screening cloud; her countenance was transfigured; a smile shone in her eyes—a smile almost triumphant; it seemed to say,

"I am glad you have been forced to discover so much of my nature; you need not so carefully moderate your language. Do you think I am myself a stranger to myself? What you tell me in terms so qualified I have known fully from a child."

She did say this as plainly as a frank and flashing glance could, but in a moment the glow of her complexion, the radiance of her aspect had subsided; if strongly conscious of her talents, she was equally conscious of her harassing defects, and the remembrance of these, obliterated for a single second, now reviving with sudden force, at once subdued the too vivid characters in which her sense of her powers had been expressed. So quick was the revulsion of feeling, I had not time to check her triumph by reproof; ere I could

H

contract my brows to a frown, she had become serious and almost mournful-looking.

"Thank you, sir," said she, rising; there was gratitude both in her voice and in the look with which she accompanied it. It was time indeed for our conference to terminate, for, when I glanced around, behold all the boarders (the day-scholars had departed) were congregated within a yard or two of my desk, and stood staring with eyes and mouth wide open; the three maîtresses formed a whispering knot in one corner, and close at my elbow was the directress, sitting on a low chair, calmly clipping the tassels of her finished purse.

CHAPTER XVII.

AFTER all, I had profited but imperfectly by the opportunity I had so boldly achieved of speaking to Mdlle. Henri. It was my intention to ask her how she came to be possessed of two English baptismal names, Frances and Evans, in addition to her French surname; also, whence she derived her good accent. I had forgotten both points, or, rather, our colloquy had been so brief that I had not had time to bring them forward; moreover, I had not half tested her powers of speaking English; all I had drawn from her in that language were the words " Yes," and " Thank you, sir." " No matter," I reflected; " what has been left incomplete now shall be finished another day." Nor did I fail to keep the promise thus made to myself. It was difficult to get even a few words of particular conversation with one pupil among so many; but, according to the old proverb, "Where there is a will there is a way," and again and again I managed to find an opportunity for exchanging a few words with Mdlle. Henri, regardless that envy stared and detraction whispered whenever I approached her.

"Your book an instant." Such was the mode in which I often began these brief dialogues; the time was always just at the conclusion of the lesson; and motioning to her to rise, I installed myself in her place, allowing her to stand deferentially at my side, for I esteemed it wise and right in her case to enforce strictly all forms ordinarily in use between master and pupil, the rather because I perceived that in proportion as my manner grew austere and magisterial, hers became easy and self-possessed—an odd contradiction, doubtless, to the ordinary effect in such cases, but so it was.

"A pencil," said I, holding out my hand without looking at her. (I am now about to sketch a brief report of the first of these conferences.) She gave me one, and while I underlined some errors in a grammatical exercise she had written, I observed,

"You are not a native of Belgium ?"

"No."

"Nor of France ?"

"No."

"Where, then, is your birth-place ?"

"I was born at Geneva."

"You don't call Frances and Evans Swiss names, I presume ?"

"No, sir, they are English names."

"Just so ; and is it the custom of the Genevese to give their children English appellatives ?"

"Non, Monsieur ; mais—"

"Speak English, if you please."

"Mais—"

"English—"

"But—" (slowly and with embarrassment)—"my parents were not all the two Genevese."

"Say *both* instead of ' all the two,' Mademoiselle." ·

"Not *both* Swiss ; my mother was English."

"Ah ! and of English extraction ?"

"Yes ; her ancestors were all English."

"And your father ?"

"He was Swiss."

"What besides?   What was his profession ?"

"Ecclesiastic—pastor—he had a church."

"Since your mother is an English woman, why do you not speak English with more facility ?"

"Maman est morte, il y a dix ans."

"And you do homage to her memory by forgetting her language.   Have the goodness to put French out of your mind so long as I converse with you ; keep to English."

"C'est si difficile, Monsieur, quand on n'en a plus l' habitude."

"You had the habitude formerly, I suppose ?   Now answer me in your mother tongue."

"Yes, sir, I spoke the English more than the French when I was a child."

"Why do you not speak it now ?"

"Because I have no English friends."

"You live with your father, I suppose ?"

" My father is dead."

" You have brothers and sisters ?"

" Not one."

" Do you live alone ?"

" No, I have an aunt—ma tante Julienne."

" Your father's sister ?"

" Justement, Monsieur."

" Is that English?"

" No ; but I forget—"

" For which, Mademoiselle, if you were a child, I should certainly devise some slight punishment; at your age—you must be two or three-and-twenty, I should think ?"

" Pas encore, Monsieur—en un mois j'aurai dix-neuf ans."

" Well, nineteen is a mature age, and, having attained it, you ought to be so solicitous for your own improvement that it should not be needful for a master to remind you twice of the expediency of your speaking English whenever practicable."

To this wise speech I received no answer ; and, when I looked up, my pupil was smiling to herself a much-meaning though not very gay smile ; it seemed to say " He talks of he knows not what ;" it said this so plainly that I determined to request information on the point concerning which my ignorance seemed to be thus tacitly affirmed.

" Are you solicitous for your own improvement ?"

" Rather."

" How do you prove it, Mademoiselle ?"

An odd question, and bluntly put ; it excited a second smile.

"Why, Monsieur, I am not inattentive, am I? I learn my lessons well—"

"Oh, a child can do that; and what more do you do?"

"What more can I do?"

"Oh, certainly, not much; but you are a teacher, are you not, as well as a pupil?"

"Yes."

"You teach lace-mending?"

"Yes."

"A dull, stupid occupation; do you like it?"

"No; it is tedious."

"Why do you pursue it? Why do you not rather teach history, geography, grammar, even arithmetic?"

"Is Monsieur certain that I am myself thoroughly acquainted with these studies?"

"I don't know; you ought to be, at your age."

"But I never was at school, Monsieur—"

"Indeed! What, then, were your friends—what was your aunt about? She is very much to blame."

"No, Monsieur, no—my aunt is good—she is not to blame—she does what she can; she lodges and nourishes me" (I report Mdlle. Henri's phrases literally, and it was thus she translated from the French). "She is not rich; she has only an annuity of twelve hundred francs, and it would be impossible for her to send me to school."

"Rather," thought I to myself on hearing this; but I continued, in the dogmatical tone I had adopted,

"It is sad, however, that you should be brought up in ignorance of the most ordinary branches of education. Had you known something of history and grammar, you might, by degrees, have relinquished your lace-mending drudgery and risen in the world."

"It is what I mean to do."

. "How? By a knowledge of English alone? That will not suffice ; no respectable family will receive a governess whose whole stock of knowledge consists in a familiarity with one foreign language."

"Monsieur, I know other things."

"Yes, yes, you can work with Berlin wools, and embroider handkerchiefs and collars : that will do little for you."

Mdlle. Henri's lips were unclosed to answer, but she checked herself, as thinking the discussion had been sufficiently pursued, and remained silent.

"Speak," I continued, impatiently ; "I never like the appearance of acquiescence when the reality is not there, and you had a contradiction at your tongue's end."

"Monsieur, I have had many lessons both in grammar, history, geography, and arithmetic. I have gone through a course of each study." ◆

"Bravo! but how did you manage it, since your aunt could not afford to send you to school?"

"By lace-mending—by the thing Monsieur despises so much."

"Truly! And now, Mademoiselle, it will be a good exercise for you to explain to me in English how such a result was produced by such means."

"Monsieur, I begged my aunt to have me taught lace-mending soon after we came to Brussels, because I knew it was a métier, a trade which was easily learned, and by which I could earn some money very

soon. I learned it in a few days, and I quickly got
work, for all the Brussels ladies have old lace—very
precious—which must be mended all the times it is
washed. I earned money a little, and this money I
gave for lessons in the studies I have mentioned; some
of it I spent in buying books—English books especially; soon I shall try to find a place of governess
or school-teacher, when I can write and speak English
well; but it will be difficult, because those who know
I have been a lace-mender will despise me, as the pupils here despise me. Pourtant j'ai mon projet," she
added, in a lower tone.

"What is it?"

"I will go and live in England; I will teach French
there."

The words were pronounced emphatically. She said
"England" as you might suppose an Israelite of Mo-
ses' days would have said Canaan.

"Have you a wish to see England?"

"Yes, and an intention."

And here a voice—the voice of the directress—interposed:

"Mademoiselle Henri, je crois qu'il va pleuvoir;
vous feriez bien, ma bonne amie, de retourner chez
vous tout de suite."

In silence, without a word of thanks for this officious
warning, Mdlle. Henri collected her books; she moved
to me respectfully, endeavored to move to her superior,
though the endeavor was almost a failure, for her head
seemed as if it would not bend, and thus departed.

Where there is one grain of perseverance or willfulness in the composition, trifling obstacles are ever

known rather to stimulate than discourage. Mdlle. Reuter might as well have spared herself the trouble of giving that intimation about the weather (by-the-by, her prediction was falsified by the event: it did not rain that evening). At the close of the next lesson I was again at Mdlle. Henri's desk. Thus did I accost her:

"What is your idea of England, Mademoiselle? Why do you wish to go there?"

Accustomed by this time to the calculated abruptness of my manner, it no longer discomposed or surprised her, and she answered with only so much of hesitation as was rendered inevitable by the difficulty she experienced in improvising the translation of her thoughts from French to English.

"England is something unique, as I have heard and read; my idea of it is vague, and I want to go there to render my idea clear—definite."

"Hum! How much of England do you suppose you could see if you went there in the capacity of a teacher? A strange notion you must have of getting a clear and definite idea of a country. All you could see of Great Britain would be the interior of a school, or, at most, of one or two private dwellings."

"It would be an English school; they would be English dwellings."

"Indisputably; but what then? What would be the value of observations made on a scale so narrow?"

"Monsieur, might not one learn something by analogy? An—échantillon—a—a sample often serves to give an idea of the whole; besides, narrow and wide are words comparative, are they not? All my life would

H 2

perhaps seem narrow in your eyes; all the life of a—
that little animal subterranean—une taupe—comment
dit-on ?"

"Mole."

"Yes—a mole, which lives under ground, would
seem narrow even to me."

"Well, Mademoiselle, what then ?   Proceed."

"Mais, Monsieur, vous me comprenez—"

"Not in the least; have the goodness to explain."

"Why, Monsieur, it is just so.   In Switzerland
I have done but little, learned but little, and seen
but little.   My life there was in a circle.   I walked
the same round every day; I could not get out of it.
Had I rested—remained there even till my death, I
should never have enlarged it, because I am poor and
not skillful—I have not great acquirements.   When
I was quite tired of this round, I begged my aunt to
go to Brussels.   My existence is no larger here, because I am no richer or higher; I walk in as narrow
a limit, but the scene is changed; it would change
again if I went to England.   I knew something of the
bourgeois of Geneva, now I know something of the
bourgeois of Brussels; if I went to London I should
know something of the bourgeois of London.   Can
you make any sense out of what I say, Monsieur, or
is it all obscure ?"

"I see, I see; now let us advert to another subject.
You propose to devote your life to teaching, and you
are a most unsuccessful teacher; you can not keep
your pupils in order."

A flush of painful confusion was the result of this

harsh remark. She bent her head to the desk, but soon raising it, replied,

"Monsieur, I am not a skillful teacher, it is true, but practice improves; besides, I work under difficulties. Here I only teach sewing; I can show no power in sewing, no superiority; it is a subordinate art; then I have no associates in this house; I am isolated; I am, too, a heretic, which deprives me of influence."

"And in England you would be a foreigner; that, too, would deprive you of influence—would effectually separate you from all around you. In England you would have as few connections, as little importance as you have here."

"But I should be learning something; for the rest, there are probably difficulties for such as I every where, and if I must contend, and perhaps be conquered, I would rather submit to English pride than to Flemish coarseness; besides, Monsieur—"

She stopped, not evidently from any difficulty in finding words to express herself, but because discretion seemed to say, "You have said enough."

"Finish your phrase," I urged.

"Besides, Monsieur, I long to live once more among Protestants; they are more honest than Catholics. A Romish school is a building with porous walls, a hollow floor, a false ceiling. Every room in this house, Monsieur, has eye-holes and ear-holes, and what the house is the inhabitants are, very treacherous: they all think it lawful to tell lies; they all call it politeness to profess friendship where they feel hatred."

"All?" said I; "you mean the pupils—the mere children—inexperienced, giddy things, who have not learned to distinguish the difference between right and wrong?"

" On the contrary, Monsieur, the children are the most sincere; they have not yet had time to become accomplished in duplicity; they will tell lies, but they do it inartificially, and you know they are lying; but the grown-up people are very false; they deceive strangers—they deceive each other—"

A servant here entered:

"Mdlle. Henri, Mdlle. Reuter vous prie de vouloir bien conduire la petite de Dorlodot chez elle, elle vous attend dans le cabinet de Rosalie la portière—c'est que sa bonne n'est pas venue la chercher—voyez-vous."

" Eh bien; est-ce que je suis sa bonne—moi?" demanded Mdlle. Henri; then smiling with that same bitter, derisive smile I had seen on her lips once before, she hastily rose and made her exit.

CHAPTER XVIII.

THE young Anglo-Swiss evidently derived both pleasure and profit from the study of her mother tongue. In teaching her, I did not, of course, confine myself to the ordinary school routine. I made instruction in English a channel for instruction in literature. I prescribed to her a course of reading. She had a little selection of English classics, a few of which had been left her by her mother, and the others she had purchased with her own penny-fee. I lent her some more modern works: all these she read with avidity, giving me, in writing, a clear summary of each work when she had perused it. Composition, too, she delighted in. Such occupation seemed the very breath of her nostrils, and soon her improved productions wrung from me the avowal that those qualities in her I had termed taste and fancy ought rather to have been denominated judgment and imagination. When I intimated so much, which I did, as usual, in dry and stinted phrase, I looked for the radiant and exulting smile my one word of eulogy had elicited before; but Frances colored. If she did smile, it was very softly and shyly; and instead of looking up to me with a conquering glance, her eye rested on my hand, which, stretched over her shoulder, was writing some directions with a pencil on the margin of her book.

"Well, are you pleased that I am satisfied with your progress?" I asked.

"Yes," said she, slowly, gently, the blush that had half subsided returning.

"But I do not say enough, I suppose?" I continued. "My praises are too cool?"

She made no answer, and, I thought, looked a little sad. I divined her thoughts, and should much have liked to have responded to them, had it been expedient so to do. She was not now very ambitious of my admiration—not eagerly desirous of dazzling me; a little affection—ever so little—pleased her better than all the panegyrics in the world. Feeling this, I stood a good while behind her, writing on the margin of her book. I could hardly quit my station or relinquish my occupation. Something retained me bending there,. my head very near hers, and my hand near hers too;

but the margin of a copy-book is not an illimitable
space; so, doubtless, the directress thought; and she
took occasion to walk past in order to ascertain by
what art I prolonged so disproportionately the period
necessary for filling it. I was obliged to go. Dis-
tasteful effort—to leave what we most prefer!

  Frances did not become pale or feeble in consequence of her sedentary employment; perhaps the
stimulus it communicated to her mind counterbalanced
the inaction it imposed on her body. She changed,
indeed, changed obviously and rapidly, but it was for
the better. When I first saw her, her countenance
was sunless, her complexion colorless. She looked
like one who had no source of enjoyment, no store of
bliss any where in the world; now the cloud had
passed from her mien, leaving space for the dawn of
hope and interest, and those feelings rose like a clear
morning, animating what had been depressed, tinting
what had been pale. Her eyes, whose color I had not
at first known, so dim were they with repressed tears,
so shadowed with ceaseless dejection, now, lit by a ray
of the sunshine that cheered her heart, revealed irids
of bright hazel—irids large and full, screened with long
lashes—and pupils instinct with fire. That look of
wan emaciation which anxiety or low spirits often
communicates to a thoughtful, thin face, rather long
than round, having vanished from hers, a clearness of
skin almost bloom, and a plumpness almost embon-
point, softened the decided lines of her features. Her
figure shared in this beneficial change; it became
rounder; and as the harmony of her form was complete and her stature of the graceful middle height,

one did not regret (or at least *I* did not regret) the absence of confirmed fullness in contours still slight, though compact, elegant, flexible; the exquisite turning of waist, wrist, hand, foot, and ankle satisfied completely my notions of symmetry, and allowed a lightness and freedom of movement which corresponded with my ideas of grace.

Thus improved, thus wakened to life, Mdlle. Henri began to take a new footing in the school. Her mental power, manifested gradually but steadily, ere long extorted recognition even from the envious; and when the young and healthy saw that she could smile brightly, converse gayly, move with vivacity and alertness, they acknowledged in her a sisterhood of youth and health, and tolerated her as of their kind accordingly.

To speak truth, I watched this change much as a gardener watches the growth of a precious plant, and I contributed to it too, even as the said gardener contributes to the development of his favorite. To me it was not difficult to discover how I could best foster my pupil, cherish her starved feelings, and induce the outward manifestation of that inward vigor which sunless drought and blighting blast had hitherto forbidden to expand. Constancy of attention; a kindness as mute as watchful, always standing by her, cloaked in the rough garb of austerity, and making its real nature known only by a rare glance of interest, or a cordial and gentle word; real respect masked with seeming imperiousness, directing, urging her actions, yet helping her too, and that with devoted care—these were the means I used, for these means best suited Frances' feelings, as susceptible as deep-vibrating— her nature, at once proud and shy.

The benefits of my system became apparent also in her altered demeanor as a teacher. She now took her place among her pupils with an air of spirit and firmness which assured them at once that she meant to be obeyed, and obeyed she was. They felt they had lost their power over her. If any girl had rebelled, she would no longer have taken her rebellion to heart. She possessed a source of comfort they could not drain, a pillar of support they could not overthrow: formerly, when insulted, she wept; now, she smiled.

The public reading of one of her devoirs achieved the revelation of her talents to all and sundry; I remember the subject—it was an emigrant's letter to his friends at home. It opened with simplicity. Some natural and graphic touches disclosed to the reader the scene of virgin forest, and great, New-World river, barren of sail and flag, amid which the epistle was supposed to be indited. The difficulties and dangers that attend a settler's life were hinted at; and in the few words said on the subject, Mdlle. Henri failed not to render audible the voice of resolve, patience, endeavor. The disasters which had driven him from his native country were alluded to; stainless honor, inflexible independence, indestructible self-respect there took the word. Past days were spoken of; the grief of parting, the regrets of absence, were touched upon; feeling, forcible and fine, breathed eloquent in every period. At the close, consolation was suggested; religious faith became there the speaker, and she spoke well.

The devoir was powerfully written in language at once chaste and choice, in a style nerved with vigor and graced with harmony.

Mdlle. Reuter was quite sufficiently acquainted with English to understand it when read or spoken in her presence, though she could neither speak nor write it herself. During the perusal of this devoir, she sat placidly busy, her eyes and fingers occupied with the formation of a " rivière," or open-work hem round a cambric handkerchief. She said nothing, and her face and forehead, clothed with a mask of purely negative expression, were as blank of comment as her lips. As neither surprise, pleasure, approbation, nor interest were evinced in her countenance, so no more were disdain, envy, annoyance, weariness; if that inscrutable mien said any thing, it was simply this:

"The matter is too trite to excite an emotion or call forth an opinion."

As soon as I had done, a hum rose; several of the pupils, pressing round Mdlle. Henri, began to beset her with compliments; the composed voice of the directress was now heard:

"Young ladies, such of you as have cloaks and umbrellas will hasten to return home before the shower becomes heavier" (it was raining a little), " the remainder will wait till their respective servants arrive to fetch them." And the school dispersed, for it was four o'clock.

"Monsieur, a word," said Mdlle. Reuter, stepping on to the estrade, and signifying, by a movement of the hand, that she wished me to relinquish, for an instant, the castor I had clutched.

" Mademoiselle, I am at your service."

" Monsieur, it is, of course, an excellent plan to encourage effort in young people by making conspicuous the progress of any particularly industrious pupil, but do you not think that in the present instance Mdlle. Henry can hardly be considered as a concurrent with the other pupils ? She is older than most of them, and has had advantages of an exclusive nature for acquiring a knowledge of English ; on the other hand, her sphere of life is somewhat beneath theirs ; under these circumstances, a public distinction, conferred upon Mdlle. Henri, may be the means of suggesting comparisons, and exciting feelings such as would be far from advantageous to the individual forming their object. The interest I take in Mdlle. Henri's real welfare makes me desirous of screening her from annoyances of this sort ; besides, Monsieur, as I have before hinted to you, the sentiment of *amour propre* has a somewhat marked preponderance in her character; celebrity has a tendency to foster this sentiment, and in her it should be rather repressed ; she rather needs keeping down than bringing forward ; and then I think, Monsieur—it appears to me that ambition, *literary* ambition especially, is not a feeling to be cherished in the mind of a woman. Would not Mdlle. Henri be much safer and happier if taught to believe that in the quiet discharge of social duties consists her real vocation, than if stimulated to aspire after applause and publicity ? She may never marry ; scanty as are her resources, obscure as are her connections, uncertain as is her health (for I think her consumptive ; her mother died of that complaint), it is more than probable she never will ; I do not see how she can rise to a position whence such a step would be possible ; but even in celibacy it would be better for her to retain the character and habits of a respectable, decorous female."

"Indisputably, Mademoiselle," was my answer. "Your opinion admits of no doubt;" and, fearful of the harangue being renewed, I retreated under cover of that cordial sentence of assent.

At the date of a fortnight after the little incident noted above, I find it recorded in my diary that a hiatus occurred in Mdlle. Henri's usually regular attendance in class. The first day or two I wondered at her absence, but did not like to ask an explanation of it. I thought, indeed, some chance word might be dropped which would afford me the information I wished to obtain, without my running the risk of exciting silly smiles and gossiping whispers by demanding it. But when a week passed, and the seat at the desk near the door still remained vacant, and when no allusion was made to the circumstance by any individual of the class—when, on the contrary, I found that all observed a marked silence on the point, I determined, *coûte qui coûte*, to break the ice of this silly reserve. I selected Sylvie as my informant, because from her I knew that I should at least get a sensible answer, unaccompanied by wriggle, titter, or other flourish of folly.

"Où donc est Mdlle. Henri?" I said one day as I returned an exercise-book I had been examining.

"Elle est partie, Monsieur."

"Partie! et pour combien de temps? Quand reviendra-t-elle?"

"Elle est partie pour toujours, Monsieur; elle ne reviendra plus."

"Ah!" was my involuntary exclamation; then, after a pause:

"En êtes-vous bien sûre, Sylvie?"

"Oui, oui, Monsieur; Mademoiselle la Directrice nous l'a dit elle-même il y a deux ou trois jours."

And I could pursue my inquiries no further; time, place, and circumstances forbade my adding another word. I could neither comment on what had been said, nor demand further particulars. A question as to the reason of the teacher's departure, as to whether it had been voluntary or otherwise, was indeed on my lips, but I suppressed it: there were listeners all round. An hour after, in passing Sylvie in the corridor as she was putting on her bonnet, I stopped short and asked,

"Sylvie, do you know Mdlle. Henri's address? I have some books of hers," I added carelessly, "and I should wish to send them to her."

"No, Monsieur," replied Sylvie; "but perhaps Rosalie, the portress, will be able to give it you."

Rosalie's cabinet was just at hand. I stepped in and repeated the inquiry. Rosalie—a smart French grisette—looked up from her work with a knowing smile, precisely the sort of smile I had been so desirous to avoid exciting. Her answer was prepared; she knew nothing whatever of Mdlle. Henri's address —had never known it. Turning from her with impatience—for I believed she lied and was hired to lie—I almost knocked down some one who had been standing at my back: it was the directress. My abrupt movement made her recoil two or three steps. I was obliged to apologize, which I did more concisely than politely. No man likes to be dogged, and in the very irritable mood in which I then was the sight of Mdlle. Reuter thoroughly incensed me. At the moment I

turned her countenance looked hard, dark, and inquis-
itive; her eyes were bent upon me with an expression
of almost hungry curiosity. I had scarcely caught
this phase of physiognomy ere it had vanished; a
bland smile played on her features; my harsh apology
was received with good-humored facility.

"Oh, don't mention it, Monsieur; you only touched
my hair with your elbow; it is no worse, only a little
disheveled." She shook it back, and, passing her fingers through her curls, loosened them into more numerous and flowing ringlets. Then she went on with
vivacity:

"Rosalie, I was coming to tell you to go instantly
and close the windows of the salon; the wind is rising, and the muslin curtains will be covered with dust."

Rosalie departed. "Now," thought I, "this will
not do. Mdlle. Reuter thinks her meanness in eaves-
dropping is screened by her art in devising a pretext,
whereas the muslin curtains she speaks of are not
more transparent than this same pretext." An impulse came over me to thrust the flimsy screen aside,
and confront her craft with a word or two of plain
truth. "The rough-shod foot treads most firmly on
slippery ground," thought I, so I began:

"Mademoiselle Henri has left your establishment—
been dismissed, I presume?"

"Ah! I wished to have a little conversation with
you, Monsieur," replied the directress, with the most
natural and affable air in the world; "but we can
not talk quietly here; will Monsieur step into the garden a minute?" And she preceded me, stepping out
through the glass door I have before mentioned.

" There," said she, when we had reached the centre
of the middle alley, and when the foliage of shrubs
and trees, now in their summer pride, closing behind
and around us, shut out the view of the house, and
thus imparted a sense of seclusion even to this little
plot of ground in the very core of a capital, "there;
one feels quiet and free when there are only pear-trees
and rose-bushes about one; I dare say you, like me,
Monsieur, are sometimes tired of being eternally in the
midst of life—of having human faces always round
you, human eyes always upon you, human voices always in your ear.　I am sure I often wish intensely
for liberty to spend a whole month in the country at
some little farm-house, bien gentille, bien propre, tout
entourée de champs et de bois; quelle vie charmante
que la vie champêtre!　N'est-ce pas, Monsieur?"

" Cela dépend, Mademoiselle."

" Que le vent est bon et frais!" continued the directress; and she was right there, for it was a south
wind, soft and sweet.　I carried my hat in my hand,
and this gentle breeze, passing through my hair,
soothed my temples like balm.　Its refreshing effect,
however, penetrated no deeper than the mere surface
of the frame; for, as I walked by the side of Mdlle.
Reuter, my heart was still hot within me, and while
I was musing the fire burned; then spake I with my
tongue:

" I understand Mdlle. Henri is gone from hence,
and will not return?"

" Ah! true.　I meant to have named the subject
to you some days ago, but my time is so completely
taken up I can not do half the things I wish.　Have

you never experienced what it is, Monsieur, to find the
day too short by twelve hours for your numerous duties ?"

"Not often. Mdlle. Henri's departure was not voluntary, I presume? If it had been, she would certainly have given me some intimation of it, being my
pupil."

"Oh, did she not tell you? that was strange. For
my part, I never thought of adverting to the subject.
When one has so many things to attend to, one is apt
to forget little incidents that are not of primary importance."

"You consider Mdlle. Henri's dismission, then, as a
very insignificant event?"

"Dismission? Ah! she was not dismissed; I can
say with truth, Monsieur, that since I became the head
of this establishment, no master or teacher has ever
been *dismissed* from it."

"Yet some have left it, Mademoiselle?"

"Many; I have found it necessary to change frequently—a change of instructors is often beneficial to
the interests of a school; it gives life and variety to
the proceedings; it amuses the pupils, and suggests to
the parents the idea of exertion and progress."

"Yet, when you are tired of a professor or maîtresse,
you scruple to dismiss them?"

"No need to have recourse to such extreme measures, I assure you. Allons, Monsieur le Professeur—
asseyons-nous; je vais vous donner une petite leçon
dans votre état d'instituteur." (I wish I might write
all she said to me in French; it loses sadly by being
translated into English.) We had now reached *the*

garden chair; the directress sat down, and signed me
to sit by her, but I only rested my knee on the seat,
and stood leaning my head and arm against the em-
bowering branch of a huge laburnum, whose golden
flowers, blent with the dusky green leaves of a lilac-
bush, formed a mixed arch of shade and sunshine over
the retreat.   Mdlle. Reuter sat silent a moment; some
novel movements were evidently working in her mind,
and they showed their nature on her astute brow;
she was meditating some *chef d'œuvre* of policy.   Convinced by several months' experience that the affectation of virtues she did not possess was unavailing to
ensnare me—aware that I had read her real nature, .
and would believe nothing of the character she gave
out as being hers—she had determined, at last, to try
a new key, and see if the lock of my heart would yield
to that; a little audacity, a word of truth, a glimpse
of the real. "Yes, I will try," was her inward resolve; and then her blue eye glittered upon me—it did
not flash—nothing of flame ever kindled in its temperate gleam.

"Monsieur fears to sit by me?" she inquired, play-
fully.

"I have no wish to usurp Pelet's place," I answered, for I had got the habit of speaking to her bluntly;
a habit begun in anger, but continued because I saw
that, instead of offending, it fascinated her.   She cast
down her eyes and drooped her eyelids; she sighed
uneasily; she turned with an anxious gesture, as if she
would give me the idea of a bird that flutters in its
cage, and would fain fly from its jail and jailer, and
seek its natural mate and pleasant nest.

"Well—and your lesson?" I demanded, briefly.

"Ah!" she exclaimed, recovering herself, "you are so young, so frank and fearless, so talented, so impatient of imbecility, so disdainful of vulgarity, you need a lesson; here it is, then: Far more is to be done in this world by dexterity than by strength; but perhaps you knew that before, for there is delicacy as well as power in your character—policy as well as pride."

"Go on," said I; and I could hardly help smiling, the flattery was so piquant, so finely seasoned. She caught the prohibited smile, though I passed my hand over my mouth to conceal it; and again she made room for me to sit beside her. I shook my head, though temptation penetrated to my senses at the moment, and once more I told her to go on.

"Well, then, if ever you are at the head of a large establishment, dismiss nobody. To speak truth, Monsieur (and to you I will speak truth), I despise people who are always making rows, blustering, sending off one to the right, and another to the left, urging, and hurrying circumstances. I'll tell you what I like best to do, Monsieur, shall I?" She looked up again; she had compounded her glance well this time—much archness, more deference, a spicy dash of coquetry, an unveiled consciousness of capacity. I nodded; she treated me like the great Mogul; so I became the great Mogul as far as she was concerned.

"I like, Monsieur, to take my knitting in my hands, and to sit quietly down in my chair; circumstances defile past me; I watch their march; so long as they follow the course I wish, I say nothing and do nothing;

I

I don't clap my hands, and cry out 'Bravo! How lucky I am!' to attract the attention and envy of my neighbors; I am merely passive; but when events fall out ill—when circumstances become adverse—I watch very vigilantly; I knit on still, and still I hold my tongue; but every now and then, Monsieur, I just put my toe out—so—and give the rebellious circumstance a little secret push, without noise, which sends it the way I wish, and I am successful after all, and nobody has seen my expedient. So, when teachers or masters become troublesome and inefficient—when, in short, the interests of the school would suffer from their retaining their places, I mind my knitting, events progress, circumstances glide past; I see one which, if pushed ever so little awry, will render untenable the post I wish to have vacated—the deed is done—the stumbling-block removed—and no one saw me; I have not made an enemy, I am rid of an incumbrance."

A moment since, and I thought her alluring; this speech concluded, I looked on her with distaste. "Just like you," was my cold answer. "And in this way you have ousted Mdlle. Henry: you wanted her office, therefore you rendered it intolerable for her?"

"Not at all, Monsieur; I was merely anxious about Mdlle. Henri's health; no, your moral sight is clear and piercing, but there you have failed to discover the truth. I took—I have always taken a real interest in Mdlle. Henri's welfare. I did not like her going out in all weathers. I thought it would be more advantageous for her to obtain a permanent situation; besides, I considered her now qualified to do something more than teach sewing. I reasoned with her;

left the decision to herself; she saw the correctness of my views, and adopted them."

"Excellent! and now, Mademoiselle, you will have the goodness to give me her address."

"Her address?" and a sombre and stony change came over the mien of the directress. "Her address? Ah! well, I wish I could oblige you, Monsieur, but I can not, and I will tell you why; whenever I myself asked her for her address, she always evaded the inquiry. I thought—I may be wrong—but I *thought* her motive for doing so was a natural though mistaken reluctance to introduce me to some, probably, very poor abode. Her means were narrow, her origin obscure; she lives somewhere, doubtless, in the 'basse ville.' "

"I'll not lose sight of my best pupil yet," said I, "though she were born of beggars and lodged in a cellar; for the rest, it is absurd to make a bugbear of her origin to me. I happen to know that she was a Swiss pastor's daughter, neither more nor less; and as to her narrow means, I care nothing for the poverty of her purse so long as her heart overflows with affluence."

"Your sentiments are perfectly noble, Monsieur," said the directress, affecting to suppress a yawn. Her sprightliness was now extinct, her temporary candor shut up; the little, red-colored, piratical-looking pennon of audacity she had allowed to float a minute in the air was furled, and the broad, soberhued flag of dissimulation again hung low over the citadel. I did not like her thus, so I cut short the *tête-à-tête* and departed.

CHAPTER XIX.

NOVELISTS should never allow themselves to weary of the study of real life. If they observed this duty conscientiously, they would give us fewer pictures checkered with vivid contrasts of light and shade; they would seldom elevate their heroes and heroines to the heights of rapture, still seldomer sink them to the depths of despair; for, if we rarely taste the fullness of joy in this life, we yet more rarely savor the acrid bitterness of hopeless anguish; unless, indeed, we have plunged like beasts into sensual indulgence, abused, strained, stimulated, again overstrained, and, at last, destroyed our faculties for enjoyment; then, truly, we may find ourselves without support, robbed of hope. Our agony is great, and how can it end? We have broken the spring of our powers; life must be all suffering—too feeble to conceive faith; death must be darkness; God, spirits, religion can have no place in our collapsed minds, where linger only hideous and polluting recollections of vice; and time brings us on to the brink of the grave, and dissolution flings us in, a rag eaten through and through with disease, wrung together with pain, stamped into the church-yard sod by the inexorable heel of despair.

But the man of regular life and rational mind never despairs. He loses his property—it is a blow—he staggers a moment; then his energies, roused by the smart, are at work to seek a remedy; activity soon mitigates regret. Sickness affects him; he takes patience—endures what he can not cure. Acute pain racks him; his writhing limbs know not where to find rest; he lean's on Hope's anchor. Death takes from him what he loves; roots up and tears violently away the stem round which his affections were twined —a dark, dismal time, a frightful wrench; but some morning Religion looks into his desolate house with sunrise, and says that in another world, another life, he shall meet his kindred again. She speaks of that world as a place unsullied by sin—of that life as an era unimbittered by suffering; she mightily strengthens her consolation by connecting with it two ideas— which mortals can not comprehend, but on which they love to repose—Eternity, Immortality; and the mind of the mourner being filled with an image, faint yet glorious, of heavenly hills all light and peace—of a spirit resting there in bliss—of a day when his spirit shall also alight there, free and disembodied—of a re-union perfected by love, purified from fear, he takes courage—goes out to encounter the necessities and discharge the duties of life; and, though sadness may never lift her burden from his mind, Hope will enable him to support it.

Well, and what suggested all this? and what is the inference to be drawn therefrom? What suggested it is the circumstance of my best pupil—my treasure—being snatched from my hands, and put away out of my reach; the inference to be drawn from it is that, being a steady, reasonable man, I did not allow the resentment, disappointment, and grief engendered in my mind by this evil chance to grow

there to any monstrous size, nor did I allow them to
monopolize the whole space of my heart; I pent
them, on the contrary, in one strait and secret nook.
In the daytime, too, when I was about my duties, I
put them on the silent system; and it was only after
I had closed the door of my chamber at night that I
somewhat relaxed my severity toward these morose
nurslings, and allowed vent to their language of murmurs; then, in revenge, they sat on my pillow, haunted my bed, and kept me awake with their long, midnight cry.

A week passed. I had said nothing more to Mdlle.
Reuter. I had been calm in my demeanor to her,
though stony cold and hard. When I looked at her
it was with the glance fitting to be bestowed on one
who I knew had consulted jealousy as an adviser, and
employed treachery as an instrument—the glance of
quiet disdain and rooted distrust. On Saturday evening, ere I left the house, I stepped into the *salle-à-
manger*, where she was sitting alone, and, placing myself before her, I asked, with the same tranquil tone
and manner that I should have used had I put the
question for the first time,

"Mademoiselle, will you have the goodness to give
me the address of Frances Evans Henri?"

A little surprised, but not disconcerted, she smiling-
ly disclaimed any knowledge of that address, adding,
"Monsieur has perhaps forgotten that I explained all
about that circumstance before—a week ago?"

"Mademoiselle," I continued, "you would greatly
oblige me by directing me to that young person's
abode."

She seemed somewhat puzzled; and at last, looking up with an admirably counterfeited air of naïvete,
she demanded, " Does Monsieur think I am telling an
untruth ?"

Still avoiding to give her a direct answer, I said,
" Is it not, then, your intention, Mademoiselle, to
oblige me in this particular ?"

" But, Monsieur, how can I tell you what I do not
know ?"

" Very well; I understand you perfectly, Mademoiselle; and now I have-only two or three words to say.
This is the last week in July; in another month the
vacation will commence; have the goodness to avail
yourself of the leisure it will afford you to look out for
another English master—at the close of August, I
shall be under the necessity of resigning my post in
your establishment."

I did not wait for her comments on this announcement, but bowed and immediately withdrew.

That same evening, soon after dinner, a servant
brought me a small packet; it was directed in a hand
I knew, but had not hoped so soon to see again. Being in my own apartment and alone, there was nothing
to prevent my immediately opening it; it contained
four five-franc pieces, and a note in English.

"MONSIEUR,—I came to Mdlle. Reuter's house yesterday, at the time when I knew you would be just
about finishing your lesson, and I asked if I might go
into the school-room and speak to you. Mdlle. Reuter
came out and said you were already gone; it had not
yet struck four, so I thought she must be mistaken,

but concluded it would be vain to call another day on
the same errand. In one sense, a note will do as well;
it will wrap up the 20 francs, the price of the lessons
I have received from you; and if it will not fully express the thanks I owe you in addition—if it will not
bid you good-by as I could wish to have done—if it
will not tell you, as I long to do, how sorry I am that
I shall probably never see you more—why, spoken
words would hardly be more adequate to the task.
Had I seen you, I should probably have stammered
out something feeble and unsatisfactory—something
belying my feelings rather than explaining them; so
it is perhaps as well that I was denied admission to
your presence. You often remarked, Monsieur, that
my devoirs dwelt a great deal on fortitude in bearing
grief; you said I introduced that theme too often; I
find, indeed, that it is much easier to write about a
severe duty than to perform it, for I am oppressed
when I see and feel to what a reverse fate has con-
demned me. You were kind to me, Monsieur—very
kind; I am afflicted—I am heart-broken to be quite
separated from you; soon I shall have no friend on
earth. But it is useless troubling you with my dis-
tresses. What claim have I on your sympathy?
None; I will then say no more.

" Farewell, Monsieur. F. E. HENRI."

I put up the note in my pocket-book; I slipped the
five-franc pieces into my purse; then I took a turn
through my narrow chamber.

" Mdlle. Reuter talked about her poverty," said I,
" and she is poor; yet she pays her debts, and more.

I have not yet given her a quarter's lessons, and she has sent me a quarter's due. I wonder of what she deprived herself to scrape together the twenty francs ; I wonder what sort of a place she has to live in, and what sort of a woman her aunt is, and whether she is likely to get employment to supply the place she has lost. No doubt she will have to trudge about long enough from school to school, to inquire here and apply there—be rejected in this place, disappointed in that. Many an evening she'll go to her bed tired and unsuccessful. And the directress would not let her in to bid me good-by ? I might not have the chance of standing with her for a few minutes at a window in the school-room, and exchanging some half dozen sentences—getting to know where she lived—putting matters in train for having all things arranged to my mind? No address on the note," I continued, drawing it again from the pocket-book and examining it on each side of the two leaves : "women are women, that is certain, and always do business like women ; men mechanically put a date and address to their communications. And these five-franc pieces"—(I hauled them forth from my purse)—"if she had offered me them herself instead of tying them up with a thread of green silk in a kind of Liliputian packet, I could have thrust them back into her little hand, and shut up the small, taper fingers over them—so—and compelled her shame, her pride, her shyness all to yield to a little bit of determined will. Now where is she? How can I get at her ?"

Opening my chamber door, I walked down into the kitchen.

I 2

"Who brought the packet?" I asked of the servant who had delivered it to me.

"Un petit commissionnaire, Monsieur."

"Did he say any thing?"

"Rien."

And I wended my way up the back stairs, wondrously the wiser for my inquiries.

"No matter," said I to myself, as I again closed the door, "no matter; I'll seek her through Brussels."

And I did. I sought her day by day, whenever I had a moment's leisure, for four weeks; I sought her on Sundays all day long; I sought her on the Boulevards, in the Allée Verte, in the Park; I sought her in Ste. Gudule and St. Jacques; I sought her in the two Protestant chapels; I attended these latter at the German, French, and English services, not doubting that I should meet her at one of them. All my researches were absolutely fruitless; my security on the last point was proved by the event to be equally groundless with my other calculations. I stood at the door of each chapel after the service, and waited till every individual had come out, scrutinizing every gown draping a slender form, peering under every bonnet covering a young head. In vain; I saw girlish figures pass me, drawing their black scarfs over their sloping shoulders, but none of them had the exact turn and air of Mdlle. Henri's; I saw pale and thoughtful faces "encadrées" in bands of brown hair, but I never found her forehead, her eyes, her eyebrows. All the features of all the faces I met seemed frittered away, because my eye failed to recognize the peculiarities it was bent upon; an ample space of brow, and a large, dark, and seri-

ous eye, with a fine but decided line of eyebrow traced
above.

"She has probably left Brussels—perhaps is gone
to England, as she said she would," muttered I, inwardly, as, on the afternoon of the fourth Sunday, I
turned from the door of the chapel royal which the
doorkeeper had just closed and locked, and followed in
the wake of the last of the congregation, now dispersed
and dispersing over the square. I had soon outwalk-
ed the couples of English gentlemen and ladies. (Gracious goodness! why don't they dress better? My eye
is yet filled with visions of the high-flounced, slovenly,
and tumbled dresses in costly silk and satin; of the
large, unbecoming collars in expensive lace; of the ill-
cut coats and strangely-fashioned pantaloons which
every Sunday, at the English service, filled the choirs
of the chapel royal, and after it, issuing forth into the
square, came into disadvantageous contrast with freshly and trimly attired foreign figures, hastening to attend salut at the church of Coburg.) I had passed these
pairs of Britons, and the groups of pretty British children, and the British footmen and waiting-maids; I
had crossed the Place Royale, and got into the Rue
Royale; thence I had diverged into the Rue de Louvain—an old and quiet street. I remember that, feeling a little hungry, and not desiring to go back and
take my share of the "goûter" now on the refectory-
table at Pelet's—to wit, pistolets and water—I stepped into a baker's and refreshed myself on a *couc* (?)
(it is a Flemish word; I don't know how to spell it)
à Corinthe—Anglice, a currant bun—and a cup of
coffee; and then I strolled on toward the Porte de

Louvain. Very soon I was out of the city, and, slowly mounting the hill which ascends from the gate, I
took my time, for the afternoon, though cloudy, was
very sultry, and not a breeze stirred to refresh the atmosphere. No inhabitant of Brussels need wander far
to search for solitude ; let him but move half a league
from his own city, and he will find her brooding still
and blank over the wide fields, so drear though so fertile, spread out treeless and trackless round the capital
of Brabant. Having gained the summit of the hill,
and having stood and looked long over the cultured
but lifeless campaign, I felt a wish to quit the high
road, which I had hitherto followed, and get in among
those tilled grounds—fertile as the beds of a Brobdig-
nagian kitchen-garden—spreading far and wide even to
the boundaries of the horizon, where, from a dusk green,
distance changed them to a sullen blue, and confused
their tints with those of the livid and thunderous-look-
ing sky. Accordingly, I turned up a by-path to the
right. I had not followed it far ere it brought me, as
I expected, into the fields, amid which, just before me,
stretched a long and lofty white wall, inclosing, as it
seemed from the foliage showing above, some thickly-
planted nursery of yew and cypress, for of that species
were the branches resting on the pale parapets, and
crowding gloomily about a massive cross, planted
doubtless on a central eminence, and extending its
arms, which seemed of black marble, over the summits
of those sinister trees. I approached, wondering to
what house this well-protected garden appertained ; I
turned the angle of the wall, thinking to see some stately residence ; I was close upon great iron gates ; there

was a hut serving for a lodge near, but I had no occasion to apply for the key: the gates were open; I pushed one leaf back; rain had rusted its hinges, for it groaned dolefully as they revolved. Thick planting embowered the entrance. Passing up the avenue, I saw objects on each hand which, in their own mute language of inscription and sign, explained clearly to what abode I had made my way. This was the house appointed for all living; crosses, monuments, and garlands of everlastings announced, "The Protestant Cemetery, outside the gate of Louvain."

The place was large enough to afford half an hour's strolling without the monotony of treading continually the same path, and, for those who love to peruse the annals of grave-yards, here was variety of inscription enough to occupy the attention for double or treble that space of time. Hither people of many kindreds, tongues, and nations had brought their dead for interment; and here, on pages of stone, of marble, and of brass, were written names, dates, last tributes of pomp or love, in English, in French, in German, and Latin. Here the Englishman had erected a marble monument over the remains of his Mary Smith or Jane Brown, and inscribed it only with her name. There the French widower had shaded the grave of his Elmire or Celestine with a brilliant thicket of roses, amid which a little tablet, rising, bore an equally bright testimony to her countless virtues. Every nation, tribe, and kindred mourned after its own fashion, and how soundless was the mourning of all! My own tread, though slow and upon smooth-rolled paths, seemed to startle, because it formed the sole break to a silence

otherwise total. Not only the winds, but the very fitful wandering airs were that afternoon, as by common
consent, all fallen asleep in their various quarters:
the north was hushed, the south silent, the east sobbed
not, nor did the west whisper. The clouds in heaven
were condensed and dull, but apparently quite motionless. Under the trees of this cemetery nestled a warm,
breathless gloom, out of which the cypresses stood up
straight and mute, above which the willows hung low
and still; where the flowers, as languid as fair, waited
listless for night dew or thunder-shower; where the
tombs, and those they hid, lay impassible to sun or
shadow, to rain or drought.

Importuned by the sound of my own footsteps, I
turned off upon the turf, and slowly advanced to a
grove of yews. I saw something stir among the stems.
I thought it might be a broken branch swinging. My
short-sighted vision had caught no form, only a sense
of motion; but the dusky shade passed on, appearing
and disappearing at the openings in the avenue. I soon
discerned it was a living thing, and a human thing;
and, drawing nearer, I perceived it was a woman, pac-
ing slowly to and fro, and evidently deeming herself
alone, as I had deemed myself alone, and meditating
as I had been meditating. Ere long she returned to a
seat which I fancy she had but just quitted, or I should
have caught sight of her before. It was in a nook
screened by a clump of trees; there was the white wall
before her, and a little stone set up against the wall,
and at the foot of the stone was an allotment of turf
freshly turned up—a new-made grave. I put on my
spectacles, and passed softly close behind her. Glanc-

ing at the inscription on the stone, I read, "Julienne Henri, died at Brussels, aged sixty. August 10th, 18—." Having perused the inscription, I looked down at the form sitting bent and thoughtful just under my eyes, unconscious of any living thing; it was a slim, youthful figure, in mourning apparel of the plainest black stuff, with a little simple black crape bonnet. I felt as well as saw who it was, and, moving neither hand nor foot, stood some moments enjoying the security of conviction. I had sought her for a month, and had never discovered one of her traces—never met a hope, or seized a chance of encountering her any where. I had been forced to loosen my grasp on expectation, and, but an hour ago, had sunk slackly under the discouraging thought that the current of life and the impulse of destiny had swept her forever from my reach ; and behold, while bending sullenly earthward beneath the pressure of despondency—while following with my eyes the track of sorrow on the turf of a grave-yard, here was my lost jewel dropped on the tear-fed herbage, nestling in the mossy and mouldy roots of yew-trees.

Frances sat very quiet, her elbow on her knee, and her head on her hand. I knew she could retain a thinking attitude a long time without change. At last a tear fell. She had been looking at the name on the stone before her, and her heart had no doubt endured one of those constrictions with which the desolate living, regretting the dead, are at times so sorely oppressed. Many tears rolled down, which she wiped away, again and again, with her handkerchief; some distressed sobs escaped her, and then, the paroxysm over, she sat quiet as before. I put my hand gently on her shoulder. No need further to prepare her, for she was neither hysterical nor liable to fainting-fits; a sudden push, indeed, might have startled her, but the contact of my quiet touch merely woke attention as I wished; and, though she turned quickly, yet so lightning-swift is thought—in some minds especially—I believe the wonder of what—the consciousness of who it was that thus stole unawares on her solitude, had passed through her brain and flashed into her heart even before she had effected that hasty movement; at least, Amazement had hardly opened her eyes and raised them to mine, ere Recognition informed their irids with most speaking brightness. Nervous surprise had hardly discomposed her features ere a sentiment of most vivid joy shone clear and warm on her whole countenance. I had hardly time to observe that she was wasted and pale ere called to feel a responsive inward pleasure by the sense of most full and exquisite pleasure glowing in the animated flush, and shining in the expansive light now diffused over my pupil's face. It was the summer sun flashing out after the heavy summer shower; and what fertilizes more rapidly than that beam, burning almost like fire in its ardor?

I hate boldness—that boldness which is of the brassy brow and insensate nerves; but I love the courage of the strong heart, the fervor of the generous blood; I loved with passion the light of Frances Evans' clear hazel eye when it did not fear to look straight into mine; I loved the tones with which she uttered the words "Mon maître! mon maître!"

I loved the movement with which she confided her

hand to my hand; I loved her as she stood there, penniless and parentless; for a sensualist charmless, for me a treasure; my best object of sympathy on earth, thinking such thoughts as I thought, feeling such feelings as I felt; my ideal of the shrine in which to seal my stores of love; personification of discretion and forethought, of diligence and persever- ance, of self-denial and self-control—those guardians, those trusty keepers of the gift I longed to confer on her—the gift of all my affections; model of truth and honor, of independence and conscientiousness—those refiners and sustainers of an honest life; silent pos- sessor of a well of tenderness, of a flame as genial as still, as pure as quenchless, of natural feeling, natural passion—those sources of refreshment and comfort to the sanctuary of home. I knew how quietly and how deeply the well bubbled in her heart; I knew how the more dangerous flame burned safely under the eye of Reason; I had seen when the fire shot up a mo- ment high and vivid, when the accelerated heat troub- led life's current in its channels; I had seen Reason reduce the rebel, and humble its blaze to embers. I had confidence in Frances Evans; I had respect for her; and, as I drew her arm through mine, and led her out of the cemetery, I felt I had another sentiment, as strong as confidence, as firm as respect, more fervid than either—that of love.

"Well, my pupil," said I, as the ominous-sound- ing gate swung to behind us, "well, I have found you again; a month's search has seemed long, and I little thought to have discovered my lost sheep straying among graves."

Never had I addressed her but as "Mademoiselle" before, and to speak thus was to take up a tone new to both her and me.   Her answer apprised me that this language ruffled none of her feelings, woke no discord in her heart.

"Mon maître," she said, "have you troubled yourself to seek me ?   I little imagined you would think much of my absence, but I grieved bitterly to be taken away from you.   I was sorry for that circumstance when heavier troubles ought to have made me forget it."

"Your aunt is dead ?"

"Yes, a fortnight since ; and she died full of regret, which I could not chase from her mind.   She kept repeating, even during the last night of her existence, 'Frances, you will be so lonely when I am gone, so friendless.'   She wished, too, that she could have been buried in Switzerland, and it was I who persuaded her in her old age to leave the banks of Lake Leman, and to come, only as it seems to die, in this flat region of Flanders.   Willingly would I have observed her last wish, and taken her remains back to our own country, but that was impossible.   I was forced to lay her here."

"She was ill but a short time, I presume ?"

"But three weeks.   When she began to sink, I asked Mdlle. Reuter's leave to stay with her and wait on her.   I readily got leave."

"Do you return to the pensionnat ?" I demanded, hastily.

"Monsieur, when I had been at home a week, Mdlle. Reuter called one evening, just after I had got my aunt

to bed. She went into her room to speak to her, and
was extremely civil and affable, as she always is ; afterward she came and sat with me a long time, and,
just as she rose to go away, she said, ' Mademoiselle,
I shall not soon cease to regret your departure from
my establishment, though indeed it is true that you
have taught your class of pupils so well that they are
all quite accomplished in the little works you manage
so skillfully, and have not the slightest need of further
instruction. My second teacher must in future supply your place, with regard to the younger pupils, as
well as she can, though she is indeed an inferior ar-
tiste to you, and doubtless it will be your part now to
assume a higher position in your calling. I am sure
you will every where find schools and families willing
to profit by your talents.' And then she paid me my
last quarter's salary. I asked, as Mademoiselle would
no doubt think, very bluntly, if she designed to discharge me from the establishment. She smiled at my
inelegance of speech, and answered that ' our connection as employer and employed was certainly dissolved, but that she hoped still to retain the pleasure
of my acquaintance ; she should always be happy to
see me as a friend ;' and then she said something
about the excellent condition of the streets, and the
long continuance of fine weather, and went away quite
cheerful."

I laughed inwardly ; all this was so like the directress—so like what I had expected and guessed of her
conduct ; and then the exposure and proof of her lie,
unconsciously afforded by Frances : " She had frequently applied for Mdlle. Henri's address," forsooth ;

"Mdlle. Henri had always evaded giving it," &c., &c., and here I found her a visitor at the very house of whose locality she had professed absolute ignorance!

Any comments I might have intended to make on my pupil's communication were checked by the plashing of large rain-drops on our faces and on the path, and by the muttering of a distant but coming storm. The warning obvious in stagnant air and leaden sky had already induced me to take the road leading back to Brussels, and now I hastened my own steps and those of my companion, and, as our way lay down hill, we got on rapidly. There was an interval after the fall of the first broad drops before heavy rain came on; in the mean time we had passed through the Porte de Louvain, and were again in the city.

"Where do you live?" I asked; "I will see you safe home."

"Rue Notre Dame aux Neiges," answered Frances.

It was not far from the Rue de Louvain, and we stood on the door-steps of the house we sought ere the clouds, severing with loud peal and shattered cataract of lightning, emptied their livid folds in a torrent, heavy, prone, and broad.

"Come in! come in!" said Frances, as, after putting her into the house, I paused ere I followed; the word decided me; I stepped across the threshold, shut the door on the rushing, flashing, whitening storm, and followed her up stairs to her apartments. Neither she nor I were wet; a projection over the door had warded off the straight-descending flood; none but the first large drops had touched our garments; one minute more, and we should not have had a dry thread on us.

Stepping over a little mat of green wool, I found myself in a small room, with a painted floor and a square of green carpet in the middle; the articles of furniture were few, but all bright and exquisitely clean; order reigned through its narrow limits—such order as it soothed my punctilious soul to behold. And I had hesitated to enter the abode, because I apprehended, after all, that Mdlle. Reuter's hint about its extreme poverty might be too well founded, and I feared to embarrass the lace-mender by entering her lodgings unawares. Poor the place might be; poor truly it was; but its neatness was better than elegance, and, had but a bright little fire shone on that clean hearth, I should have deemed it more attractive than a palace. No fire was there, however, and no fuel laid ready to light; the lace-mender was unable to allow herself that indulgence, especially now, when, deprived by death of her sole relative, she had only her own unaided exertions to rely on. Frances went into an inner room to take off her bonnet, and she came out a model of frugal neatness, with her well-fitting black stuff dress, so accurately defining her elegant bust and taper waist, with her spotless white collar turned back from a fair and shapely neck, with her plenteous brown hair arranged in smooth bands on her temples, and in a large Grecian plat behind. Ornaments she had none—neither brooch, ring, nor ribbon; she did well enough without them: perfection of fit, proportion of form, grace of carriage, agreeably supplied their place. Her eye, as she re-entered the small sitting-room, instantly sought mine, which was just then lingering on the hearth. I knew she read at once the sort of inward ruth and pitying pain which the chill vacancy of that hearth stirred in my soul. Quick to penetrate, quick to determine, and quicker to put in practice, she had in a moment tied a Holland apron round her waist; then she disappeared, and reappeared with a basket; it had a cover; she opened it, and produced wood and coal; deftly and compactly she arranged them in the grate.

"It is her whole stock, and she will exhaust it out of hospitality," thought I.

"What are you going to do?" I asked: "not surely to light a fire this hot evening? I shall be smothered." &

"Indeed, Monsieur, I feel it very chilly since the rain began; besides, I must boil the water for my tea, for I take tea on Sundays. You will be obliged to try and bear the heat."

She had struck a light; the wood was already in a blaze; and, truly, when contrasted with the darkness, the wild tumult of the tempest without, that peaceful glow which began to beam on the now animated hearth seemed very cheering. A low, purring sound from some quarter announced that another being besides myself was pleased with the change; a black cat, roused by the light from its sleep on a little cushioned foot-stool, came and rubbed its head against Frances' gown as she knelt. She caressed it, saying it had been a favorite with her "pauvre tante Julienne."

The fire being lit, the hearth swept, and a small kettle of a very antique pattern, such as I thought I remembered to have seen in old farm-houses in England, placed over the now ruddy flame, Frances' hands were washed, and her apron removed in an instant; then she opened a cupboard, and took out a tea-tray, on which she had soon arranged a china tea-equipage, whose pattern, shape, and size denoted a remote antiquity; a little old-fashioned silver spoon was deposited in each saucer, and a pair of silver-tongs, equally old-fashioned, were laid on the sugar-basin; from the cupboard, too, was produced a tidy silver cream-ewer, not larger than an egg-shell. While making these preparations, she chanced to look up, and, reading curiosity in my eyes, she smiled and asked,

"Is this like England, Monsieur?",

"Like the England of a hundred years ago," I replied.

"Is it, truly? Well, every thing on this tray is at least a hundred years old: these cups, these spoons, this ewer, are all heir-looms; my great-grandmother left them to my grandmother, she to my mother, and my mother brought them with her from England to Switzerland, and left them to me; and, ever since I was a little girl, I have thought I should like to carry them back to England, whence they came."

She put some pistolets on the table; she made the tea as foreigners do make tea—*i. e.*, at the rate of a teaspoonful to half a dozen cups; she placed me a chair, and, as I took it, she asked, with a sort of exultation,

"Will it make you think yourself at home for a moment?"

"If I had a home in England, I believe it would recall it," I answered; and, in truth, there was a sort of illusion in seeing the fair-complexioned, English-looking girl presiding at the English meal, and speaking in the English language.

"You have, then, no home?" was her remark.

"None, nor ever had. If ever I possess a home, it must be of my own making, and the task is yet to begin." And, as I spoke, a pang, new to me, shot across my heart: it was a pang of mortification at the humility of my position and the inadequacy of my means; while with that pang was born a desire to do more, earn more, be more, possess more; and in the increased possessions, my roused and eager spirit panted to include the home I had never had, the wife I inwardly vowed to win.

Frances' tea was little better than hot water, sugar, and milk; but I liked it, and it cheered me; and her pistolets, with which she could not offer me butter, were sweet to my palate as manna.

The repast over, and the treasured plate and porcelain being washed and put by, the bright table rubbed still brighter, "le chat de ma tante Julienne" also being fed with provisions brought forth on a plate for its special use, a few stray cinders, and a scattering of ashes too, being swept from the hearth, Frances at last sat down; and then, as she took a chair opposite to me, she betrayed, for the first time, a little embarrassment; and no wonder, for indeed I had unconsciously watched her rather too closely, followed all her steps and all her movements a little too perseveringly with my eyes, for she mesmerized me by the grace and alertness of her action—by the deft, cleanly, and even decorative effect resulting from each touch of her slight and fine fingers; and when, at last, she subsided to

stillness, the intelligence of her face seemed beauty to
me, and I dwelt on it accordingly. Her color, however, rising rather than settling with repose, and her
eyes remaining downcast, though I kept waiting for
the lids to be raised that I might drink a ray of the
light I loved—a light where fire dissolved in softness,
where affection tempered penetration, where, just now
at least, pleasure played with thought—this expectation not being gratified, I began at last to suspect that
I had probably myself to blame for the disappointment. I must cease gazing, and begin talking, if I
wished to break the spell under which she now sat
motionless; so, recollecting the composing effect which
an authoritative tone and manner had ever been wont
to produce on her, I said,

"Get one of your English books, Mademoiselle, for
the rain yet falls heavily, and will probably detain me
half an hour longer."

Released and set at ease, up she rose, got her book,
and accepted at once the chair I placed for her at my
side. She had selected "Paradise Lost" from her
shelf of classics, thinking, I suppose, the religious
character of the book best adapted it to Sunday. I
told her to begin at the beginning; and while she
read Milton's invocation to that heavenly muse, who
on the "secret top of Oreb or Sinai" had taught the
Hebrew shepherd how in the womb of chaos the conception of a world had originated and ripened, I enjoyed, undisturbed, the treble pleasure of having her
near me, hearing the sound of her voice—a sound
sweet and satisfying in my ear—and looking, by intervals, at her face. Of this last privilege I chiefly
K

availed myself when I found fault with an intonation, a pause, or an emphasis; as long as I dogmatized, I might also gaze, without exciting too warm a flush.

"Enough," said I, when she had gone through some half dozen pages (a work of time with her, for she read slowly, and paused often to ask and receive information)—"enough; and now the rain is ceasing, and I must soon go;" for, indeed, at that moment, looking toward the window, I saw it all blue; ·the thunderclouds were broken and scattered, and the setting August sun sent a gleam like the reflection of rubies through the lattice. I got up; I drew on my gloves.

"You have not yet found another situation to supply the place of that from which you were dismissed by Mdlle. Reuter?"

"No, Monsieur; I have made inquiries every where, but they all ask me for references; and, to speak truth, I do not like to apply to the directress, because I consider she acted neither justly nor honorably toward me. She used underhand means to set my pupils against me, and thereby render me unhappy while I held my place in her establishment, and she eventually deprived me of it by a masked and hypocritical manœuvre, pretending that she was acting for my good, but really snatching from me my chief means of subsistence at a crisis when not only my own life, but that of another, depended on my exertions: of her I will never more ask a favor."

"How, then, do you propose to get on? How do you live now?"

"I have still my lace-mending trade; with care, it will keep me from starvation, and I doubt not, by dint

of exertion, to get better employment yet; it is only
a fortnight since I began to try; my courage or hopes
are by no means worn out yet."

"And if you get what you wish, what then? What
are your ultimate views?"

"To save enough to cross the Channel; I always
look to England as my Canaan."

"Well, well, ere long I shall pay you another visit;
good-evening now," and I left her rather abruptly. I
had much ado to resist a strong inward impulse urging
me to take a warmer, a more expressive leave. What
so natural as to fold her for a moment in a close embrace, to imprint one kiss on her cheek or forehead?
I was not unreasonable: that was all I wanted; satisfied in that point, I could go away content, and Reason denied me even this. She ordered me to turn my
eyes from her face, and my steps from her apartment
—to quit her as dryly and coldly as I would have
quitted old Madame Pelet. I obeyed, but I swore
rancorously to be avenged one day. "I'll earn a right
to do as I please in this matter, or I'll die in the contest. I have one object before me now—to get that
Genevese girl for my wife; and my wife she shall be
—that is, provided she has as much, or half as much
regard for her master as he has for her. And would
she be so docile, so smiling, so happy under my instructions if she had not? Would she sit at my side
when I dictate or correct with such a still, contented,
halcyon mien?" For I had ever remarked that, however sad or harassed her countenance might be when I
entered a room, yet, after I had been near her, spoken
to her a few words, given her some directions, uttered

perhaps some reproofs, she would, all at once, nestle into a nook of happiness, and look up serene and revived. The reproofs suited her best of all. While I scolded she would chip away with her penknife at a pencil or a pen; fidgeting a little, pouting a little, defending herself by monosyllables, and when I deprived her of the pen or pencil, fearing it would be all cut away, and when I interdicted even the monosyllabic defense for the purpose of working up the subdued excitement a little higher, she would at last raise her eyes and give me a certain glance, sweetened with gayety, and pointed with defiance, which, to speak truth, thrilled me as nothing had ever done, and made me,. in a fashion (though happily she did not know it), her subject, if not her slave. After such little scenes, her spirits would maintain their flow often for some hours, and, as I remarked before, her health therefrom took a sustenance and vigor which, previously to the event of her aunt's death and her dismissal, had almost recreated her whole frame.

It has taken me several minutes to write these last sentences, but I had thought all their purport during the brief interval of descending the stairs from Frances' room. Just as I was opening the outer door, I remembered the twenty francs which I had not restored. I paused: impossible to carry them away with me; difficult to force them back on their original owner; I had now seen her in her own humble abode, witnessed the dignity of her poverty, the pride of order, the fastidious care of conservatism obvious in the arrangement and economy of her little home; I was sure she would not suffer herself to be excused paying her debts;

I was certain the favor of indemnity would be accepted from no hand, perhaps least of all from mine; yet these four five-franc pieces were a burden to my self-respect, and I must get rid of them. An expedient— a clumsy one, no doubt, but the best I could devise— suggested itself to me. I darted up the stairs, knocked, re-entered the room as if in haste:

"Mademoiselle, I have forgotten one of my gloves. I must have left it here."

She instantly rose to seek it. As she turned her back, I, being now at the hearth, noiselessly lifted a little vase, one of a set of china ornaments as old-fashioned as the tea-cups, slipped the money under it, then saying "Oh, here is my glove; I had dropped it within the fender; good-evening, Mademoiselle," I made my second exit.

Brief as my impromptu return had been, it had afforded me time to pick up a heart-ache. I remarked that Frances had already removed the red embers of her cheerful little fire from the grate. Forced to calculate every item, to save in every detail, she had, instantly on my departure, retrenched a luxury too expensive to be enjoyed alone.

"I am glad it is not yet winter," thought I; "but in two months more come the winds and rains of November; would to God that before then I could earn the right and the power to shovel coals into that grate *ad libitum !*"

Already the pavement was drying. A balmy and fresh breeze stirred the air, purified by lightning. I left the west behind me, where spread a sky like opal; azure immingled with crimson: the enlarged sun, glo-

rious in Tyrian tints, dipped his brim already. Stepping, as I was, eastward, I faced a vast bank of
clouds, but also I had before me the arch of an evening rainbow—a perfect rainbow—high, wide, vivid. I
looked long; my eye drank in the scene, and I suppose my brain must have absorbed it; for that night,
after lying awake in pleasant fever a long time, watching the silent sheet-lightning, which still played among
the retreating clouds, and flashed silvery over the stars,
I at last fell asleep, and then, in a dream, were repro-
duced the setting sun, the bank of clouds, the mighty
rainbow.   I stood, methought, on a terrace; I leaned
over a parapeted wall; there was space below me,
depth I could not fathom, but hearing an endless dash
of waves, I believed it to be the sea; sea spread to the
horizon; sea of changeful green and intense blue: all
was soft in the distance—all vapor-veiled. A spark
of gold glistened on the line between water and air,
floated up, approached, enlarged, changed; the object
hung midway between heaven and earth, under the
arch of the rainbow, the soft but dusk clouds diffused
behind. It hovered as on wings; pearly, fleecy, gleam-
ing air streamed like raiment round it; light, tinted
with carnation, colored what seemed face and limbs;
a large star shone with still lustre on an angel's forehead; an upraised arm and hand, glancing like a ray,
pointed to the bow overhead, and a voice in my heart
whispered,

"Hope smiles on effort!"

CHAPTER XX.

A COMPETENCY was what I wanted; a competency it was now my aim and resolve to secure; but never had I been farther from the mark. With August the school-year (l'année scolaire) closed, the examinations concluded, the prizes were adjudged, the schools dispersed, the gates of all colleges, the doors of all pensionnats shut, not to be reopened till the beginning or middle of October. The last day of August was at hand, and what was my position? Had I advanced a step since the commencement of the past quarter? On the contrary, I had receded one. By renouncing my engagement as English master in Mdlle. Reuter's establishment, I had voluntarily cut off £20 from my yearly income; I had diminished my £60 per annum to £40, and even that sum I now held by a very precarious tenure.

It is some time since I made any reference to M. Pelet. The moonlight walk is, I think, the last incident recorded in this narrative where that gentleman cuts any conspicuous figure. The fact is, since that event, a change had come over the spirit of our intercourse. He, indeed, ignorant that the still hour, a cloudless moon, and an open lattice had revealed to me the secret of his selfish love and false friendship, would have continued smooth and complaisant as ever; but I grew spiny as a porcupine, and inflexible as a black-thorn

cudgel; I never had a smile for his raillery, never a
moment for his society; his invitations to take coffee
with him in his parlor were invariably rejected, and
very stiffly and sternly rejected too; his jesting allusions to the directress (which he still continued) were
heard with a grim calm very different from the petulant pleasure they were formerly wont to excite. For
a long time Pelet bore with my frigid demeanor very
patiently; he even increased his attentions; but, finding that even a cringing politeness failed to thaw or
move me, he at last altered too; in his turn he cooled;
his invitations ceased; his countenance became sus-
picious and overcast, and I read in the perplexed yet
brooding aspect of his brow a constant examination
and comparison of premises, and an anxious endeavor
to draw thence some explanatory inference. Ere long,
I fancy, he succeeded, for he was not without penetration; perhaps, too, Mdlle. Zoraïde might have aided
him in the solution of the enigma; at any rate, I soon
found that the uncertainty of doubt had vanished from
his manner. Renouncing all pretense of friendship
and cordiality, he adopted a reserved, formal, but still
scrupulously polite deportment. This was the point
to which I had wished to bring him, and I was now
again comparatively at my ease. I did not, it is true,
like my position in his house, but, being freed from the
annoyance of false professions and double-dealing I
could endure it, especially as no heroic sentiments of
hatred or jealousy of the director distracted my philo-
sophical soul. He had not, I found, wounded me in a
very tender point, the wound was so soon and so radically healed, leaving only a sense of contempt for the

treacherous fashion in which it had been inflicted, and
a lasting mistrust of the hand which I had detected
attempting to stab in the dark.

This state of things continued till about the middle
of July, and then there was a little change. Pelet
came home one night, an hour after his usual time, in
a state of unequivocal intoxication, a thing anomalous
with him; for, if he had some of the worst faults of
his countrymen, he had also one at least of their virtues, *i. e.*, sobriety. So drunk, however, was he upon
this occasion that, after having roused the whole establishment (except the pupils, whose dormitory, being
over the classes in a building apart from the dwelling-
house, was consequently out of the reach of disturb-
ance) by violently ringing the hall bell and ordering
lunch to be brought in immediately, for he imagined
it was noon, whereas the city bells had just tolled midnight—after having furiously rated the servants for
their want of punctuality, and gone near to chastise
his poor old mother, who advised him to go to bed, he
began raving dreadfully about "le maudit Anglais,
Creemsvort." I had not yet retired. Some German
books I had got hold of had kept me up late. I heard
the uproar below, and could distinguish the director's
voice exalted in a manner as appalling as it was unusual. Opening my door a little, I became aware of
a demand on his part for " Creemsvort" to be brought
down to him, that he might cut his throat on the hall
table, and wash his honor, which he affirmed to be in
a dirty condition, in infernal British blood. " He is
either mad or drunk," thought I, " and in either case
the old woman and the servants will be the better of

K 2

a man's assistance;" so I descended straight to the
hall. I found him staggering about, his eyes in a fine
phrensy rolling; a pretty sight he was, a just medium
between the fool and the lunatic.

"Come, M. Pelet," said I, "you had better go to
bed," and I took hold of his arm. His excitement,
of course, increased greatly at sight and touch of the
individual for whose blood he had been making application. He struggled and struck with fury; but a
drunken man is no match for a sober one; and, even
in his normal state, Pelet's worn-out frame could not
have stood against my sound one. I got him up stairs,
and, in process of time, to bed. During the operation
he did not fail to utter comminations which, though
broken, had a sense in them. While stigmatizing me
as the treacherous spawn of a perfidious country, he
in the same breath anathematized Zoraïde Reuter; he
termed her "femme sotte et vicieuse," who, in a fit of
lewd caprice, had thrown herself away on an unprincipled adventurer, directing the point of the last appellation by a furious blow obliquely aimed at me. I
left him in the act of bounding elastically out of the
bed into which I had tucked him; but, as I took the
precaution of turning the key in the door behind me,
I retired to my own room, assured of his safe custody
till the morning, and free to draw undisturbed con-
clusions from the scene I had just witnessed.

Now it was precisely about this time that the directress, stung by my coldness, bewitched by my scorn,
and excited by the preference she suspected me of
cherishing for another, had fallen into a snare of her
own laying—was herself caught in the meshes of the

very passion with which she wished to entangle me. Conscious of the state of things in that quarter, I gathered, from the condition in which I saw my employer, that his ladye-love had betrayed the alienation of her affections—inclinations, rather, I would say; affection is a word at once too warm and too pure for the subject—had let him see that the cavity of her hollow heart, emptied of his image, was now occupied by that of his usher. It was not without some surprise that I found myself obliged to entertain this view of the case. Pelet, with his old-established school, was so convenient, so profitable a match—Zoraïde was so calculating, so interested a woman—I wondered mere personal preference could, in her mind, have prevailed for a moment over worldly advantage; yet it was evident, from what Pelet said, that not only had she repulsed him, but had even let slip expressions of partiality for me. One of his drunken exclamations was, "And the jade dotes on your youth, you raw blockhead! and talks of your noble deportment, as she calls your accursed English formality—and your pure morals, forsooth! des mœurs de Caton a-t-elle dit—sotte!" Hers, I thought, must be a curious soul, where, in spite of a strong natural tendency to estimate unduly advantages of wealth and station, the sardonic disdain of a fortuneless subordinate had wrought a deeper impression than could be imprinted by the most flattering assiduities of a prosperous *chef d'institution*. I smiled inwardly; and, strange to say, though my *amour propre* was excited not disagreeably by the conquest, my better feelings remained untouched. Next day, when I saw the directress, and when she made an excuse to meet me in the corridor, and besought my notice by a demeanor and look subdued to Helot humility, I could not love, I could scarcely pity her. To answer briefly and dryly some interesting inquiry about my health—to pass her by with a stern bow— was all I could. Her presence and manner had then, and for some time previously and consequently, a singular effect upon me : they sealed up all that was good, elicited all that was noxious in my nature; sometimes they enervated my senses, but they always hardened my heart. I was aware of the detriment done, and quarreled with myself for the change. I had ever hated a tyrant ; and, behold, the possession of a slave, self-given, went near to transform me into what I abhorred. There was at once a sort of low gratification in receiving this luscious incense from an attractive and still young worshiper, and an irritating sense of degradation in the very experience of the pleasure. When she stole about me with the soft step of a slave, I felt at once barbarous and sensual as a pacha. I endured her homage sometimes ; sometimes I rebuked it. My indifference or harshness served equally to increase the evil I desired to check.

"Que le dédain lui sied bien !" I once overheard her say to her mother: "il est beau comme Apollon quand il sourit de son air hautain."

And the jolly old dame laughed, and said she thought her daughter was bewitched; for I had no point of a handsome man about me, except being straight and without deformity. "Pour moi," she continued, "il me fait tout l'effet d'un chat-huant, avec ses bésicles."

Worthy old girl! I could have gone and kissed her

had she not been a little too old, too fat, and too red-
faced, her sensible, truthful words seemed so wholesome, contrasted with the morbid illusions of her daughter.

When Pelet awoke on the morning after his phrensy fit, he retained no recollection of what had happened the previous night, and his mother fortunately had
the discretion to refrain from informing him that I had
been a witness of his degradation. He did not again
have recourse to wine for curing his griefs, but even in
his sober mood he soon showed that the iron of jealousy had entered into his soul. A thorough Frenchman, the national characteristic of ferocity had not
been omitted by nature in compounding the ingre-
dients of his character. It had appeared first in his
access of drunken wrath, when some of his demonstra-
tions of hatred to my person were of a truly fiendish
character, and now it was more covertly betrayed by
momentary contractions of the features, and flashes of
fierceness in his light blue eyes, when their glance
chanced to encounter mine. He absolutely avoided
speaking to me. I was now spared even the falsehood of his politeness. In this state of our mutual
relations, my soul rebelled, sometimes almost ungov-
ernably, against living in the house and discharging
the service of such a man; but who is free from the
constraint of circumstances? At that time I was not.
I used to rise each morning eager to shake off his yoke,
and go out with my portmanteau under my arm, if a
beggar, at least a freeman; and in the evening, when
I came back from the pensionnat de demoiselles, a certain pleasant voice in my ear; a certain face, so intelli-

gent, yet so docile, so reflective, yet so soft, in my eyes;
a certain cast of character, at once proud and pliant,
sensitive and sagacious, serious and ardent, in my head;
a certain tone of feeling, fervid and modest, refined and
practical, pure and powerful, delighting and troubling
my memory—visions of new ties I longed to contract,
of new duties I longed to undertake, had taken the rover
and the rebel out of me, and had shown endurance of
my hated lot in the light of a Spartan virtue.

But Pelet's fury subsided; a fortnight·sufficed for
its rise, progress, and extinction; in that space of time
the dismissal of the obnoxious teacher had been effected in the neighboring house, and in the same interval
I had declared my resolution to follow and find out
my pupil, and upon my application for her address being refused, I had summarily resigned my own post.
This last act seemed at once to restore Mdlle. Reuter
to her senses. Her sagacity, her judgment, so long
misled by a fascinating delusion, struck again into the
right track the moment that delusion vanished. By
the right track I do not mean the steep and difficult
path of principle; in that path she never trod; but the
plain highway of common sense, from which she had
of late widely diverged. When there, she carefully
sought, and having found, industriously pursued the
trail of her old suitor, M. Pelet. She soon overtook
him. What arts she employed to soothe and blind
him I know not, but she succeeded both in allaying
his wrath and hoodwinking his discernment, as was
soon proved by the alteration in his mien and manner.
She must have managed to convince him that I neither was, nor ever had been, a rival of his, for the fort-

night of fury against me terminated in a fit of exceeding graciousness and amenity, not unmixed with a dash
of exulting self-complacency, more ludicrous than irritating. Pelet's bachelor's life had been passed in prop-
er French style, with due disregard to moral restraint,
and I thought his married life promised to be very
French also. He often boasted to me what a terror
he had been to certain husbands of his acquaintance.
I perceived it would not now be difficult to pay him
back in his own coin.

The crisis drew on. No sooner had the holidays
commenced than note of preparation for some moment-
ous event sounded all through the premises of Pelet:
painters, polishers, and upholsterers were immediately
set to work, and there was talk of "la chambre de
Madame," "le salon de Madame." Not deeming it
probable that the old duenna at present graced with
that title in our house had inspired her son with such
enthusiasm of filial piety as to induce him to fit up
apartments expressly for her use, I concluded, in common with the cook, the two housemaids, and the kitch-
en scullion, that a new and more juvenile Madame was
destined to be the tenant of these gay chambers.

Presently official announcement of the coming event
was put forth. In another week's time, M. François
Pelet, directeur, and Mdlle. Zoraïde Reuter, directrice,
were to be joined together in the bands of matrimony.
Monsieur, in person, heralded the fact to me, terminat-
ing his communication by an obliging expression of
his desire that I should continue, as heretofore, his
ablest assistant and most trusted friend, and a prop-
osition to raise my salary by an additional two hund-

red francs per annum. I thanked him, gave no con-
clusive answer at the time, and, when he had left me,
threw off my blouse, put on my coat, and set out on a
long walk outside the porte de Flandre, in order, as I
thought, to cool my blood, calm my nerves, and shake
my disarranged ideas into some order. In fact, I had
just received what was virtually my dismissal. I
could not conceal, I did not desire to conceal from myself the conviction that, being now certain that Mdlle.
Reuter was destined to become Madame Pelet, it would
not do for me to remain a dependent dweller in the
house which was soon to be hers. Her present demeanor toward me was deficient neither in dignity nor
propriety, but I knew her former feeling was unchanged. Decorum now repressed, and Policy masked it, but Opportunity would be too strong for either
of these; Temptation would shiver their restraints.

I was no pope—I could not boast infallibility; in
short, if I staid, the probability was that, in three
months' time, a practical modern French novel would
be in full process of concoction under the roof of the
unsuspecting Pelet. Now modern French novels are
not to my taste, either practically or theoretically.
Limited as had yet been my experience of life, I had
once had the opportunity of contemplating, near at
hand, an example of the results produced by a course
of interesting and romantic domestic treachery. No
golden halo of fiction was about this example; I saw
it bare and real, and it was very loathsome. I saw a
mind degraded by the practice of mean subterfuge, by
the habit of perfidious deception, and a body depraved
by the infectious influence of the vice-polluted soul. I

had suffered much from the forced and prolonged view
of this spectacle ; those sufferings I did not now regret, for their simple recollection acted as a most
wholesome antidote to temptation. They had inscribed on my reason the conviction that unlawful
pleasure, trenching on another's rights, is delusive and
envenomed pleasure; its hollowness disappoints at the
time, its poison cruelly tortures afterward, its effects
deprave forever.

From all this resulted the conclusion that I must
leave Pelet's, and that instantly ; " but," said Prudence, " you know not where to go nor how to live ;"
and then the dream of true love came over me : Frances Henri seemed to stand at my side ; her slender
waist to invite my arm ; her hand to court my hand;
I felt it was made to nestle in mine; I could not relinquish my right to it, nor could I withdraw my eyes
forever from hers, where I saw so much happiness,
such a correspondence of heart with heart ; over whose
expression I had such influence ; where I could kindle bliss, infuse awe, stir deep delight, rouse sparkling
spirit, and sometimes waken pleasurable dread. My
hopes to win and possess, my resolutions to work and
rise, rose in array against me ; and here I was about
to plunge into the gulf of absolute destitution ; " and
all this," suggested an inward voice, "because you fear
an evil which may never happen !" "It will happen ;
you *know* it will," answered that stubborn monitor,
Conscience. " Do what you feel is right ; obey me,
and even in the sloughs of want I will plant for you
firm footing." And then, as I walked fast along the
road, there rose upon me a strange, inly-felt idea of

some Great Being, unseen, but all present, who, in his
beneficence, desired only my welfare, and now watched the struggle of good and evil in my heart, and waited to see whether I should obey his voice, heard in
the whispers of my conscience, or lend an ear to the
sophisms by which his enemy and mine, the Spirit of
Evil, sought to lead me astray.   Rough and steep
was the path indicated by divine suggestion ; mossy
and declining the green way along which Temptation
strewed flowers ; but whereas, methought, the Deity
of love, the Friend of all that exists, would smile
well-pleased were I to gird up my loins and address
myself to the rude ascent, so, on the other hand, each
inclination to the velvet declivity seemed to kindle a
gleam of triumph on the brow of the man-hating, God-
defying demon.   Sharp and short I turned round ;
fast I retraced my steps ; in half an hour I was again
at M. Pelet's : I sought him in his study ; brief parley, concise explanation sufficed ; my manner proved
that I was resolved ; he, perhaps, at heart approved
my decision.   After twenty minutes' conversation I
re-entered my own room, self-deprived of the means
of living, self-sentenced to leave my present home,
with the short notice of a week in which to provide
another.

CHAPTER XXI.

DIRECTLY as I closed the door, I saw laid on the table two letters. My thought was that they were notes of invitation from the friends of some of my pupils. I had received such marks of attention occasionally, and with me, who had no friends, correspondence of more interest was out of the question; the postman's arrival had never yet been an event of interest to me since I came to Brussels. I laid my hand carelessly on the documents, and, coldly and slowly glancing at them, prepared to break the seals. My eye was arrested, and my hand too; I saw what excited me, as if I had found a vivid picture where I expected only to discover a blank page. On one cover was an English post-mark; on the other, a lady's clear, fine autograph: the last I opened first:

"MONSIEUR,—I found out what you had done the very morning after your visit to me. You might be sure I should dust the china every day; and, as no one but you had been in my room for a week, and as fairy-money is not current in Brussels, I could not doubt who left the twenty francs on the chimney-piece. I thought I heard you stir the vase when I was stooping to look for your glove under the table, and I wondered you should imagine it had got into such a little cup. Now, Monsieur, the money is not mine, and I shall not keep it; I will not send it in this note, because it might be lost; besides, it is heavy; but I will restore it to you the first time I see you, and you must make no difficulties about taking it, because, in the first place, I am sure, Monsieur, you can understand that one likes to pay one's debts; that it is satisfactory to owe no man any thing; and, in the second place, I can now very well afford to be honest, as I am provided with a situation. This last circumstance is, indeed, the reason of my writing to you, for it is pleasant to communicate good news; and, in these days, I have only my master to whom I can tell any thing.

" A week ago, Monsieur, I was sent for by a Mrs. Wharton, an English lady. Her eldest daughter was going to be married, and some rich relation having made her a present of a veil and dress in costly old lace, as precious, they said, almost as jewels, but a little damaged by time, I was commissioned to put them in repair. I had to do it at the house; they gave me, besides, some embroidery to complete, and nearly a week elapsed before I had finished every thing. While I worked, Miss Wharton often came into the room and sat with me, and so did Mrs. Wharton; they made me talk English; asked how I had learned to speak it so well; then they inquired what I knew besides— what books I had read; soon they seemed to make a sort of wonder of me, considering me, no doubt, as a learned grisette. One afternoon Mrs. Wharton brought in a Parisian lady to test the accuracy of my knowledge of French; the result of it was that, owing probably, in a great degree, to the mother's and daughter's good-humor about the marriage, which inclined them to do beneficent deeds, and partly, I think, because they are naturally benevolent people, they decided that the wish I had expressed to do something more than mend lace was a very legitimate one, and the same day they took me in their carriage to Mrs. D.'s, who is the directress of the first English school at Brussels. It seems she happened to be in want of a French lady to give lessons in geography, history, grammar, and composition in the French language. Mrs. Wharton recommended me very warmly; and, as two of her younger daughters are pupils in the house, her patronage availed to get me the place. It was settled that I am to attend six hours daily (for, happily, it was not required that I should live in the house; I should have been sorry to leave my lodgings), and for this Mrs. D. will give me twelve hundred francs per annum.

"You see, therefore, Monsieur, that I am now rich —richer almost than I ever hoped to be. I feel thankful for it, especially as my sight was beginning to be injured by constant working at fine lace; and I was getting, too, very weary of sitting up late at nights, and yet not being able to find time for reading or study. I began to fear that I should fall ill, and be unable to pay my way; this fear is now, in a great measure, removed; and, in truth, Monsieur, I am very grateful to God for the relief; and I feel it necessary, almost, to speak of my happiness to some one who is kind-hearted enough to derive joy from seeing others joyful. I could not, therefore, resist the temptation of writing to you. I argued with myself it is very pleasant for me to write, and it will not be exactly painful, though it may be tiresome to Monsieur to read.

Do not be too angry with my circumlocution and inel-
egancies of expression, and believe me your attached
pupil,   F. E. HENRI."

Having read this letter, I mused on its contents for
a few moments—whether with sentiments pleasurable
or otherwise I will hereafter note—and then took up
the other. It was directed in a hand to me unknown
—small, and rather neat; neither masculine nor exactly feminine; the seal bore a coat of arms, concerning which I could only decipher that it was not that
of the Seacome family, consequently the epistle could
be from none of my almost forgotten and certainly
quite forgetting patrician relations. From whom, then,
was it? I removed the envelope; the note folded within ran as follows:

"I have no doubt in the world that you are doing
well in that greasy Flanders; living probably on the
fat of the unctuous land; sitting like a black-haired,
tawny-skinned, long-nosed Israelite by the flesh-pots
of Egypt, or like a rascally son of Levi near the brass
caldrons of the sanctuary, and every now and then
plunging in a consecrated hook, and drawing out of the
sea of broth the fattest of heave-shoulders and the
fleshiest of wave-breasts. I know this, because you
never write to any one in England, thankless dog that
you are! I, by the sovereign efficacy of my recommendation, got you the place where you are now living
in clover, and yet not a word of gratitude, or even acknowledgment, have you ever offered in return; but I
am coming to see you, and small conception can you,

with your addled aristocratic brains, form of the sort
of moral kicking I have ready packed in my carpet-
bag, destined to be presented to you immediately on
my arrival.

"Meantime, I know all about your affairs, and have
just got information, by Brown's last letter, that you
are said to be on the point of forming an advantageous
match with a pursy little Belgian schoolmistress—a
Mdlle. Zénobie, or some such name. Won't I have a
look at her when I come over? And this you may rely
on: if she pleases my taste, or if I think it worth while
in a pecuniary point of view, I'll pounce on your prize
and bear her away triumphant in spite of your teeth.
Yet I don't like dumpies either, and Brown says she
is little and stout—the better fitted for a wiry, starved-
looking chap like you.

"Be on the look-out, for you know neither the day
nor hour when your —— (I don't wish to blaspheme,
so I'll leave a blank) cometh.

"Yours truly, HUNSDEN YORKE HUNSDEN."

"Humph!" said I; and, ere I laid the letter down,
I again glanced at the small, neat handwriting, not a
bit like that of a mercantile man, nor, indeed, of any
man except Hunsden himself. They talk of affinities
between the autograph and the character: what affinity
was there here? I recalled the writer's peculiar face,
and certain traits I suspected, rather than knew, to ap-
pertain to his nature, and I answered, "A great deal."

Hunsden, then, was coming to Brussels, and coming
I knew not when; coming charged with the expectation of finding me on the summit of prosperity, about

to be married, to step into a warm nest, to lie comfortably down by the side of a snug, well-fed little mate.

" I wish him joy of the fidelity of the picture he has painted," thought I. " What will he say when, instead of a pair of plump turtle-doves, billing and cooing in a bower of roses, he finds a single lean cormorant, standing mateless and shelterless on poverty's bleak cliff? Oh, confound him! Let him come, and let him laugh at the contrast between rumor and fact. Were he the devil himself, instead of being merely very like him, I'd not condescend to get out of his way, or to forge a smile or a cheerful word wherewith to avert his sarcasm."

Then I recurred to the other letter: that struck a chord whose sound I could not deaden by thrusting my fingers into my ears, for it vibrated within; and though its swell might be exquisite music, its cadence was a groan.

That Frances was relieved from the pressure of want, that the curse of excessive labor was taken off her, filled me with happiness; that her first thought in prosperity should be to augment her joy by sharing it with me, met and satisfied the wish of my heart. Two results of her letter were then pleasant, sweet as two draughts of nectar; but applying my lips for the third time to the cup, and they were excoriated as with vinegar and gall.

Two persons whose desires are moderate may live well enough in Brussels on an income which would scarcely afford a respectable maintenance for one in London; and that, not because the necessaries of life are so much dearer in the latter capital, or taxes so much higher than in the former, but because the En-

glish surpass in folly all the nations on God's earth,
and are more abject slaves to custom, to opinion, to
the desire to keep up a certain appearance, than the
Italians are to priestcraft, the French to vainglory, the
Russians to their Czar, or the Germans to black beer.
I have seen a degree of sense in the modest arrangement of one homely Belgian household that might put
to shame the elegance, the superfluities, the luxuries,
the strained refinements of a hundred genteel English
mansions. In Belgium, provided you can make money, you may save it; this is scarcely possible in England; ostentation there lavishes in a month what industry has earned in a year. More shame to all classes in that most bountiful and beggarly country for their
servile following of Fashion. I could write a chapter
or two on this subject, but must forbear, at least for
the present. Had I retained my £60 per annum, I
could, now that Frances was in possession of £50, have
gone straight to her this very evening, and spoken out
the words which, repressed, kept fretting my heart with
fever; our united income would, as we should have
managed it, have sufficed well for our mutual support,
since we lived in a country where economy was not
confounded with meanness, where frugality in dress,
food, and furniture was not synonymous with vulgarity in these various points. But the placeless usher,
bare of resource, and unsupported by connections, must
not think of this; such a sentiment as love, such a
word as marriage, were misplaced in his heart and on
his lips. Now, for the first time, did I truly feel what
it was to be poor; now did the sacrifice I had made in
casting from me the means of living put on a new as-

T.

pect; instead of a correct, just, honorable act, it seemed a deed at once light and fanatical.   I took several
turns in my room, under the goading influence of most
poignant remorse; I walked a quarter of an hour from
the wall to the window; and at the window, Self-re-
proach seemed to face me; at the wall, Self-disdain:
all at once out spoke Conscience:

"Down, stupid tormentors!" cried she; "the man
has done his duty.   You shall not bait him thus by
thoughts of what might have been; he relinquished a
temporary and contingent good to avoid a permanent
and certain evil; he did well.   Let him reflect now,
and when your blinding dust and deafening hum subside, he will discover a path."

I sat down; I propped my forehead on both my
hands; I thought and thought an hour—two hours—
vainly.   I seemed like one sealed in a subterranean
vault, who gazes at utter blackness—at blackness in-
sured by yard-thick stone walls around, and by piles
of building above, expecting light to penetrate through
granite, and through cement firm as granite.   But
there are chinks, or there may be chinks, in the best
adjusted masonry; there was a chink in my cavernous
cell; for eventually I saw, or seemed to see, a ray—
pallid, indeed, and cold, and doubtful, but still a ray,
for it showed that narrow path which Conscience had
promised.   After two, three hours' torturing research
in brain and memory, I disinterred certain remains of
circumstances, and conceived a hope that by putting
them together an expedient might be framed and a resource discovered.   The circumstances were briefly
these:

Some three months ago M. Pelet had, on the occasion of his fête, given the boys a treat, which treat consisted in a party of pleasure to a certain place of public resort in the outskirts of Brussels, of which I do not at this moment remember the name, but near it were several of those lakelets called étangs; and there was one étang larger than the rest, where on holidays people were accustomed to amuse themselves by rowing round it in little boats. The boys, having eaten an unlimited quantity of " gaufres," and drunk several bottles of Louvain beer, amid the shades of a garden made and provided for such crams, petitioned the director for leave to take a row on the étang. Half a dozen of the eldest succeeded in obtaining leave, and I was commissioned to accompany them as surveillant. Among the half dozen happened to be a certain Jean Baptiste Vandenhuten, a most ponderous young Flamand, not tall, but even now, at the early age of sixteen possessing a breadth and depth of personal development truly national. It chanced that Jean was the first lad to step into the boat. He stumbled, rolled to one side, the boat revolted at his weight, and capsized. Vandenhuten sank like lead, rose, sank again. My coat and waistcoat were off in an instant. I had not been brought up at Eton, and boated, and bathed, and swum there ten long years for nothing; it was a natural and easy act for me to leap to the rescue. The lads and the boatman yelled; they thought there would be two deaths by drowning instead of one; but as Jean rose the third time, I clutched him by one leg and the collar, and in three minutes more both he and I were safe landed. To speak heaven's truth, my merit in the

action was small indeed, for I had run no risk, and
subsequently did not even catch cold from the wet-
ting; but when M. and Madame Vandenhuten, of
whom Jean Baptiste was the sole hope, came to hear
of the exploit, they seemed to think I had evinced a
bravery and devotion which no thanks could sufficiently repay. Madame, in particular, was " certain
I must have dearly loved their sweet son, or I would
not thus have hazarded my own life to save his."
Monsieur, an honest-looking though phlegmatic man,
said very little, but he would not suffer me to leave
the room till I had promised that, in case I ever stood
in need of help, I would, by applying to him, give him
a chance of discharging the obligation under which he
affirmed I had laid him.   These words, then, were my
glimmer of light ; it was here I found my sole outlet ;
and, in truth, though the cold light roused, it did not
cheer me, nor did the outlet seem such as I should
like to pass through. Right I had none to M. Vandenhuten's good offices ; it was not on the ground of
merit I could apply to him ; no, I must stand on that
of necessity : I had no work ; I wanted work ; my
best chance of obtaining it lay in securing his recommendation.   This I knew could be had by asking for
it ; not to ask, because the request revolted my pride
and contradicted my habits, would, I felt, be an indulgence of false and indolent fastidiousness. I might
repent the omission all my life ; I would not, then, be
guilty of it.

  That evening I went to M. Vandenhuten's ; but I
had bent the bow and adjusted the shaft in vain ; the
string broke. I rang the bell at the great door (it

was a large, handsome house in an expensive part of
the town) ; a man-servant opened ; I asked for M. Vandenhuten ; M. Vandenhuten and family were all out
of town—gone to Ostend—did not know when they
would be back. I left my card and retraced my steps.

CHAPTER XXII.

A WEEK is gone ; *le jour des noces* arrived ; the
marriage was solemnized at St. Jacques ; Mdlle. Zoraïde became Madame Pelet, *née* Reuter; and, in about
an hour after this transformation, "the happy pair,"
as newspapers phrase it, were on their way to Paris,
where, according to previous arrangement, the honeymoon was to be spent. The next day I quitted the
pensionnat. Myself and my chattels (some books
and clothes) were soon transferred to a modest lodging I had hired in a street not far off. In half an
hour my clothes were arranged in a commode, my
books on a shelf, and the "flitting" was effected. I
should not have been unhappy that day had not one
pang tortured me—a longing to go to the Rue Notre
Dame aux Neiges, resisted, yet irritated by an inward
resolve to avoid that street till such time as the mist
of doubt should clear from my prospects.

It was a sweet September evening—very mild, very
still ; I had nothing to do ; at that hour I knew
Frances would be equally released from occupation ;
I thought she might possibly be wishing for her master ; I knew I wished for my pupil. Imagination be-

gan with her low whispers, infusing into my soul the
soft tale of pleasures that might be.

"You will find her reading or writing," said she;
"you can take your seat at her side; you need not
startle her peace by undue excitement; you need not
embarrass her manner by unusual action or language.
Be as you always are; look over what she has written; listen while she reads; chide her, or quietly ap-
prove; you know the effect of either system; you
know her smile when pleased, you know the play of
her looks when roused; you have the secret of awak-
ening what expression you will, and you can choose
among that pleasant variety. With you she will sit
silent as long as it suits you to talk alone; you can
hold her under a potent spell: intelligent as she is,
eloquent as she can be, you can seal her lips, and veil
her bright countenance with diffidence; yet, you know,
she is not all monotonous mildness; you have seen,
with a sort of strange pleasure, revolt, scorn, austerity,
bitterness, lay energetic claim to a place in her feelings and physiognomy; you know that few could rule
her as you do; you know she might break, but never
bend under the hand of Tyranny and Injustice, but
Reason and Affection can guide her by a sign. Try
their influence now. Go: they are not passions; you
may handle them safely."

"I will *not* go," was my answer to the sweet tempt-
ress. "A man is master of himself to a certain point,
but not beyond it. Could I seek Frances to-night,
could I sit with her alone in a quiet room, and address her only in the language of Reason and Affection?"

"No," was the brief, fervent reply of that Love which had conquered and now controlled me.

Time seemed to stagnate; the sun would not go down; my watch ticked, but I thought the hands were paralyzed.

"What a hot evening!" I cried, throwing open the lattice; for, indeed, I had seldom felt so feverish. Hearing a step ascending the common stair, I wondered whether the "locataire," now mounting to his apartments, were as unsettled in mind and condition as I was, or whether he lived in the calm of certain resources, and in the freedom of unfettered feelings. What! was he coming in person to solve the problem hardly proposed in inaudible thought? He had actually knocked at the door—at *my* door—a smart, prompt rap; and, almost before I could invite him in, he was over the threshold, and had closed the door behind him.

"And how are you?" asked an indifferent, quiet voice, in the English language; while my visitor, without any sort of bustle or introduction, put his hat on the table, and his gloves into his hat, and, drawing the only arm-chair the room afforded a little forward, seated himself tranquilly therein.

"Can't you speak?" he inquired in a few moments, in a tone whose nonchalance seemed to intimate that it was much the same thing whether I answered or not. The fact is, I found it desirable to have recourse to my good friends "les bésicles;" not exactly to ascertain the identity of my visitor, for I already knew him, confound his impudence! but to see how he looked—to get a clear notion of his mien and coun-

tenance.   I wiped the glasses very deliberately, and
put them on quite as deliberately, adjusting them so
as not to hurt the bridge of my nose, or get entangled
in my short tufts of dun hair.   I was sitting in the
window-seat, with my back to the light, and I had him
vis-à-vis, a position he would much rather have had
reversed; for, at any time, he preferred scrutinizing to
being scrutinized.   Yes, it was *he*, and no mistake,
with his six feet of length arranged in a sitting attitude ; with his dark traveling surtout with its velvet
collar, his gray pantaloons, his black stock, and *his* .
face, the most original one Nature ever modeled, yet
the least obtrusively so ; not one feature that could be
termed marked or odd, yet the effect of the whole
unique.   There is no use in attempting to describe
what is indescribable.   Being in no hurry to address
him, I sat and stared at my ease.

"Oh, that's your game, is it?" said he, at last.
"Well, we'll see which is soonest tired."   And he
slowly drew out a fine cigar-case, picked one to his
taste, lit it, took a book from the shelf convenient to
his hand, then leaning back, proceeded to smoke and
read as tranquilly as if he had been in his own room
in Grove Street, X——shire, England.   I knew he
was capable of continuing in that attitude till midnight if he conceived the whim, so I rose, and, taking
the book from his hand, said,

"You did not ask for it, and you shall not have it."

"It is silly and dull," he observed, "so I have not
lost much ;" then the spell being broken, he went on :
"I thought you lived at Pelet's ; I went there this afternoon, expecting to be starved to death by sitting in

a boarding-school drawing-room, and they told me you were gone—had departed this morning; you had left your address behind you though, which I wondered at; it was a more practical and sensible precaution than I should have imagined you capable of. Why did you leave?"

"Because M. Pelet has just married the lady whom you and Mr. Brown assigned to me as my wife."

"Oh indeed!" replied Hunsden, with a short laugh; "so you've lost both your wife and your place?"

"Precisely so."

I saw him give a quick, covert glance all round my room; he marked its narrow limits, its scanty furniture; in an instant he had comprehended the state of matters—had absolved me from the crime of prosperity. A curious effect this discovery wrought in his strange mind. I am morally certain that, if he had found me installed in a handsome parlor, lounging on a soft couch, with a pretty, wealthy wife at my side, he would have hated me; a brief, cold, haughty visit would in such a case have been the extreme limit of his civilities, and never would he have come near me more, so long as the tide of fortune bore me smoothly on its surface; but the painted furniture, the bare walls, the cheerless solitude of my room relaxed his rigid pride, and I know not what softening change had taken place both in his voice and look ere he spoke again.

"You have got another place?"

"No."

"You are in the way of getting one?"

"No."

"That is bad; have you applied to Brown?"

"No indeed."

"You had better; he often has it in his power to give useful information in such matters."

"He served me once very well; I have no claim on him, and am not in the humor to bother him again."

"Oh, if you're bashful, and dread being intrusive, you need only commission me. I shall see him to-night; I can put in a word."

"I beg you will not, Mr. Hunsden; I am in your debt already; you did me an important service when I was at X——; got me out of a den where I was dying: that service I have never repaid, and at present I decline positively adding another item to the account."

"If the wind sits that way, I'm satisfied. I thought my unexampled generosity in turning you out of that accursed counting-house would be duly appreciated some day; 'Cast your bread on the waters, and it shall be found after many days,' say the Scriptures. Yes, that's right, lad—make much of me—I'm a non-pareil; there's nothing like me in the common herd. In the mean time, to put all humbug aside and talk sense for a few moments, you would be greatly the better of a situation, and, what is more, you are a fool if you refuse to take one from any hand that offers it."

"Very well, Mr. Hunsden; now you have settled that point, talk of something else. What news from X——?"

"I have not settled that point, or at least there is another to settle before we get to X——. Is this Miss Zénobie" (Zoraïde, interposed I)—"well, Zoraïde—is she really married to Pelet?"

' I tell you yes; and if you don't believe me, go and ask the curé of St. Jacques."

" And your heart is broken ?"

" I am not aware that it is; it feels all right—beats as usual."

" Then your feelings are less superfine than I took them to be; you must be a coarse, callous character to bear such a thwack without staggering under it."

" Staggering under it ?   What the deuce is there to stagger under in the circumstance of a Belgian school-mistress marrying a French schoolmaster ?   The prog-eny will doubtless be a strange hybrid race; but that's their look out, not mine."

" He indulges in scurrilous jests, and the bride was his affianced one !"

" Who said so ?"

" Brown."

" I'll tell you what, Hunsden, Brown is an old gos-sip."

"He is; but, in the mean time, if his gossip be found-ed on less than fact—if you took no particular interest in Miss Zoraïde, why, oh youthful pedagogue! did you leave your place in consequence of her becoming Ma-dame Pelet ?"

" Because—" I felt my face grow a little hot; "be-cause—in short, Mr. Hunsden, I decline answering any more questions," and I plunged my hands deep in my breeches pocket.

Hunsden triumphed: his eyes—his laugh announced victory.

" What the deuce are you laughing at, Mr. Huns-den ?"

"At your exemplary composure. Well, lad, I'll not bore you; I see how it is; Zoraïde has jilted you— married some one richer, as any sensible woman would have done if she had had the chance."

I made no reply; I let him think so, not feeling inclined to enter into an explanation of the real state of things, and as little to forge a false account; but it was not easy to blind Hunsden; my very silence, instead of convincing him that he had hit the truth, seemed to render him doubtful about it. He went on:

"I suppose the affair has been conducted as such affairs always are among rational people: you offered her your youth and your talents—such as they are— in exchange for her position and money; I don't suppose you took appearance, or what is called *love*, into the account, for I understand she is older than you, and, Brown says, rather sensible-looking than beautiful. She, having then no chance of making a better bargain, was at first inclined to come to terms with you; but Pelet, the head of a flourishing school, stepped in with a higher bid; she accepted, and he has got her: a correct transaction—perfectly so— business-like and legitimate. And now we'll talk of something else."

"Do," said I, very glad to dismiss the topic, and especially glad to have baffled the sagacity of my cross-questioner, if, indeed, I had baffled it; for, though his words now led away from the dangerous point, his eyes, keen and watchful, seemed still preoccupied with the former idea.

"You want to hear news from X——? And what interest can you have in X——? You left no friends

there, for you made none. Nobody ever asks after
you, neither man nor woman; and if I mention your
name in company, the men look as if I had spoken of
Prester John, and the women sneer covertly. Our
X—— belles must have disliked you. How did you
excite their displeasure?"

"I don't know. I seldom spoke to them; they
were nothing to me. I considered them only as something to be glanced at from a distance. Their dresses
and faces were often pleasing enough to the eye, but I
could not understand their conversation, nor even read
their countenances. When I caught snatches of what
they said, I could never make much of it, and the play
of their lips and eyes did not help me at all."

"That was your fault, not theirs. There are sensible as well as handsome women in X——; women
it is worth any man's while to talk to, and with whom
I can talk with pleasure; but you had and have no
pleasant address; there is nothing in you to induce a
woman to be affable. I have remarked you sitting
near the door in a room full of company, bent on hearing, not on speaking; on observing, not on entertaining; looking frigidly shy at the commencement of a
party, confusingly vigilant about the middle, and in-
sultingly weary toward the end. Is that the way, do
you think, ever to communicate pleasure or excite interest? No; and if you are generally unpopular, it is
because you deserve to be so."

"Content!" I ejaculated.

"No, you are not content; you see beauty always
turning its back on you; you are mortified, and then
you sneer. I verily believe all that is desirable on

earth — wealth, reputation, love — will forever to you
be the ripe grapes on the high trellis: you'll look up
at them; they will tantalize in you the lust of the eye,
but they are out of reach; you have not the address
to fe🖤a ladder, and you'll go away calling them
sour."

Cutting as these words might have been under some
circumstances, they drew no blood now. My life was
changed; my experience had been varied since I left
X——, but Hunsden could not know this; he had
seen me only in the character of Mr. Crimsworth's
clerk—a dependent among wealthy strangers, meeting
disdain with a hard front, conscious of an unsocial and
unattractive exterior, refusing to sue for notice which
I was sure would be withheld, declining to evince an
admiration which I knew would be scorned as worth-
less. He could not be aware that, since then, youth
and loveliness had been to me every day objects; that
I had studied them at leisure and closely, and had seen
the plain texture of truth under the embroidery of appearance; nor could he, keen-sighted as he was, penetrate into my heart, search my brain, and read my
peculiar sympathies and antipathies; he had not known
me long enough or well enough to perceive how low my
feelings would ebb under some influences, powerful over
most minds; how high, how fast they would flow under other influences, that perhaps acted with the more
intense force on me, because they acted on me alone.
Neither could he suspect for an instant the history of
my communications with Mdlle. Reuter; secret to him
and to all others was the tale of her strange infatua-
tion: her blandishments, her wiles had been seen but

by me, and to me only were they known; but they
had changed me, for they had proved that I *could* impress. A sweeter secret nestled deeper in my heart;
one full of tenderness and as full of strength: it took
the sting out of Hunsden's sarcasm; it kept me un-
bent by shame and unstirred by wrath. But of all
this I could say nothing—nothing decisive, at least; uncertainty sealed my lips, and during the interval of silence by which alone I replied to Mr. Hunsden, I made
up my mind to be for the present wholly misjudged by
him, and misjudged I was. He thought he had been
rather too hard upon me, and that I was crushed by
the weight of his upbraidings; so, to reassure me, he
said doubtless I should mend some day; I was only
at the beginning of life yet; and since happily I was
not quite without sense, every false step I made would
be a good lesson.

Just then I turned my face a little to the light.
The approach of twilight and my position in the win-.
dow-seat had for the last ten minutes prevented him
from studying my countenance; as I moved, however,
he caught an expression which he thus interpreted:

"Confound it, how doggedly self-approving the lad
looks! I thought he was fit to die with shame, and
there he sits grinning smiles, as good as to say, 'Let
the world wag as it will, I've the philosopher's stone
in my waistcoat pocket, and the elixir of life in my
cupboard; I'm independent of both Fate and Fortune!'"

"Hunsden, you spoke of grapes; I was thinking of
a fruit I like better than your X—— hot-house grapes
—an unique fruit, growing wild, which I have marked

as my own, and hope one day to gather and taste. It is of no use your offering me the draught of bitterness, or threatening me with death by thirst; I have the anticipation of sweetness on my palate; the hope of freshness on my lips; I can reject the unsavory, and endure the exhausting."

"For how long?"

"Till the next opportunity for effort; and as the prize of success will be a treasure after my own heart, I'll bring a bull's strength to the struggle."

"Bad luck crushes bulls as easy as bullaces; and, I believe, the fury dogs you; you were born with a wooden spoon in your mouth, depend on it."

"I believe you; and I mean to make my wooden spoon do the work of some people's silver ladles: grasped firmly, and handled nimbly, even a wooden spoon will shovel up broth."

Hunsden rose: "I see," said he; "I suppose you're one of those who develop best unwatched, and act best unaided; work your own way. Now I'll go;" and, without another word, he was going. At the door he turned:

"Crimsworth Hall is sold," said he.

"Sold!" was my echo.

"Yes; you know, of course, that your brother failed three months ago?"

"What! Edward Crimsworth?"

"Precisely; and his wife went home to her father's. When affairs went awry, his temper sympathized with them; he used her ill; I told you he would be a tyrant to her some day; as to him—"

"Ay, as to him—what is become of him?"

"Nothing extraordinary—don't be alarmed; he put himself under the protection of the court, compounded with his creditors—tenpence in the pound; in six weeks· set up again, coaxed back his wife, and is flourishing like a green bay-tree."

"And Crimsworth Hall—was the furniture sold too?" .

"Every thing, from the grand piano down to the rolling-pin."

"And the contents of the oak dining-room—were they sold?"

"Of course; why should the sofas and chairs of that room be held more sacred than those of any other?"

"And the pictures?"

"What pictures? Crimsworth had no special collection that I know of. He did not profess to be an amateur."

"There were two portraits, one on each side the mantel-piece; you can not have forgotten them, Mr. Hunsden; you once noticed that of the lady—"

"Oh, I know—the thin-faced gentlewoman with a shawl put on like drapery. Why, as a matter of course, it would be sold among the other things. If you had been rich, you might have bought it, for I remember you said it represented your mother : you see what it is to be without a sou."

I did. "But surely," I thought to myself, "I shall not always be so poverty-stricken; I may one day buy it back yet. Who purchased it? do you know?" I asked.

"How is it likely? I never inquired who pur-

chased any thing; there spoke the unpractical man—
to imagine all the world is interested in what interests
himself! Now good-night; I'm off for Germany to-
morrow morning; I shall be back here in six weeks,
and possibly I may call and see you again. I wonder whether you'll be still out of place!" he laughed,
as mockingly, as heartlessly as Mephistophiles, and so
laughing, vanished.

Some people, however indifferent they may become
after a considerable space of absence, always contrive
to leave a pleasant impression just at parting; not so
Hunsden; a conference with him affected one like a
draught of Peruvian bark; it seemed a concentration
of the specially harsh, stringent bitter; whether, like
bark, it invigorated, I scarcely knew.

A ruffled mind makes a restless pillow. I slept little on the night after this interview; toward morning
I began to doze, but hardly had my slumber become
sleep when I was roused from it by hearing a noise in
my sitting-room, to which my bed-room adjoined—a
step, and a shoving of furniture; the movement lasted
barely two minutes; with the closing of the door it
ceased. I listened; not a mouse stirred; perhaps I
had dreamed it; perhaps a *locataire* had made a mistake, and entered my apartment instead of his own. It
was yet but five o'clock; neither I nor the day were
wide awake; I turned, and was soon unconscious.
When I did rise, about two hours later, I had forgotten the circumstance; the first thing I saw, however,
on quitting my chamber, recalled it: just pushed in at
the door of my sitting-room, and still standing on end,.
was a wooden packing-case—a rough deal affair, wide

but shallow; a porter had doubtless shoved it forward, but, seeing no occupant of the room, had left it at the entrance.

"That is none of mine," thought I, approaching; "it must be meant for somebody else." I stooped to examine the address:

"Wm. Crimsworth, Esq., No. —— —— Street, Brussels."

I was puzzled; but, concluding that the best way to obtain information was to ask within, I cut the cords and opened the case. Green baize enveloped its contents, sewn carefully at the sides; I ripped the packthread with my penknife, and still, as the seam gave way, glimpses of gilding appeared through the widening interstices. Boards and baize being at length removed, I lifted from the case a large picture, in a magnificent frame; leaning it against a chair, in a position where the light from the window fell favorably upon it, I stepped back—already I had mounted my spectacles. A portrait painter's sky (the most sombre and threatening of welkins), and distant trees of a conventional depth of hue, raised in full relief a pale, pensive-looking female face, shadowed with soft dark hair, almost blending with the equally dark clouds; large, solemn eyes looked reflectively into mine; a thin cheek rested on a delicate little hand; a shawl, artistically draped, half hid, half showed a slight figure. A listener (had there been one) might have heard me, after ten minutes' silent gazing, utter the word "Mother!" I might have said more, but with me, the first word uttered aloud in soliloquy rouses consciousness; it reminds me that only crazy people talk to themselves, and then I think out my monologue instead of speaking it. I had thought a long while, and a long while had contemplated the intelligence, the sweetness, and, alas! the sadness also of those fine gray eyes, the mental power of that forehead, and the rare sensibility of that serious mouth, when my glance, traveling downward, fell on a narrow billet, stuck in the corner of the picture, between the frame and the canvas. Then I first asked, "Who sent this picture? Who thought of me, saved it out of the wreck of Crimsworth Hall, and now commits it to the care of its natural keeper?" I took the note from its niche; thus it spoke:

"There is a sort of stupid pleasure in giving a child sweets, a fool his bells, a dog a bone. You are repaid by seeing the child besmear his face with sugar; by witnessing how the fool's ecstasy makes a greater fool of him than ever; by watching the dog's nature come out over his bone. In giving William Crimsworth his mother's picture, I give him sweets, bells, and bone, all in one. What grieves me is that I can not behold the result; I would have added five shillings more to my bid if the auctioneer could only have promised me that pleasure. H. Y. H.

"P.S.—You said last night you positively declined adding another item to your account with me; don't you think I've saved you that trouble?"

I muffled the picture in its green baize covering, restored it to the case, and, having transported the whole concern to my bed-room, put it out of sight under my bed. My pleasure was now poisoned by pungent pain.

I determined to look no more till I could look at my ease. If Hunsden had come in at that moment, I should have said to him, " I owe you nothing, Hunsden—not a fraction of a farthing; you have paid yourself in taunts."

Too anxious to remain any longer quiescent, I had no sooner breakfasted than I repaired once more to M. Vandenhuten's, scarcely hoping to find him at home, for a week had barely elapsed since my first call, but fancying I might be able to glean information as to the time when his return was expected. A better result awaited me than I had anticipated; for, though the family were yet at Ostend, M. Vandenhuten had come over to Brussels on business for the day. He received me with the quiet kindness of a sincere though not excitable man. I had not sat five minutes alone with him in his bureau before I became aware of a sense of ease in his presence such as I rarely experienced with strangers. I was surprised at my own composure; for, after all, I had come on business to me exceedingly painful, that of soliciting a favor. I asked on what basis the calm rested; I feared it might be deceptive. Ere long I caught a glimpse of the ground, and at once I felt assured of its solidity; I knew where I was.

M. Vandenhuten was rich, respected, and influential; I, poor, despised, and powerless; so we stood to the world at large as members of the world's society; but to each other, as a pair of human beings, our positions were reversed. The Dutchman (he was not Flamand, but pure Hollandais) was slow, cool, of rather dense intelligence, though sound and accurate judgment; the

Englishman far more nervous, active, quicker both to plan and to practice, to conceive and to realize. The Dutchman was benevolent, the Englishman suscepti- ble; in short, our characters dovetailed, but my mind, having more fire and action than his, instinctively as- sumed and kept the predominance.

This point settled, and my position well ascertained, I addressed him on the subject of my affairs with that genuine frankness which full confidence can alone in- spire. It was a pleasure to him to be so appealed to. He thanked me for giving him this opportunity of using a little exertion in my behalf. I went on to explain to him that my wish was not so much to be helped as to be put into the way of helping myself; of him I did not want exertion—that was to be my part—but only information and recommendation. Soon after I rose to go. He held out his hand at parting—an action of greater significance with foreigners than with En- glishmen. As I exchanged a smile with him, I thought the benevolence of his truthful face was better than the intelligence of my own. Characters of my order experience a balm-like solace in the contact of such souls as animated the honest breast of Victor Vanden- huten.

The next fortnight was a period of many alterna- tions. My existence during its lapse resembled a sky of one of those autumnal nights which are specially haunted by meteors and falling stars. Hopes and fears, expectations and disappointments, descended in glancing showers from zenith to horizon; but all were transient, and darkness followed swift each vanishing apparition. M. Vandenhuten aided me faithfully; he set me on the track of several places, and himself made efforts to secure them for me; but for a long time solicitation and recommendation were vain: the door either shut in my face when I was about to walk in, or another candidate, entering before me, rendered my further advance useless. Feverish and roused, no disappointment arrested me; defeat following fast on defeat served as stimulants to will. I forgot fastidiousness, conquered reserve, thrust pride from me: I asked, I persevered, I remonstrated, I dunned. It is so that openings are forced into the guarded circle where Fortune sits dealing favors round. My perseverance made me known; my importunity made me remarked. I was inquired about; my former pupils' parents, gathering the reports of their children, heard me spoken of as talented, and they echoed the word; the sound, bandied about at random, came at last to ears which, but for its universality, it might never have reached; and at the very crisis when I had tried my last effort and knew not what to do, Fortune looked in at me one morning; as I sat in drear and almost desperate deliberation on my bedstead, nodded with the familiarity of an old acquaintance—though God knows I had never met her before—and threw a prize into my lap.

In the second week of October, 18—, I got the appointment of English professor to all the classes of —— College, Brussels, with a salary of three thousand francs per annum, and the certainty of being able, by dint of the reputation and publicity accompanying the position, to make as much more by private lessons. The official notice which communicated this information mentioned also that it was the strong recommendation of M. Vandenhuten, negociant, which had turned the scale of choice in my favor.

No sooner had I read the announcement than I hurried to M. Vandenhuten's bureau, pushed the document under his nose, and when he had perused it, took both his hands, and thanked him with unrestrained vivacity. My vivid words and emphatic gesture moved his Dutch calm to unwonted sensation. He said he was happy—glad to have served me; but he had done nothing meriting such thanks. He had not laid out a centime—only scratched a few words on a sheet of paper.

Again I repeated to him,

"You have made me quite happy, and in a way that suits me; I do not feel an obligation irksome conferred by your kind hand; I do not feel disposed to shun you because you have done me a favor; from this day you must consent to admit me to your intimate acquaintance, for I shall hereafter recur again and again to the pleasure of your society."

"Ainsi soit-il," was the reply, accompanied by a smile of benignant content. I went away with its sunshine in my heart.

CHAPTER XXIII.

IT was two o'clock when I returned to my lodgings; my dinner, just brought in from a neighboring hotel, smoked on the table; I sat down, thinking to eat: had the plate been heaped with potsherds and broken glass instead of boiled beef and haricots, I could not have made a more signal failure; appetite had forsaken me. Impatient of seeing food which I could not taste, I put it all aside into a cupboard, and then demanded, "What shall I do till evening?" for before six P.M. it would be vain to seek the Rue Notre Dame aux Neiges; its inhabitant (for me it had but one) was detained by her vocation elsewhere. I walked in the streets of Brussels, and I walked in my own room from two o'clock till six; never once in that space of time did I sit down. I was in my chamber when the last named hour struck; I had just bathed my face and feverish hands, and was standing near the glass; my cheek was crimson, my eye was flame, still all my features looked quite settled and calm. Descending swiftly the stair and stepping out, I was glad to see Twilight drawing on in clouds; such shade was to me like a grateful screen, and the chill of latter Autumn, breathing in a fitful wind from the northwest, met me as a refreshing coolness. Still I saw it was cold to others, for the women I passed were wrapped in shawls, and the men had their coats buttoned close.

When are we quite happy? Was I so then? No; an urgent and growing dread worried my nerves, and had worried them since the first moment good tidings had reached me. How was Frances? It was ten weeks since I had seen her, six since I had heard from her or of her. I had answered her letter by a brief note, friendly but calm, in which no mention of continued correspondence or further visits was made. At that hour my bark hung on the topmost curl of a wave of fate, and I knew not on what shoal the onward rush

of the billow might hurl it; I would not then attac
her destiny to mine by the slightest thread; if door
ed to split on the rock, or run aground on the san
bank, I was resolved no other vessel should share n
disaster. But six weeks was a long time, and could
be that she was still well and doing well? Were n
all sages agreed in declaring that happiness finds 1
climax on earth? Dared I think that but half a stre
now divided me from the full cup of contentment—t]
draught drawn from waters said to flow only in heaver

I was at the door; I entered the quiet house;
mounted the stairs; the lobby was void and still—ε
the doors closed; I looked for the neat green mat;
lay duly in its place.

" Signal of hope!" I said, and advanced. " But
will be a little calmer; I am not going to rush in, ar
get up a scene directly." Forcibly staying my eag
step, I paused on the mat.

" What an absolute hush! Is she in? Is any bod
in?" I demanded to myself. A little tinkle, as of cir
ders falling from a grate, replied; ' a movement—a fi:
was gently stirred; and the slight rustle of life cor
tinuing, a step passed equably backward and forwar(
backward and forward, in the apartment. Fascinate(
I stood; more fixedly fascinated when a voice rewar(
ed the attention of my strained ear—so low, so sel
addressed, I never fancied the speaker otherwise tha
alone; solitude might speak thus in a desert, or in t]
hall of a forsaken house.

> " ' And ne'er but once, my son,' he said,
> Was yon dark cavern trod;
> In persecution's iron days,
> When the land was left by God.

From Bewley's bog, with slaughter red,
   A wanderer hither drew,
· And oft he stopped and turned his head
   As by fits the night-winds blew.
Feet trampling round by Cheviot-edge
   Were heard the troopers keen;
And frequent from the Whitelaw ridge
   The death-shot flashed between," &c., &c.

The old Scotch ballad was partly recited, then dropped; a pause ensued; then another strain followed, in
French, of which the purport, translated, ran as follows:

I gave, at first, attention close;
   Then interest warm ensued;
From interest as improvement rose,
   Succeeded gratitude.

Obedience was no effort soon,
   And labor was no pain;
If tired, a word, a glance alone
   Would give me strength again.

From others of the studious band
   Ere long he singled me;
But only by more close demand,
   And sterner urgency.

The task he from another took,
   From me he did reject;
He would no slight omission brook,
   And suffer no defect.

If my companions went astray,
   He scarce their wanderings blamed;
If I but faltered in the way,
   His anger fiercely flamed.

Something stirred in an adjoining chamber; it would
not do to be surprised eaves-dropping; I tapped hastily, and as hastily entered. Frances was just before
me. She had been walking slowly in her room, and
her step was checked by my advent. Twilight only

was with her, and tranquil, ruddy Firelight: to these
sisters, the Bright and the Dark, she had been speaking, ere I entered, in poetry. Sir Walter Scott's voice,
to her a foreign, far-off sound, a mountain echo, had uttered itself in the first stanzas; the second, I thought,
from the style and the substance, was the language of
her own heart. Her face was grave, its expression con-
centrated; she bent on me an unsmiling eye—an eye
just returning from abstraction, just awaking from
dreams. Well-arranged was her simple attire, smooth
her dark hair, orderly her tranquil room; but what—
with her thoughtful look, her serious self-reliance, her
bent to meditation and haply inspiration—what had
she to do with love? "Nothing," was the answer of
her own sad though gentle countenance; it seemed to
say, "I must cultivate fortitude and cling to poetry;
one is to be my support, and the other my solace
through life. Human affections do not bloom, nor do
human passions glow for me." Other women have
such thoughts. Frances, had she been as desolate as
she deemed, would not have been worse off than thou-
sands of her sex. Look at the rigid and formal race
of old maids—the race whom all despise; they have
fed themselves, from youth upward, on maxims of resignation and endurance. Many of them get ossified
with their dry diet. Self-control is so continually
their thought, so perpetually their object, that at last
it absorbs the softer and more agreeable qualities of
their nature, and they die mere models of austerity,
fashioned out of a little parchment and much bone.
Anatomists will tell you that there is a heart in the
withered old maid's carcass the same as in that of any

cherished wife or proud mother in the land. Can this be
so? I really don't know, but feel inclined to doubt it.

I came forward, bade Frances "good-evening," and
took my seat. The chair I had chosen was one she
had probably just left : it stood by a little table where
were her open desk and papers. I know not whether
she had fully recognized me at first, but she did so
now; and in a voice soft but quiet, she returned my
greeting. I had shown no eagerness; she took her
cue from me, and evinced no surprise. We met as
we had always met, as master and pupil—nothing
more. I proceeded to handle the papers; Frances,
observant and serviceable, stepped into an inner room,
brought a candle, lit it, placed it by me, then drew the
curtain over the lattice, and having added a little fresh
fuel to the already bright fire, she drew a second chair
to the table, and sat down at my right hand, a little
removed. The paper on the top was a translation of
some grave French author into English, but under-
neath lay a sheet with stanzas; on this I laid hands.
Frances half rose, made a movement to recover the
captured spoil, saying that was nothing—a mere copy
of verses. I put by resistance with the decision I
knew she never long opposed; but on this occasion
her fingers had fastened on the paper. I had quietly
to unloose them; their hold dissolved to my touch;
her hand shrunk away; my own would fain have followed it, but for the present I forbade such impulse.
The first page of the sheet was occupied with the
lines I had overheard; the sequel was not exactly the
writer's own experience, but a composition by portions
of that experience suggested. Thus, while egotism

was avoided, the faney was exercised and the heart
satisfied. I translate as before, and my translation is
nearly literal ; it continued thus :

> When sickness stayed a while my course,
> He seemed impatient still,
> Because his pupil's flagging force
> Could not obey his will.

> One day, when summoned to the bed
> Where Pain and I did strive,
> I heard him, as he bent his head,
> Say, "God, she *must* revive !"

> I felt his hand, with gentle stress,
> A moment laid on mine,
> And wished to mark my consciousness
> By some responsive sign.

> But pow'rless then to speak or move,
> I only felt, within,
> The sense of Hope, the strength of Love,
> Their healing work begin.

> And as he from the room withdrew,
> My heart his steps pursued ;
> I longed to prove, by efforts new,
> My speechless gratitude.

> When once again I took my place,
> Long vacant, in the class,
> Th' unfrequent smile across his face
> Did for one moment pass.

> The lessons done ; the signal made
> Of glad release and play,
> He, as he passed, an instant staid,
> One kindly word to say.

> "Jane, till to-morrow you are free
> From tedious task and rule ;
> This afternoon I must not see
> That yet pale face in school.

" Seek in the garden shades a seat,
Far from the play-ground din ;
The sun is warm, the air is sweet :
Stay till I call you in."

A long and pleasant afternoon
I passed in those green bowers ;
All silent, tranquil, and alone
With birds, and bees, and flowers.

Yet, when my master's voice I heard
Call, from the window, " Jane !"
I entered, joyful, at the word,
The busy house again.

He, in the hall, paced up and down ;
He paused as I passed by ;
His forehead stern relaxed its frown ;
He raised his deep-set eye.

" Not quite so pale," he murmured low.
" Now, Jane, go rest a while."
And as I smiled, his smoothened brow
Returned as glad a smile.

My perfect health restored, he took
His mien austere again ;
And, as before, he would not brook
The slightest fault from Jane.

The longest task, the hardest theme
Fell to my share as erst,
And still I toiled to place my name
In every study first.

He yet begrudged and stinted praise,
But I had learned to read
The secret meaning of his face,
And that was my best meed.

Even when his hasty temper spoke
In tones that sorrow stirred,
My grief was lulled as soon as woke
By some relenting word.

And when he lent some precious book,
   Or gave some fragrant flower,
I did not quail to Envy's look,
   Upheld by Pleasure's power.

At last our school ranks took their ground;
   The hard-fought field I won;
The prize, a laurel-wreath, was bound
   My throbbing forehead on.

Low at my master's knee I bent,
   The offered crown to meet;
Its green leaves through my temples sent
   A thrill as wild as sweet.

The strong pulse of Ambition struck
   In every vein I owned;
At the same instant, bleeding broke
   A secret, inward wound.

The hour of triumph was to me
   The hour of sorrow sore;
A day hence I must cross the sea,
   Ne'er to recross it more.

An hour hence, in my master's room,
   I with him sat alone,
And told him what a dreary gloom
   O'er joy had parting thrown.

He little said; the time was brief,
   The ship was soon to sail,
And while I sobbed in bitter grief,
   My master but looked pale.

They called in haste; he bade me go,
   Then snatched me back again;
He held me fast and murmured low,
   "Why will they part us, Jane?

"Were you not happy in my care?
   Did I not faithful prove?
Will others to my darling bear
   As true, as deep a love?

"O God, watch o'er my foster child!
  O guard her gentle head!
When winds are high and tempests wild,
  Protection round her spread!

"They call again; leave then my breast;
  Quit thy true shelter, Jane;
But when deceived, repulsed, oppress'd,
  Come home to me again."

I read, then dreamily made marks on the margin with my pencil, thinking all the while of other things; thinking that "Jane" was now at my side—no child, but a girl of nineteen—and she might be mine, so my heart affirmed. Poverty's curse was taken off me; Envy and Jealousy were far away, and unapprised of this our quiet meeting; the frost of the master's manner might melt; I felt the thaw coming fast, whether I would or not; no further need for the eye to practice a hard look, for the brow to compress its expanse into a stern fold: it was now permitted to suffer the outward revelation of the inward glow—to seek, demand, elicit an answering ardor. While musing thus, I thought that the grass on Hermon never drank the fresh dews of sunset more gratefully than my feelings drank the bliss of this hour.

Frances rose as if restless; she passed before me to stir the fire, which did not want stirring; she lifted and put down the little ornaments on the mantel-piece; her dress waved within a yard of me; slight, straight, and elegant, she stood erect on the hearth.

There are impulses we can control, but there are others which control us, because they attain us with a tiger-leap, and are our masters ere we have seen them. Perhaps, though, such impulses are seldom altogether

M 2

bad; perhaps Reason, by a process as brief as quiet, a process that is finished ere felt, has ascertained the sanity of the deed Instinct meditates, and feels justified in remaining passive while it is performed. I know I did not reason, I did not plan or intend; yet, whereas one moment I was sitting solus on the chair near the table, the next I held Frances on my knee, placed there with sharpness and decision, and retained with exceeding tenacity.

"Monsieur!" cried Frances, and was still; not another word escaped her lips. Sorely confounded she seemed during the lapse of the first few moments, but the amazement soon subsided; terror did not succeed, nor fury; after all, she was only a little nearer than she had ever been before to one she habitually respected and trusted. Embarrassment might have impelled her to contend, but self-respect checked resistance where resistance was useless.

"Frances, how much regard have you for me?" was my demand. No answer; the situation was yet too new and surprising to permit speech. On this consideration, I compelled myself for some seconds to tolerate her silence, though impatient of it. Presently I repeated the same question, probably not in the calmest of tones. She looked at me; my face, doubtless, was no model of composure, my eyes no still wells of tranquillity.

"Do speak," I urged; and a very low, hurried, yet still arch voice said,

"Monsieur, vous me faîtes mal; de grâce lâchez un peu ma main droite."

In truth, I became aware that I was holding the

said "main droite" in a somewhat ruthless grasp. I did as desired; and, for the third time, asked more gently,

"Frances, how much regard have you for me?"

"Mon maître, j'en ai beaucoup," was the truthful rejoinder.

"Frances, have you enough to give yourself to me as my wife—to accept me as your husband?"

I felt the agitation of the heart; I saw "the purple light of love" cast its glowing reflection on cheek, temples, neck; I desired to consult the eye, but sheltering lash and lid forbade.

"Monsieur," said the soft voice at last, "Monsieur désire savoir si je consens—si—enfin, si je veux me marier avec lui?"

"Justement."

"Monsieur sera-t-il aussi bon mari qu'il a été bon maître?"

"I will try, Frances."

A pause; then, with a new, yet still subdued inflection of the voice—an inflection which provoked while it pleased me—accompanied, too, by a "sourire à la fois fin et timide" in perfect harmony with the tone,

"C'est à dire, Monsieur sera toujours un peu entêté, exigeant, volontaire—"

"Have I been so, Frances?"

"Mais oui; vous le savez bien."

"Have I been nothing else?"

"Mais oui; vous avez été mon meilleur ami."

"And what, Frances, are you to me?"

"Votre dévouée élève, qui vous aime de tout son cœur."

" Will my pupil consent to pass her life with me?
Speak English now, Frances."

Some moments were taken for reflection; the answer, pronounced slowly, ran thus:

"You have always made me happy; I like to hear
you speak; I like to see you; I like to be near you;
I believe you are very good and very superior; I know
you are stern to those who are careless and idle, but
you are kind, very kind to the attentive and industrious, even if they are not clever. Master, I should be
glad to live with you always;" and she made a sort
of movement, as if she would have clung to me; but,
restraining herself, she only added, with earnest emphasis, "Master, I consent to pass my life with you."

"Very well, Frances."

I drew her a little nearer to my heart; I took a first
kiss from her lips, thereby sealing the compact now
framed between us; afterward she and I were silent,
nor was our silence brief. Frances' thoughts, during
this interval, I know not, nor did I attempt to guess
them; I was not occupied in searching her countenance, nor in otherwise troubling her composure. The
peace I felt I wished her to feel; my arm, it is true,
still detained her, but with a restraint that was gentle
enough, so long as no opposition tightened it. My
gaze was on the red fire; my heart was measuring its
own content; it sounded, and sounded, and found the
depth fathomless.

"Monsieur," at last said my quiet companion, as
stirless in her happiness as a mouse in its terror.
Even now in speaking she scarcely lifted her head.

"Well, Frances?" I like unexaggerated intercourse;

it is not my way to overpower with amorous epithets, any more than to worry with selfishly importunate caresses.

"Monsieur est raisonnable, n'est-ce pas ?"

"Yes, especially when I am requested to be so in English; but why do you ask me? You see nothing vehement or obtrusive in my manner; am I not tranquil enough ?"

"Ce n'est pas cela—" began Frances.

"English," I reminded her.

"Well, Monsieur, I wished merely to say that I should like, of course, to retain my employment of teaching. You will teach still, I suppose, Monsieur ?"

"Oh yes. It is all I have to depend on."

"Bon !—I mean good. Thus we shall have both the same profession. I like that; and my efforts to get on will be as unrestrained as yours—will they not, Monsieur ?"

"You are laying plans to be independent of me," said I.

"Yes, Monsieur; I must be no incumbrance to you —no burden in any way."

"But, Frances, I have not yet told you what my prospects are. I have left M. Pelet, and after nearly a month's seeking I have got another place, with a salary of three thousand francs a year, which I can easily double by a little additional exertion. Thus you see it would be useless for you to fag yourself by going out to give lessons; on six thousand francs you and I can live, and live well."

Frances seemed to consider. There is something flattering to man's strength, something consonant to his honorable pride, in the idea of becoming the providence of what he loves—feeding and clothing it, as God does the lilies of the field. So, to decide her resolution, I went on :

"Life has been painful and laborious enough to you so far, Frances; you require complete rest; your twelve hundred francs would not form a very important addition to our income, and what sacrifice of comfort to earn it! Relinquish your labors—you must be weary—and let me have the happiness of giving you rest."

I am not sure whether Frances had accorded due attention to my harangue. Instead of answering me with her usual respectful promptitude, she only sighed and said,

"How rich you are, Monsieur!" and then she stirred uneasy in my arms. "Three thousand francs," she murmured, "while I get only twelve hundred!" She went on faster. "However, it must be so for the present; and, Monsieur, were you not saying something about my giving up my place? Oh no, I shall hold it fast;" and her little fingers emphatically tightened on mine.

"Think of my marrying you to be kept by you, Monsieur! I could not do it; and how dull my days would be! You would be away teaching in close, noisy school-rooms from morning till evening, and I should be lingering at home, unemployed and solitary; I should get depressed and sullen, and you would soon tire of me."

"Frances, you could read and study—two things you like so well."

"Monsieur, I could not. I like a contemplative life,

but I like an active life better; I must act in some
way, and act with you. I have taken notice, Monsieur, that people who are only in each other's company for amusement never really like each other so
well, or esteem each other so highly, as those who
work together, and perhaps suffer together."

" You speak God's truth," said I, at last, " and you
shall have your own way, for it is the best way. Now,
as a reward for such ready consent, give me a voluntary kiss."

After some hesitation, natural to a novice in the art
of kissing, she brought her lips into very shy and gentle contact with my forehead. I took the small gift
as a loan, and repaid it promptly, and with generous
interest.

I know not whether Frances was really much altered since the time I first saw her; but, as I looked at
her now, I felt that she was singularly changed for
me; the sad eye, the pale cheek, the dejected and joyless countenance I remembered as her early attributes,
were quite gone, and now I saw a face dressed in
graces; smile, dimple, and rosy tint rounded its contours and brightened its hues. I had been accustomed to nurse a flattering idea that my strong attachment
to her proved some particular perspicacity in my nature. She was not handsome, she was not rich, she
was not even accomplished, yet was she my life's
treasure. I must, then, be a man of peculiar discernment. To-night my eyes opened on the mistake I had
made. I began to suspect that it was only my tastes
which were unique, not my power of discovering and
appreciating the superiority of moral worth over phys-

ical charms.   For me Frances had physical charms;
in her there was no deformity to get over; none of
those prominent defects of eyes, teeth, complexion,
shape, which hold at bay the admiration of the bold-
est male champions of intellect (for women can love a
downright ugly man if he be but talented); had she
been either "édentée, myope, rugueuse, ou bossue,"
my feelings toward her might still have been kindly,
but they could never have been impassioned.   I had
affection for the poor little misshapen Sylvie, but for
her I could never have had love.   It is true, Frances'
mental points had been the first to interest me, and
they still retained the strongest hold on my preference;
but I liked the graces of her person too.   I derived a
pleasure, purely material, from contemplating the clearness of her brown eyes, the fairness of her fine skin,
the purity of her well-set teeth, the proportion of her
delicate form; and that pleasure I could ill have dispensed with.   It appeared, then, that I too was a sensualist in my temperate and fastidious way.

Now, reader, during the last two pages I have been
giving you honey fresh from flowers, but you must not
live entirely on food so luscious; taste, then, a little
gall—just a drop, by way of change.

At a somewhat late hour I returned to my lodgings.
Having temporarily forgotten that man had any such
coarse cares as those of eating and drinking, I went to
bed fasting.   I had been excited and in action all day,
and had tasted no food since eight that morning; besides, for a fortnight past, I had known no rest either
of body or mind; the last few hours had been a sweet
delirium; it would not subside now, and, till long after

midnight, broke with troubled ecstasy the rest I so
much needed. At last I dozed, but not for long; it
was yet quite dark when I awoke, and my waking
was like that of Job when a spirit passed before his
face, and, like him, "the hair of my flesh stood up."
I might continue the parallel, for, in truth, though I
saw nothing, yet "a thing was secretly brought unto
me, and mine ear received a little thereof; there was
silence, and I heard a voice" saying, "In the midst of
life we are in death."

That sound, and the sensation of chill anguish accompanying it, many would have regarded as super-
natural; but I recognized it at once as the effect of
reaction. Man is ever clogged with his mortality, and
it was my mortal nature which now faltered and plain-
ed; my nerves, which jarred and gave a false sound,
because the soul, of late rushing headlong to an aim,
had overstrained the body's comparative weakness. A
horror of great darkness fell upon me; I felt my chamber invaded by one I had known formerly, but had
thought forever departed. I was temporarily a prey
to Hypochondria. ——

She had been my acquaintance, nay, my guest once
before in boyhood. I had entertained her at bed and
board for a year; for that space of time I had her to
myself in secret; she lay with me, she ate with me,
she walked out with me, showing me nooks in woods,
hollows in hills, where we could sit together, and where
she could drop her drear veil over me, and so hide sky
and sun, grass and green tree; taking me entirely to
her death-cold bosom, and holding me with arms of
bone. What tales she would tell me at such hours!

What songs she would recite in my ears! How she would discourse to me of her own country—the Grave —and again and again promise to conduct me there ere long; and, drawing me to the very brink of a black, sullen river, show me, on the other side, shores unequal with mound, monument, and tablet, standing up in a glimmer more hoary than moonlight. "Necropolis!" she would whisper, pointing to the pale piles, and add, "It contains a mansion prepared for you."

But my boyhood was lonely, parentless—uncheered by brother or sister; and there was no marvel that, just as I rose to youth, a sorceress, finding me lost in vague mental wanderings, with many affections and few objects, glowing aspirations and gloomy prospects, strong desires and slender hopes, should lift up her illusive lamp to me in the distance, and lure me to her vaulted home of horrors. No wonder her spells *then* had power; but *now*, when my course was widening, my prospect brightening; when my affections had found a rest; when my desires, folding wings, weary with long flight, had just alighted on the very lap of Fruition, and nestled there warm, content, under the caress of a soft hand, why did Hypochondria accost me now?

I repulsed her as one would a dreaded and ghastly concubine coming to imbitter a husband's heart toward his young bride; in vain; she kept her sway over me for that night and the next day, and eight succeeding days. Afterward my spirits began slowly to recover their tone; my appetite returned, and in a fortnight I was well. I had gone about as usual all the time, and had said nothing to any body of what I felt, but I was glad when the evil spirit departed from me, and I could again seek Frances, and sit at her side, freed from the dreadful tyranny of my demon.

•

CHAPTER XXIV.

ONE fine, frosty Sunday in November, Frances and I took a long walk; we made the tour of the city by the Boulevards; and afterward, Frances being a little tired, we sat down on one of those wayside seats placed under the trees at intervals for the accommodation of the weary. Frances was telling me about Switzerland; the subject animated her; and I was just thinking that her eyes spoke full as eloquently as her tongue, when she stopped and remarked,

"Monsieur, there is a gentleman who knows you."

I looked up. Three fashionably dressed men were just then passing—Englishmen, I knew by their air and gait as well as by their features. In the tallest of the trio I at once recognized Mr. Hunsden. He was in the act of lifting his hat to Frances; afterward he made a grimace at me, and passed on.

"Who is he?"

"A person I knew in England."

"Why did he bow to me? He does not know me."

"Yes, he does know you, in his way."

"How, Monsieur?" (she still called me "Monsieur;" I could not persuade her to adopt any more familiar term).

"Did you not read the expression of his eyes?"

"Of his eyes? No. What did they say?"

" To you they said, 'How do you do, Wilhelmina Crimsworth?' To me, ' So you have found your counterpart at last; there she sits, the female of your kind.'"   •

"Monsieur, you could not read all that in his eyes, he was so soon gone."

" I read that and more, Frances; I read that he will probably call on me this evening, or on some future occasion shortly; and I have no doubt he will insist on being introduced to you. Shall I bring him to your rooms?"

"If you please, Monsieur—I have no objection. I think, indeed, I should rather like to see him nearer, he looks so original."

As I had anticipated, Mr. Hunsden came that evening. The first thing he said was,

" You need not begin boasting, Monsieur le Professeur. I know about your appointment to ——— College, and all that; Brown has told me." Then he intimated that he had returned from Germany but a day or two since; afterward he abruptly demanded whether that was Madame Pelet-Reuter with whom he had seen me on the Boulevards. I was going to utter a rather emphatic negative, but, on second thoughts, checked myself, and, seeming to assent, asked what he thought of her.

" As to her, I'll come to that directly; but first I've a word for you. I see you are a scoundrel; you've no business to be promenading about with another man's wife. I thought you had sounder sense than to get mixed up in foreign hodge-podge of this sort."

" But the lady—"

" She's too good for you, evidently; she is like you,
but something better than you—no beauty, though;
yet when she rose (for I looked back to see you both
walk away) I thought her figure and carriage good.
These foreigners understand grace. What the devil
has she done with Pelet? She has not been married
to him three months. He must be a spoon!"

I would not let the mistake go too far; I did not
like it much.

"Pelet? How your head runs on M. and Madame
Pelet! You are always talking about them. I wish
to the gods you had wedded Mdlle. Zoraïde yourself!"

"Was that young gentlewoman not Mdlle. Zoraïde?"

"No; nor Madame Zoraïde either."

"Why did you tell a lie, then?"

"I told no lie; but you are in such a hurry. She
is a pupil of mine—a Swiss girl."

"And of course you are going to be married to her?
Don't deny that."

"Married! I think I shall, if Fate spares us both
ten weeks longer. That is my little wild strawberry,
Hunsden, whose sweetness made me careless of your
hot-house grapes."

"Stop! No boasting—no heroics; I wont bear
them. What is she? To what *caste* does she be-
long?"

I smiled. Hunsden unconsciously laid stress on
the word *caste*, and, in fact, republican, lord-hater as
he was, Hunsden was as proud of his old ——shire
blood, of his descent and family standing, respectable
and respected through long generations back, as any

peer in the realm of his Norman race and Conquest-
dated title. Hunsden would as little have thought of
taking a wife from a *caste* inferior to his own as a Stan-
ley would think of mating with a Cobden. I enjoyed
the surprise I should give; I enjoyed the triumph of
my practice over his theory; and leaning over the table, and uttering the words slowly but with repressed
glee, I said concisely,

" She is a lace-mender."

Hunsden examined me. He did not *say* he was
surprised, but surprised he was; he had his own notions of good breeding. I saw he suspected I was
going to take some very rash step; but, repressing
declamation or remonstrance, he only answered,

" Well, you are the best judge of your own affairs.
A lace-mender may make a good wife as well as a lady;
but, of course, you have taken care to ascertain thoroughly that, since she has not education, fortune, or
station, she is well furnished with such natural qualities as you think most likely to conduce to your happiness. Has she many relations?"

" None in Brussels."

" That is better. Relations are often the real evil
in such cases. I can not but think that a train of inferior connections would have been a bore to you to
your life's end."

After sitting in silence a little while longer, Hunsden rose, and was quietly bidding me good-evening;
the polite, considerate manner in which he offered me
his hand (a thing he had never done before) convinced
me that he thought I had made a terrible fool of myself; and that, ruined and thrown away as I was, it

was no time for sarcasm or cynism, or, indeed, for any thing but indulgence and forbearance.

"Good-night, William," he said, in a really soft voice, while his face looked benevolently compassionate. "Good-night, lad. I wish you and your future wife much prosperity; and I hope she will satisfy your fastidious soul."

I had much ado to refrain from laughing as I beheld the magnanimous pity of his mien. Maintaining, however, a grave air, I said,

"I thought you would have liked to have seen Mdlle. Henri?"

"Oh, that is the name! Yes, if it would be convenient, I should like to see her; but—" He hesitated.

"Well?"

"I should on no account wish to intrude."

"Come, then," said I. We set out. Hunsden no doubt regarded me as a rash, imprudent man thus to show my poor little grisette sweetheart in her poor little unfurnished grenier; but he prepared to act the real gentleman, having, in fact, the kernel of that character under the harsh husk it pleased him to wear by way of mental Mackintosh. He talked affably, and even gently, as we went along the street; he had never been so civil to me in his life. We reached the house, entered, ascended the stair. On gaining the lobby, Hunsden turned to mount a narrower stair which led to a higher story. I saw his mind was bent on the attics.

"Here, Mr. Hunsden," said I, quietly, tapping at Frances' door. He turned; in his genuine politeness he was a little disconcerted at having made the mistake; his eye reverted to the green mat, but he said nothing.

We walked in, and Frances rose from her seat near the table to receive us. Her mourning attire gave her a recluse, rather conventual, but, withal, very distinguished look; its grave simplicity added nothing to beauty, but much to dignity; the finish of the white collar and manchettes sufficed for a relief to the merino gown of solemn black; ornament was forsworn. Frances courtesied with sedate grace, looking, as she always did look when one first accosted her, more a woman to respect than to love. I introduced Mr. Hunsden, and she expressed her happiness at making his acquaintance in French. The pure and polished accent—the low, yet sweet and rather full voice, produced their effect immediately. Hunsden spoke French in reply. I had not heard him speak that language before: he managed it very well. I retired to the window-seat; Mr. Hunsden, at his hostess's invitation, occupied a chair near the hearth; from my position I could see them both, and the room too, at a glance. The room was so clean and bright, it looked like a little polished cabinet; a glass filled with flowers in the centre of the table, a fresh rose in each china cup on the mantel-piece, gave it an air of fête. Frances was serious, and Mr. Hunsden subdued, but both mutually polite; they got on at the French swimmingly: ordinary topics were discussed with great state and decorum; I thought I had never seen two such models of propriety, for Hunsden (thanks to the constraint of the foreign tongue) was obliged to shape his phrases and measure his sentences with a care that forbade any eccentricity. At last England was mentioned, and Frances proceeded to ask questions. Animated by degrees, she began to change, just as a grave night-sky changes at the approach of sunrise: first it seemed as if her forehead cleared, then her eyes glittered, her features relaxed, and became quite mobile; her sub-dued complexion grew warm and transparent; to me, she now looked pretty; before, she had only looked ladylike.

She had many things to say to the Englishman just fresh from his island-country, and she urged him with an enthusiasm of curiosity which ere long thawed Hunsden's reserve as fire thaws a congealed viper. I use this not very flattering comparison because he vividly reminded me of a snake waking from torpor, as he erected his tall form, reared his head, before a little declined, and putting back his hair from his broad Saxon forehead, showed unshaded the gleam of almost savage satire which his interlocutor's tone of eagerness and look of ardor had sufficed at once to kindle in his soul and elicit from his eyes: he was himself, as Frances was herself, and in none but his own language would he now address her.

"You understand English?" was the prefatory question.

"A little."

"Well, then, you shall have plenty of it; and, first, I see you've not much more sense than some others of my acquaintance" (indicating me with his thumb), "or else you'd never turn rabid about that dirty little country called England, for rabid I see you are; I

N

read Anglophobia in your looks, and hear it in your words. Why, Mademoiselle, is it possible that any body with a grain of rationality should feel enthusiasm about a mere name, and that name England? I thought you were a lady abbess five minutes ago, and respected you accordingly; and now I see you are a sort of Swiss sibyl, with High-Tory and High-Church principles."

" England is your country ?" asked Frances.

" Yes."

" And you don't like it ?"

" I'd be sorry to like it. A little, corrupt, venal, lord-and-king-cursed nation, full of mucky pride (as they say in ——shire) and helpless pauperism ; rotten with abuses, worm-eaten with prejudices !"

" You might say so of almost every state ; there are abuses and prejudices every where, and I thought fewer in England than in other countries."

" Come to England and see. Come to Birmingham and Manchester; come to St. Giles' in London, and get a practical notion of how our system works. Examine the footprints of our august aristocracy ; see how they walk in blood, crushing hearts as they go. Just put your head in at English cottage doors; get a glimpse of Famine crouched torpid on black hearthstones ; of Disease lying bare on beds without coverlets ; of Infamy wantoning viciously with Ignorance, though indeed Luxury is her favorite paramour, and princely halls are dearer to her than thatched hovels—"

" I was not thinking of the wretchedness and vice in England ; I was thinking of the good side—of what is elevated in your character as a nation."

"There is no good side—none, at least, of which you can have any knowledge; for you can not appreciate the efforts of industry, the achievements of enterprise, or the discoveries of science. Narrowness of education and obscurity of position quite incapacitate you from understanding those points; and as to historical and poetical associations, I will not insult you, Mademoiselle, by supposing that you alluded to such humbug."

"But I did, partly."

Hunsden laughed—his laugh of unmitigated scorn.

"I did, Mr. Hunsden. Are you of the number of those to whom such associations give no pleasure?"

"Mademoiselle, what is an association? I never saw one. What is its length, breadth, weight, value—ay, *value?* What price will it bring in the market?"

"Your portrait, to any one who loved you, would, for the sake of association, be without price."

That inscrutable Hunsden heard this remark, and felt it rather acutely, too, somewhere, for he colored—a thing not unusual with him when hit unawares on a tender point. A sort of trouble momentarily darkened his eye, and I believe he filled up the transient pause succeeding his antagonist's home-thrust by a wish that some one did love him as he would like to be loved—some one whose love he could unreservedly return.

The lady pursued her temporary advantage.

"If your world is a world without associations, Mr. Hunsden, I no longer wonder that you hate England so. I don't clearly know what Paradise is, and what angels are; yet, taking it to be the most glorious region I can conceive, and angels the most elevated ex- ·

istence, if one of them—if Abdiel the Faithful himself" (she was thinking of Milton) "were suddenly
stripped of the faculty of association, I think he would
soon rush forth from 'the ever-during gates,' leave
heaven, and seek what he had lost in hell—yes, in the
very hell from which he turned 'with retorted scorn.'"

Frances' tone in saying this was as marked as her
language, and it was when the word "hell" twanged
off from her lips with a somewhat startling emphasis
that Hunsden deigned to bestow one slight glance of
admiration.   He liked something strong, whether in
man or woman; he liked whatever dared to clear conventional limits.   He had never before heard a lady
say "hell" with that uncompromising sort of accent,
and the sound pleased him from a lady's lips; he would
fain have had Frances to strike the string again, but
it was not in her way.   The display of eccentric vigor
never gave her pleasure, and it only sounded in her
voice or flashed in her countenance when extraordinary
circumstances—and those generally painful—forced it
out of the depths where it burned latent.   To me,
once or twice, she had in intimate conversation uttered
venturous thoughts in nervous language; but when
the hour of such manifestation was past, I could not
recall it; it came of itself, and of itself departed.
Hunsden's excitations she put by soon with a smile,
and recurring to the theme of disputation, said,

"Since England is nothing, why do the Continental
nations respect her so?"

"I should have thought no child would have asked
that question," replied Hunsden, who never at any
time gave information without reproving for stupidity

those who asked it of him; "if you had been my pupil, as I suppose you once had the misfortune to be
that of a deplorable character not a hundred miles off,
I would have put you in the corner for such a confes-
sion of ignorance. Why, Mademoiselle, can't you see
that it is our *gold* which buys us French politeness,
German good-will, and Swiss servility?" And he
sneered diabolically.

"Swiss!" said Frances, catching the word "servility." "Do you call my countrymen servile?" And
she started up. I could not suppress a low laugh:
there was ire in her glance, and defiance in her attitude. "Do you abuse Switzerland to me, Mr. Hunsden? Do you think I have no associations? Do you
calculate that I am prepared to dwell only on what
vice and degradation may be found in Alpine villages,
and to leave quite out of my heart the social greatness
of my countrymen, and our blood-earned freedom, and
the natural glories of our mountains? You're mistaken—you're mistaken."

"Social greatness—call it what you will, your countrymen are sensible fellows; they make a marketable
article of what to you is an abstract idea; they have,
ere this, sold their social greatness and also their
blood-earned freedom to be the servants of foreign
kings."

"You never were in Switzerland?"

"Yes, I have been there twice."

"You know nothing of it."

"I do."

"And you say the Swiss are mercenary, as a par-
rot says 'Poor Poll,' or as the Belgians here say the

English are not brave, or as the French accuse them of being perfidious: there is no justice in your dictums."

"There is truth."

"I tell you, Mr. Hunsden, you are a more unpractical man than I am an unpractical woman, for you don't acknowledge what really exists. You want to annihilate individual patriotism and national greatness as an Atheist would annihilate God and his own soul, by denying their existence."

"Where are you flying to? You are off at a tangent. I thought we were talking about the mercenary nature of the Swiss."

"We were; and if you proved to me that the Swiss are mercenary to-morrow (which you can not do), I should love Switzerland still."

"You would be mad, then—mad as a March hare —to indulge in a passion for millions of ship-loads of soil, timber, snow, and ice."

"Not so mad as you, who love nothing."

"There's a method in my madness; there's none in yours."

"Your method is to squeeze the sap out of creation, and make manure of the refuse by way of turning it to what you call use."

"You can not reason at all," said Hunsden; "there's no logic in you."

"Better to be without logic than without feeling," retorted Frances, who was now passing backward and forward from her cupboard to the table, intent, if not on hospitable thoughts, at least on hospitable deeds, for she was laying the cloth, and putting plates, knives, and forks thereon.

"Is that a hit at me, Mademoiselle? Do you suppose I am without feeling?"

"I suppose you are always interfering with your own feelings and those of other people, and dogmatizing about the irrationality of this, that, and the other sentiment, and then ordering it to be suppressed because you imagine it to be inconsistent with logic."

"I do right."

Frances had stepped out of sight into a sort of little pantry; she soon reappeared.

"You do right? Indeed, no; you are much mistaken if you think so. Just be so good as to let me get to the fire, Mr. Hunsden; I have something to cook." (An interval occupied in settling a casserole on the fire; then, while she stirred its contents), "Right! as if it were right to crush any pleasurable sentiment that God has given to man, especially any sentiment that, like patriotism, spreads man's selfishness in wider circles" (fire stirred, dish put down before it).

"Were you born in Switzerland?"

"I should think so, or else why should I call it my country?"

"And where did you get your English features and figure?"

"I am English too; half the blood in my veins is English; thus I have a right to a double power of patriotism, possessing an interest in two noble, free, and fortunate countries."

"You had an English mother?"

"Yes, yes; and you, I suppose, had a mother from the moon or from Utopia, since not a nation in Europe has a claim on your interest."

"On the contrary, I'm a universal patriot, if you could understand me rightly; my country is the world."

"Sympathies so widely diffused must be very shallow: will you have the goodness to come to table? Monsieur" (to me, who appeared to be now absorbed in reading by moonlight)—"Monsieur, supper is served."

This was said in quite a different voice to that in which she had been bandying phrases with Mr. Hunsden—not so short, graver and softer.

"Frances, what do you mean by preparing supper? we had no intention of staying."

"Ah, Monsieur, but you have staid, and supper is prepared; you have only the alternative of eating it."

The meal was a foreign one, of course: it consisted of two small but tasty dishes of meat, prepared with skill and served with nicety; a salad and "fromage François" completed it. The business of eating interposed a brief truce between the belligerents, but no sooner was supper disposed of than they were at it again. The fresh subject of dispute ran on the spirit of religious intolerance which Mr. Hunsden affirmed to exist strongly in Switzerland, notwithstanding the professed attachment of the Swiss to freedom. Here Frances had greatly the worst of it, not only because she was unskilled to argue, but because her own real opinions on the point in question happened to coincide pretty nearly with Mr. Hunsden's, and she only contradicted him out of opposition. At last she gave in, confessing that she thought as he thought, but bidding him take notice that she did not consider herself beaten.

"No more did the French at Waterloo," said Hunsden.

"There is no comparison between the cases," rejoined Frances; "mine was a sham-fight."

"Sham or real, it's up with you."

"No; though I have neither logic nor wealth of words, yet in a case where my opinion really differed from yours, I would adhere to it when I had not another word to say in its defense; you should be baffled by dumb determination. You speak of Waterloo; your Wellington ought to have been conquered there, according to Napoleon; but he persevered in spite of the laws of war, and was victorious in defiance of military tactics. I would do as he did."

"I'll be bound for it you would; probably you have some of the same sort of stubborn stuff in you."

"I should be sorry if I had not; he and Tell were brothers, and I'd scorn the Swiss, man or woman, who had none of the much-enduring nature of our heroic William in his soul."

"If Tell was like Wellington, he was an ass."

"Does not *ass* mean *baudet?*" asked Frances, turning to me.

"No, no," I replied, "it means an *esprit-fort;* and now," I continued, as I saw that fresh occasion of strife was brewing between these two, "it is high time to go."

Hunsden rose. "Good-by," said he to Frances; "I shall be off for this glorious England to-morrow, and it may be twelve months or more before I come to Brussels again; whenever I do come I'll seek you out, and you shall see if I don't find means to make you

N 2

fiercer than a dragon. You've done pretty well this evening, but next interview you shall challenge me outright. Meantime you're doomed to become Mrs. William Crimsworth, I suppose. Poor young lady! but you have a spark of spirit; cherish it, and give the Professor the full benefit thereof."

"Are you married, Mr. Hunsden?" asked Frances, suddenly.

"No. I should have thought you might have guessed I was a Benedick by my look."

"Well, whenever you marry, don't take a wife out of Switzerland; for if you begin blaspheming Helvetia, and cursing the cantons—above all, if you mention the word *ass* in the same breath with the name Tell (for ass *is* baudet, I know, though Monsieur is pleased to translate it *esprit-fort*), your mountain maid will some night smother her Breton-bretonnant, even as your own Shakspeare's Othello smothered Desdemona."

"I am warned," said Hunsden; "and so are you, lad" (nodding to me). "I hope yet to hear of a travesty of the Moor and his gentle lady, in which the parts shall be reversed according to the plan just sketched—you, however, being in my night-cap. Farewell, Mademoiselle." He bowed on her hand, absolutely like Sir Charles Grandison on that of Harriet Byron; adding, "Death from such fingers would not be without charms."

"Mon Dieu!" murmured Frances, opening her large eyes, and lifting her distinctly arched brows; "c'est qu'il fait des compliments! je ne m'y suis pas attendu." She smiled half in ire, half in mirth, courtesied with foreign grace, and so they parted.

No sooner had we got into the street than Hunsden collared me.

"And that is your lace-mender?" said he; "and you reckon you have done a fine, magnanimous thing in offering to marry her? You, a scion of Seacombe, have proved your disdain of social distinctions by taking up with an *ouvrière!* And I pitied the fellow, thinking his feelings had misled him, and that he had hurt himself by contracting a low match!"

"Just let go my collar, Hunsden."

On the contrary, he swayed me to and fro; so I grappled him round the waist. It was dark; the street lonely and lampless. We had then a tug for it; and after we had both rolled on the pavement and with difficulty picked ourselves up, we agreed to walk on more soberly.

"Yes, that's my lace-mender," said I; "and she is to be mine for life, God willing."

"God is not willing—you can't suppose it. What business have you to be suited so well with a partner? And she treats you with a sort of respect too, and says 'Monsieur,' and modulates her tone in addressing you as if you were something superior! She could not evince more deference to such a one as me, were she favored by Fortune to the supreme extent of being my choice instead of yours."

"Hunsden, you're a puppy. But you've only seen the title-page of my happiness; you don't know the tale that follows; you can not conceive the interest, and sweet variety, and thrilling excitement of the narrative."

Hunsden—speaking low and deep, for we had now

entered a busier street—desired me to hold my peace, threatening to do something dreadful if I stimulated his wrath further by boasting. I laughed till my sides ached. We soon reached his hotel; before he entered it he said,

"Don't be vainglorious. Your lace-mender is too good for you, but not good enough for me; neither physically nor morally does she come up to my ideal of a woman. No; I dream of something far beyond that pale-faced, excitable little Helvetian (by-the-by, she has infinitely more of the nervous, mobile Parisienne in her than of the robust 'jungfrau'). Your Mdlle. Henri is in person *chétive*, in mind sans *caractère*, compared with the queen of my visions. You, indeed, may put up with that *minois chiffonné;* but when I marry I must have straighter and more harmonious features, to say nothing of a nobler and better developed shape than that perverse, ill-thriven child can boast."

"Bribe a seraph to fetch you a coal of fire from heaven if you will," said I, "and with it kindle life in the tallest, fattest, most boneless, fullest-blooded of Rubens' painted women—leave me only my Alpine peri, and I'll not envy you."

With a simultaneous movement, each turned his back to the other. Neither said "God bless you," yet on the morrow the sea was to roll between us.

CHAPTER XXV.

In two months more Frances had fulfilled the time of mourning for her aunt. One January morning—the first of the new-year holidays—I went in a fiacre, accompanied only by M. Vandenhuten, to the Rue Notre Dame aux Neiges, and having alighted alone and walked up stairs, I found Frances apparently waiting for me, dressed in a style scarcely appropriate to that cold, · bright, frosty day. Never till now had I seen her attired in any other than black or sad-colored stuff; and there she stood by the window, clad all in white, and white of a most diaphanous texture. Her array was very simple, to be sure, but it looked imposing and festal because it was so clear, full, and floating; a veil shadowed her head, and hung below her knee; a little wreath of pink flowers fastened it to her thickly-tressed Grecian plat, and thence it fell softly on each side of her face. Singular to state, she was or had been crying. When I asked her if she were ready, she said "yes, Monsieur" with something very like a checked sob; and when I took a shawl, which lay on the table, and folded it round her, not only did tear after tear course unbidden down her cheek, but she shook to my ministration like a reed. I said I was sorry to see her in such low spirits, and requested to be allowed an insight into the origin thereof. She only said "it was impossible to help it," and then voluntarily though hurriedly putting her hand into mine, accompanied me out of the room, and ran down stairs with a quick, uncertain step, like one who was eager to get some formidable piece of business over. I put her into the fiacre. M. Vandenhuten received her and seated her beside himself; we drove all together to the Protestant chapel, went through a certain service in the Common Prayer-Book, and she and I came out married. M. Vandenhuten had given the bride away.

We took no bridal trip; our modesty, screened by the peaceful obscurity of our station, and the pleasant isolation of our circumstances, did not exact that additional precaution. We repaired at once to a small house I had taken in the faubourg nearest that part of the city where the scene of our avocations lay.

Three or four hours after the wedding ceremony, Frances, divested of her bridal snow, and attired in a pretty lilac gown of warmer materials, a piquant black silk apron, and a lace collar with some finishing decoration of lilac ribbon, was kneeling on the carpet of a neatly-furnished though not spacious parlor, arranging on the shelves of a chiffonière some books which I handed to her from the table. It was snowing fast out of doors; the afternoon had turned out wild and cold; the leaden sky seemed full of drifts, and the street was already ankle-deep in the white down-fall. Our fire burned bright, our new habitation looked brilliantly clean and fresh, the furniture was all arranged, and there were but some articles of glass, china, books, &c., to put in order. Frances found in this business occupation till tea-time, and then, after I had distinctly instructed her how to make a cup of tea in rational En-

glish style, and after she had got over the dismay occasioned by seeing such an extravagant amount of material put into the pot, she administered to me a prop-
er British repast, at which there wanted neither candles nor urn, firelight nor comfort.

Our week's holiday glided by, and we readdressed
ourselves to labor. Both my wife and I began in good
earnest with the notion that we were working people,
destined to earn our bread by exertion, and that of the
most assiduous kind. Our days were thoroughly occupied. We used to part every morning at eight
o'clock, and not meet again till five P.M.; but into
what sweet rest did the turmoil of each busy day decline! Looking down the vista of memory, I see the
evenings passed in that little parlor like a long string
of rubies circling the dusk brow of the past. Unva-
ried were they as each cut gem, and like each gem brilliant and burning.

A year and a half passed. One morning (it was a
fête, and we had the day to ourselves) Frances said
to me, with a suddenness peculiar to her when she
had been thinking long on a subject, and at last, having come to a conclusion, wished to test its soundness
by the touchstone of my judgment,

"I don't work enough."

"What now?" demanded I, looking up from my
coffee, which I had been deliberately stirring while
enjoying, in anticipation, a walk I proposed to take
with Frances that fine summer day (it was June) to a
certain farm-house in the country where we were to
dine. "What now?" and I saw at once, in the serious ardor of her face, a project of vital importance.

"I am not satisfied," returned she: "you are now earning eight thousand francs a year" (it was true; my efforts, punctuality, the fame of my pupils' progress, the publicity of my station, had so far helped me on), "while I am still at my miserable twelve hundred francs. I *can* do better, and I *will*."

"You work as long and as diligently as I do, Frances."

"Yes, Monsieur, but I am not working in the right way, and I am convinced of it."

"You wish to change—you have a plan for progress in your mind; go and put on your bonnet, and, while we take our walk, you shall tell me of it."

"Yes, Monsieur."

She went, as docile as a well-trained child. She was a curious mixture of tractability and firmness. I sat thinking about her, and wondering what her plan could be, when she re-entered.

"Monsieur, I have given Minnie" (our bonne) "leave to go out too, as it is so very fine; so will you be kind enough to lock the door, and take the key with you?"

"Kiss me, Mrs. Crimsworth," was my not very apposite reply; but she looked so engaging in her light summer dress and little cottage bonnet, and her manner in speaking to me was then, as always, so unaffectedly and suavely respectful, that my heart expanded at the sight of her, and a kiss seemed necessary to content its importunity.

"There, Monsieur."

"Why do you always call me 'Monsieur?' Say William."

"I can not pronounce your W; besides, 'Monsieur' belongs to you; I like it best."

Minnie having departed in clean cap and smart shawl, we too set out, leaving the house solitary and silent—silent, at least, but for the ticking of the clock. We were soon clear of Brussels; the fields received us, and then the lanes, remote from carriage-resounding *chaussées*. Ere long we came upon a nook, so rural, green, and secluded, it might have been a spot in some pastoral English province. A bank of short and mossy grass, under a hawthorn, offered a seat too tempting to be declined. We took it, and when we had admired and examined some English-looking wild-flowers growing at our feet, I recalled Frances' attention and my own to the topic touched on at breakfast.

"What was her plan?" A natural one—the next step to be mounted by us, or, at least, by her, if she wanted to rise in her profession. She proposed to begin a school. We already had the means for commencing on a careful scale, having lived greatly within our income. We possessed too, by this time, an extensive and eligible connection, in the sense advantageous to our business; for, though our circle of visiting acquaintance continued as limited as ever, we were now widely known in schools and families as teachers. When Frances had developed her plan, she intimated, in some closing sentences, her hopes for the future. If we only had good health and tolerable success, we might, she was sure, in time realize an independency, and that, perhaps, before we were too old to enjoy it; and then both she and I would rest; and what was

to hinder us from going to live in England? Ei
was still her Promised Land.

I put no obstacle in her way—raised no obje
I knew she was not one who could live quiesce:
inactive, or even comparatively inactive. Duti
must have to fulfill, and important duties; wo
do, and exciting, absorbing, profitable work;
faculties stirred in her frame, and they demand
nourishment, free exercise: mine was not the
ever to starve or cramp them; no, I delighted in
ing them sustenance, and in clearing them wider
for action.

"You have conceived a plan, Frances," s:
"and a good plan; execute it; you have my fre
sent; and wherever and whenever my assista:
wanted, ask and you shall have it."

Frances' eyes thanked me almost with tears
a sparkle or two, soon brushed away; she pos:
herself of my hand too, and held it for some tim
close clasped in both her own, but she said no
than "thank you, Monsieur."

We passed a divine day, and came home late,
ed by a full summer moon.

Ten years rush now upon me with dusty, vibr
unresting wings; years of bustle, action, unsl
endeavor; years in which I and my wife, h
launched ourselves in the full career of progre
progress whirls on in European capitals, scarcely
repose, were strangers to amusement, never th
of indulgence, and yet, as our course ran side by
as we marched hand in hand, we neither murn
repented, nor faltered. Hope indeed cheered us; l

kept us up; harmony of thought and deed smoothed many difficulties, and finally, success bestowed every now and then encouraging reward on diligence. Our school became one of the most popular in Brussels, and as by degrees we raised our terms and elevated our system of education, our choice of pupils grew more select, and at length included the children of the best families in Belgium. We had, too, an excellent connection in England, first opened by the unsolicited recommendation of Mr. Hunsden, who having been over, and having abused me for my prosperity in set terms, went back, and soon after sent a leash of young ——shire heiresses—his cousins, as he said—" to be polished off by Mrs. Crimsworth."

As to this same Mrs. Crimsworth, in one sense she was become another woman, though in another she remained unchanged. So different was she under different circumstances, I seemed to possess two wives. The faculties of her nature already disclosed when I married her remained fresh and fair, but other faculties shot up strong, branched out broad, and quite altered the external character of the plant. Firmness, activity, and enterprise covered with grave foliage poetic feeling and fervor; but these flowers were still there, preserved pure and dewy under the umbrage of later growth and hardier nature. Perhaps I only in the world knew the secret of their existence, but to me they were ever ready to yield an exquisite fragrance and present a beauty as chaste as radiant.

In the daytime my house and establishment were conducted by Madame the Directress, a stately and elegant woman, bearing much anxious thought on her

large brow, much calculated dignity in her
mien. Immediately after breakfast I used
with this lady : I went to my college, she
school-room. Returning for an hour in the co
the day, I found her always in class, intentl
pied, silence, industry, observance attending
presence. When not actually teaching, she wa
looking and guiding by eye and gesture; she t
peared vigilant and solicitous. When commun
instruction, her aspect was more animated; sh
ed to feel a certain enjoyment in the occupation
language in which she addressed her pupils,
simple and unpretending, was never trite or dr
did not speak from routine-formulas ; she ma
own phrases as she went on, and very nervo
impressive phrases they frequently were; ofter
elucidating favorite points of history or geograp
would wax genuinely eloquent in her earne
Her pupils, or at least the elder and more int
among them, recognized well the language of a
rior mind ; they felt too, and some of them r
the impression of elevated sentiments. The
little fondling between mistress and girls, but s
Frances' pupils in time learned to love her sin
all of them beheld her with respect : her gene
meanor toward them was serious ; sometimes
nant when they pleased her with their progress
tention, always scrupulously refined and consi
In cases where reproof or punishment was call
she was usually forbearing enough ; but if an
advantage of that forbearance, which sometime
pened, a sharp, sudden, and lightning-like s

taught the culprit the extent of the mistake commit-
ted. Sometimes a gleam of tenderness softened her
eyes and manner, but this was rare; only when a pupil was sick, or when it pined after home, or in the
case of some little motherless child, or of one much
poorer than its companions, whose scanty wardrobe
and mean appointments brought on it the contempt
of the jeweled young countesses and silk-clad misses.
Over such feeble fledglings the directress spread a
wing of kindliest protection : it was to their bedsides
she came at night to tuck them warmly in ; it was
after them she looked in winter to see that they always had a comfortable seat by the stove ; it was
they who by turns were summoned to the salon to receive some little dole of cake or fruit—to sit on a foot-
stool at the fireside—to enjoy home-comforts, and almost home-liberty, for an evening together—to be
spoken to gently and softly, comforted, encouraged,
cherished ; and when bedtime came, dismissed with a
kiss of true tenderness. As to Julia and Georgiana
G——, daughters of an English baronet, as to Mdlle.
Mathilde de ——, heiress of a Belgian count, and sundry other children of patrician race, the directress was
careful of them as of the others, anxious for their progress as for that of the rest, but it never seemed to enter her head to distinguish them by a mark of preference. One girl, of noble blood, she loved dearly—a
young Irish baroness—Lady Catharine ——; but it
was for her enthusiastic heart and clever head, for her
generosity and her genius ; the title and rank went for
nothing.

My afternoons were spent also in college, with the

exception of an hour which my wife daily exacted of
me for her establishment, and with which she would
not dispense. She said that I must spend that time
among her pupils to learn their characters, to be "*au
courant*" with every thing that was passing in the
house, to become interested in what interested her, to
be able to give her my opinion on knotty points when
she required it, and this she did constantly, never allowing my interest in the pupils to fall asleep, and
never making any change of importance without my
cognizance and consent. She delighted to sit by me
when I gave my lessons (lessons in literature), her
hands folded on her knee, the most fixedly attentive
of any present. She rarely addressed me in class ;
when she did, it was with an air of marked deference ;
it was her pleasure, her joy to make me still the master in all things.

At six o'clock P.M. my daily labors ceased. I then
came home, for my home was my heaven. Ever at
that hour, as I entered our private sitting-room, the
lady-directress vanished from before my eyes, and Frances Henri, my own little lace-mender, was magically
restored to my arms. Much disappointed she would
have been if her master had not been as constant to
the tryste as herself, and if his truthful kiss had not
been prompt to answer her soft "Bon soir, Monsieur."

Talk French to me she would, and many a punishment she has had for her willfulness. I fear the choice
of chastisement must have been injudicious, for, instead
of correcting the fault, it seemed to encourage its renewal. Our evenings were our own ; that recreation
was necessary to refresh our strength for the due dis-

charge of our duties. Sometimes we spent them all in conversation; and my young Genevese, now that she was thoroughly accustomed to her English professor, now that she loved him too absolutely to fear him much, reposed in him a confidence so unlimited that topics of conversation could no more be wanting with him than subjects for communion with her own heart. In those moments, happy as a bird with its mate, she would show me what she had of vivacity, of mirth, of originality in her well-dowered nature. She would show, too, some stores of raillery, of "malice," and would vex, tease, pique me sometimes about what she called my "bizarreries Anglaises," my "caprices insu-laires," with a wild and witty wickedness that made a perfect white demon of her while it lasted. This was rare, however, and the elfish freak was always short. Sometimes, when driven a little hard in the war of words, for her tongue did ample justice to the pith, the point, the delicacy of her native French, in which language she always attacked me, I used to turn upon her with my old decision, and arrest bodily the sprite that teased me. Vain idea! no sooner had I grasped hand or arm than the elf was gone; the provocative smile quenched in the expressive brown eyes, and a ray of gentle homage shone under the lids in its place. I had seized a mere vexing fairy, and found a submissive and supplicating little mortal woman in my arms. Then I made her get a book, and read English to me for an hour by way of penance. I frequently dosed her with Wordsworth in this way, and Wordsworth steadied her soon; she had a difficulty in comprehend-ing his deep, serene, and sober mind; his language, too, was not facile to her; she had to ask questions, to sue for explanations, to be like a child and a novice, and to acknowledge me as her senior and director. Her instinct instantly penetrated and possessed the meaning of more ardent and imaginative writers. Byron excited her; Scott she loved; Wordsworth only she puzzled at, wondered over, and hesitated to pronounce an opinion upon.

But whether she read to me or talked with me; whether she teased me in French or entreated me in English; whether she jested with wit or inquired with deference; narrated with interest or listened with attention; whether she smiled *at* me or *on* me, always at nine o'clock I was left—abandoned. She would extricate herself from my arms, quit my side, take her lamp, and be gone. Her mission was up stairs. I have followed her sometimes and watched her. First she opened the door of the dortoir (the pupils' chamber); noiselesly she glided up the long room between the two rows of white beds, and surveyed all the sleepers; if any were wakeful, especially if any were sad, spoke to them and soothed them; stood some minutes to ascertain that all was safe and tranquil; trimmed the watch-light which burned in the apartment all night; then withdrew, closing the door behind her without sound. Thence she glided to our own chamber: it had a little cabinet within; this she sought; there, too, appeared a bed, but one, and that a very small one; her face (the night I followed and observed her) changed as she approached this tiny couch; from grave it warmed to earnest; she shaded with one hand the lamp she held in the other; she bent above the pillow and hung over a child asleep; its slumber (that evening at least, and usually, I believe) was sound and calm; no tear wet its dark eyelashes; no fever heated its round cheek; no ill dream discomposed its budding features. Frances gazed; she did not smile, and yet the deepest delight filled, flushed her face; feeling, pleasurable, powerful, worked in her whole frame, which still was motionless. I saw, indeed, her heart heave; her lips were a little apart; her breathing grew somewhat hurried; the child smiled; then at last the mother smiled too, and said in a low soliloquy, "God bless my little son!" She stooped closer over him, breathed the softest of kisses on his brow, covered his minute hand with hers, and at last started up and came away. I regained the parlor before her. Entering it two minutes later, she said, quietly, as she put down her extinguished lamp,

"Victor rests well: he smiled in his sleep; he has your smile, Monsieur."

The said Victor was, of course, her own boy, born in the third year of our marriage. His Christian name had been given him in honor of M. Vandenhuten, who continued always our trusty and well-beloved friend.

Frances was then a good and dear wife to me, because I was to her a good, just, and faithful husband. What she would have been had she married a harsh, envious, careless man—a profligate, a prodigal, a drunkard, or a tyrant, is another question, and one which I once propounded to her. Her answer, given after some reflection, was,

"I should have tried to endure the evil or cure it for a while; and when I found it intolerable and incurable, I should have left my torturer suddenly and silently.

"And if law or might had forced you back again?"

"What, to a drunkard, a profligate, a selfish spendthrift, an unjust fool?" •

"Yes."

"I would have gone back; again assured myself whether or not his vice and my misery were capable of remedy, and if not, have left him again."

"And if again forced to return and compelled to abide?"

"I don't know," she said, hastily. "Why do you ask me, Monsieur?"

I would have an answer, because I saw a strange kind of spirit in her eye, whose voice I determined to waken.

"Monsieur, if a wife's nature loathes that of the man she is wedded to, marriage must be slavery. Against slavery all right thinkers revolt; and though torture be the price of resistance, torture must be dared; though the only road to freedom lie through the gates of death, those gates must be passed, for freedom is indispensable. Then, Monsieur, I would resist as far as my strength permitted; when that strength failed I should be sure of a refuge. Death would certainly screen me both from bad laws and their consequences."

"Voluntary death, Frances?"

"No, Monsieur. I'd have courage to live out every throe of anguish Fate assigned me, and principle to contend for justice and liberty to the last."

"I see you would have made no patient Grizzle.

And now, supposing Fate had merely assigned you the lot of an old maid, what then? How would you have liked celibacy?"

"Not much, certainly. An old maid's life must doubtless be void and vapid—her heart strained and empty. Had I been an old maid, I should have spent existence in efforts to fill the void and ease the aching. I should have probably failed, and died weary and disappointed, despised and of no account, like other single women. But I'm not an old maid," she added, quickly. "I should have been, though, but for my master. I should never have suited any man but Professor Crimsworth; no other gentleman, French, English, or Belgian, would have thought me amiable or handsome; and I doubt whether I should have cared for the approbation of many others, if I could have obtained it. Now I have been Professor Crimsworth's wife eight years, and what is he in my eyes? Is he honorable, beloved—" She stopped; her voice was cut off, her eyes suddenly suffused. She and I were standing side by side. She threw her arms around me, and strained me to her heart with passionate earnestness: the energy of her whole being glowed in her dark and then dilated eye, and crimsoned her animated cheek; her look and movement were like inspiration; in one there was such a flash, in the other such a power. Half an hour afterward, when she had become calm, I asked where all that wild vigor was gone which had transformed her erewhile, and made her glance so thrilling and ardent—her action so rapid and strong. She looked down, smiling softly and passively:

"I can not tell where it is gone, Monsieur," said

she, "but I know that, whenever it is wanted, it will·
come back again."

Behold us now at the close of ten years, and we
have realized an independency. The rapidity with
which we have attained this end had its origin in three
reasons: Firstly, we worked so hard for it; secondly,
we had no incumbrances to delay success; thirdly, as
soon as we had capital to invest, two well-skilled
counselors, one in Belgium, one in England, viz., Vandenhuten and Hunsden, gave us each a word of advice as to the sort of investment to be chosen. The
suggestion made was judicious; and, being promptly
acted on, the result proved gainful—I need not say
how gainful; I communicated details to Messrs. Vandenhuten and Hunsden; nobody else can be interested
in hearing them.

Accounts being wound up, and our professional connection disposed of, we both agreed that, as Mammon
was not our master, nor his service that in which we
desired to spend our lives; as our desires were temperate, and our habits unostentatious, we had now
abundance to live on—abundance to leave our boy,
and should, besides, always have a balance on hand,
which, properly managed by right sympathy and un-
selfish activity, might help Philanthropy in her enter-
prises, and put solace into the hand of Charity.

To England we now resolved to take wing. We
arrived there safely; Frances realized the dream of
her lifetime. We spent a whole summer and autumn
in traveling from end to end of the British islands, and
afterward passed a winter in London. Then we
thought it high time to fix our residence. My heart

yearned toward my native county of ——shire, and it is in ——shire I now live; it is in the library of my own home I am now writing. That home lies amid a sequestered and rather hilly region, thirty miles removed from X——; a region whose verdure the smoke of mills has not yet sullied, whose waters still run pure, whose swells of moorland preserve in some ferny glens that lie between them the very primal wildness of nature—her moss, her bracken, her blue-bells; her scents of reed and heather; her free and fresh breezes. My house is a picturesque and not too spacious dwelling, with low and long windows, a trellised and leaf-veiled porch over the front door, just now, on this summer evening, looking like an arch of roses and ivy. The garden is chiefly laid out in lawn, formed of the sod of the hills, with herbage short and soft as moss, full of its own peculiar flowers, tiny and starlike, imbedded in the minute embroidery of their fine foliage. At the bottom of the sloping garden there is a wicket, which opens upon a lane as green as the lawn, very long, shady, and little frequented; on the turf of this lane generally appear the first daisies of spring, whence its name, Daisy Lane, serving also as a distinction to the house.

It terminates (the lane I mean) in a valley full of wood, which wood—chiefly oak and beech—spreads shadowy about the vicinage of a very old mansion, one of the Elizabethan structures, much larger, as well as more antique than Daisy Lane, the property and residence of an individual familiar both to me and to the reader. Yes, in Hunsden Wood—for so are those glades and that gray building, with many gables and more chimneys, named—abides Yorke Hunsden, still unmarried; never, I suppose, having yet found his ideal, though I know at least a score of young ladies within a circuit of forty miles who would be willing to assist him in the search.

The estate fell to him by the death of his father five years since. He has given up trade, after having made by it sufficient to pay off some incumbrances by which the family heritage was burdened. I say he abides here, but I do not think he is resident above five months out of the twelve; he wanders from land to land, and spends some part of each winter in town; he frequently brings visitors with him when he comes to ——shire, and these visitors are often foreigners: sometimes he has a German metaphysician, sometimes a French savant; he had once a dissatisfied and savage-looking Italian, who neither sang nor played, and of whom Frances affirmed that he had "tout l'air d'un conspirateur."

What English guests Hunsden invites are all either men of Birmingham or Manchester—hard men, seemingly knit up in one thought, whose talk is of free trade. The foreign visitors, too, are politicians: they take a wider theme—European progress—the spread of liberal sentiments over the Continent; on their mental tablets, the names of Russia, Austria, and the Pope are inscribed in red ink. I have heard some of them talk vigorous sense—yea, I have been present at polyglot discussions in the old, oak-lined dining-room at Hunsden Wood, where a singular insight was given of the sentiments entertained by resolute minds respecting old northern despotisms, and older southern super-

stitions; also I have heard much twaddle, enounced
chiefly in French and Deutsch, but let that pass.
Hunsden himself tolerated the driveling theorists; with
the practical men he seemed leagued hand and heart.

When Hunsden is staying alone at the Wood (which
seldom happens), he generally finds his way two or
three times a week to Daisy Lane. He has a philan-
thropic motive for coming to smoke his cigar in our
porch on summer evenings : he says he does it to kill
the earwigs among the roses, with which insects, but
for his benevolent fumigations, he intimates we should
certainly be overrun.   On wet days, too, we are almost sure to see him.   According to him, it gets on
time to work me into lunacy by treading on my mental corns, or to force from Mrs. Crimsworth revelations
of the dragon within her by insulting the memory of
Hofer and Tell.

We also go frequently to Hunsden Wood, and both
I and Frances relish a visit there highly.   If there are
other guests, their characters are an interesting study;
their conversation is exciting and strange; the absence
of all local narrowness both in the host and his chosen
society gives a metropolitan, almost a cosmopolitan
freedom and largeness to the talk.   Hunsden himself
is a polite man in his own house.   He has, when he
chooses to employ it, an inexhaustible power of entertaining guests.   His very mansion, too, is interesting;
the rooms look storied, the passages legendary, the
low-ceiled chambers, with their long rows of diamond-
paned lattices, have an Old-World, haunted air.   In
his travels he has collected store of articles of *virtu*,
which are well and tastefully disposed in his panel-

ed or tapestried rooms. I have seen there one or two pictures, and one or two pieces of statuary which many an aristocratic connoisseur might have envied.

When I and Frances have dined and spent an evening with Hunsden, he often walks home with us. His wood is large, and some of the timber is old and of huge growth. There are winding ways in it, which, pursued through glade and brake, make the walk back to Daisy Lane a somewhat long one. Many a time, when we have had the benefit of a full moon, and when the night has been mild and balmy; when, moreover, a certain nightingale has been singing, and a certain stream, hid in alders, has lent the song a soft accompaniment, the remote church-bell of the one hamlet in a district of ten miles has tolled midnight ere the lord of the wood left us at our porch. Free-flowing was his talk at such hours, and far more quiet and gentle than in the daytime and before numbers. He would then forget politics and discussion, and would dwell on the past times of his house, on his family history, on himself and his own feelings—subjects each and all invested with a peculiar zest, for they were each and all unique. One glorious night in June, after I had been taunting him about his ideal bride, and asking him when she would come and graft her foreign beauty on the old Hunsden oak, he answered suddenly,

"You call her ideal; but see, here is her shadow; and there can not be a shadow without a substance."

He had led us from the depth of the "winding way" into a glade from whence the beeches withdrew, leaving it open to the sky; an unclouded moon poured her light into this glade, and Hunsden held out under her beam an ivory miniature.

Frances, with eagerness, examined it first; then she gave it to me, still, however, pushing her little face close to mine, and seeking in my eyes what I thought of the portrait. I thought it represented a very handsome and very individual-looking female face, with, as he had once said, "straight and harmonious features." It was dark; the hair, raven-black, swept not only from the brow, but from the temples, seemed thrust away carelessly, as if such beauty dispensed with, nay, despised arrangement. The Italian eye looked straight into you, and an independent, determined eye it was; the mouth was as firm as fine; the chin ditto. On the back of the miniature was gilded "Lucia."

"That is a real head," was my conclusion.

Hunsden smiled.

"I think so," he replied. "All was real in Lucia."

"And she was somebody you would have liked to marry, but could not?"

"I should certainly have liked to marry her, and that I *have* not done so is a proof that I *could* not."

He repossessed himself of the miniature, now again in Frances' hand, and put it away.

"What do *you* think of it?" he asked of my wife, as he buttoned his coat over it.

"I am sure Lucia once wore chains and broke them," was the strange answer. "I do not mean matrimonial chains," she added, correcting herself, as if she feared misinterpretation, "but social chains of some sort. The face is that of one who has made an effort, and a successful and triumphant effort, to wrest

O 2

some vigorous and valued faculty from insupportable constraint; and when Lucia's faculty got free, I am certain it spread wide pinions and carried her higher than—" She hesitated.

"Than what?" demanded Hunsden.

"Than 'les convenances' permitted you to follow."

"I think you grow spiteful—impertinent."

"Lucia has trodden the stage," continued Frances. "You never seriously thought of marrying her. You admired her originality, her fearlessness, her energy of body and mind; you delighted in her talent, whatever that was, whether song, dance, or dramatic represent- ation; you worshiped her beauty, which was of the sort after your own heart; but I am sure she filled a sphere from whence you would never have thought of taking a wife."

"Ingenious," remarked Hunsden; "whether true or not is another question. Meantime, don't you feel your little lamp of a spirit wax very pale beside such a girandole as Lucia's?"

"Yes."

"Candid, at least; and the Professor will soon be dissatisfied with the dim light you give?"

"Will you, Monsieur?"

"My sight was always too weak to endure a blaze, Frances," and we had now reached the wicket.

I said, a few pages back, that this is a sweet sum- mer evening; it is: there has been a series of lovely days, and this is the loveliest; the hay is just carried from my fields, its perfume still lingers in the air. Frances proposed to me, an hour or two since, to take tea out on the lawn; I see the round table, loaded with china, placed under a certain beech; Hunsden is expected—nay, I hear he is come; there is his voice laying down the law on some point with authority; that of Frances replies: she opposes him, of course. They are disputing about Victor, of whom Hunsden affirms that his mother is making a milksop. Mrs. Crimsworth retaliates:

"Better a thousand times he should be a milksop than what he, Hunsden, calls 'a fine lad;' and, moreover, she says that if Hunsden were to become a fixture in the neighborhood, and were not a mere comet, coming and going, no one knows how, when, where, or why, she would be quite uneasy till she had got Victor away to a school at least a hundred miles off; for that, with his mutinous maxims and unpractical dogmas, he would ruin a score of children."

I have a word to say of Victor ere I shut this manuscript in my desk, but it must be a brief one, for I hear the tinkle of silver on porcelain.

Victor is as little of a pretty child as I am of a handsome man, or his mother of a fine woman; he is pale and spare, with large eyes, as dark as those of Frances, and as deeply set as mine. His shape is symmetrical enough, but slight; his health is good. I never saw a child smile less than he does, nor one who knits such a formidable brow when sitting over a book that interests him, or while listening to tales of adventure, peril, or wonder narrated by his mother, Hunsden, or myself. But, though still, he is not unhappy; though serious, not morose: he has a susceptibility to pleasurable sensations almost too keen, for it amounts to enthusiasm. He learned to read in the

old-fashioned way out of a spelling-book at his mother's knee, and as he got on without driving by that
method, she thought it unnecessary to buy him ivory
letters, or to try any of the other inducements to learning now deemed indispensable. When he could read
he became a glutton of books, and is so still. His
toys have been few, and he has never wanted more;
for those he possesses he seems to have contracted a
partiality amounting to affection: this feeling, directed
toward one or two living animals of the house, strengthens almost to a passion.

Mr. Hunsden gave him a mastiff cub, which he called Yorke, after the donor. It grew to a superb dog,
whose fierceness, however, was much modified by the
companionship and caresses of its young master. He
would go nowhere, do nothing without Yorke; Yorke
lay at his feet while he learned his lessons, played with
him in the garden, walked with him in the lane and
wood, sat near his chair at meals, was fed always by
his own hand, was the first thing he sought in the
morning, the last he left at night. Yorke accompanied
Mr. Hunsden one day to X——, and was bitten in the
street by a dog in a rabid state. As soon as Hunsden
had brought him home, and had informed me of the
circumstance, I went into the yard and shot him where
he lay licking his wound: he was dead in an instant;
he had not seen me level the gun—I stood behind him.
I had scarcely been ten minutes in the house when
my ear was struck with sounds of anguish. I repaired to the yard once more, for they proceeded thence.
Victor was kneeling beside his dead mastiff, bent over
it, embracing its bull-like neck, and lost in a passion
of the wildest woe. He saw me.

"Oh, papa, I'll never forgive you! I'll never forgive you!" was his exclamation. "You shot Yorke; I saw it from the window. I never believed you could be so cruel; I can love you no more!"

I had much ado to explain to him, with steady voice, the stern necessity of the deed. He still, with that inconsolable and bitter accent which I can not render, but which pierced my heart, repeated,

"He might have been cured—you should have tried—you should have burnt the wound with a hot iron, or covered it with caustic. You gave no time; and now it is too late: he is dead!"

He sank fairly down on the senseless carcass. I waited patiently a long while, till his grief had somewhat exhausted him, and then I lifted him in my arms and carried him to his mother, sure that she would comfort him best. She had witnessed the whole scene from a window. She would not come out for fear of increasing my difficulties by her emotion, but she was ready now to receive him. She took him to her kind heart, and on to her gentle lap; consoled him but with her lips, her eyes, her soft embrace, for some time; and then, when his sobs diminished, told him that Yorke had felt no pain in dying, and that, if he had been left to expire naturally, his end would have been most horrible; above all, she told him that I was not cruel (for that idea seemed to give exquisite pain to poor Victor); that it was my affection for Yorke and him which had made me act so, and that I was now almost heartbroken to see him weep thus bitterly.

Victor would have been no true son of his father had these considerations, these reasons, breathed in so

low, so sweet a tone—married to caresses so benign,
so tender—to looks so inspired with pitying sympathy, produced no effect on him. They did produce an
effect: he grew calmer, rested his face on her shoulder,
and lay still in her arms. Looking up shortly, he
asked his mother to tell him over again what she had
said about Yorke having suffered no pain, and my not
being cruel; the balmy words being repeated, he again
pillowed his cheek on her breast, and was again tranquil.

Some hours after, he came to me in my library,
asked if I forgave him, and desired to be reconciled.
I drew the lad to my side, and there I kept him a good
while, and had much talk with him, in the course of
which he disclosed many points of feeling and thought
I approved of in my son. I found, it is true, few elements of the "good fellow" or the "fine fellow" in
him; scant sparkles of the spirit which loves to flash
over the wine-cup, or which kindles the passions to a
destroying fire; but I saw in the soil of his heart
healthy and swelling germs of compassion, affection,
fidelity. I discovered in the garden of his intellect a
rich growth of wholesome principles—reason, justice,
moral courage, promised, if not blighted, a fertile bearing. So I bestowed on his large forehead and on his
cheek—still pale with tears—a proud and contented
kiss, and sent him away comforted. Yet I saw him
the next day laid on the mound under which Yorke
had been buried, his face covered with his hands. He
was melancholy for some weeks; and more than a
year elapsed before he would listen to any proposal
of having another dog.

Victor learns fast. He must soon go to Eton, where, I suspect, his first year or two will be utter wretchedness : to leave me, his mother, and his home, will give his heart an agonized wrench; then the fagging will not suit him; but emulation, thirst after knowledge, the glory of success, will stir and reward him in time. Meantime, I feel in myself a strong repugnance to fix the hour which will uproot my sole olive-branch, and transplant it far from me; and, when I speak to Frances on the subject, I am heard with a kind of patient pain, as though I alluded to some fearful operation, at which her nature shudders, but from which her fortitude will not permit her to re-coil. The step must, however, be taken, and it *shall* be; for, though Frances will not make a milksop of her son, she will accustom him to a style of treat-ment, a forbearance, a congenial tenderness he will meet with from no one else. She sees, as I also see, a something in Victor's temper—a kind of electrical ardor and power—which emits, now and then, ominous sparks. Hunsden calls it his spirit, and says it should not be curbed. I call it the leaven of the offending Adam, and consider that it should be, if not *whipped* out of him, at least soundly disciplined ; ànd that he will be cheap of any amount of either bodily or men-tal suffering which will ground him radically in the art of self-control. Frances gives this *something* in her son's marked character no name; but when it appears in the grinding of his teeth, in the glittering of his eye, in the fierce revolt of feeling against disappointment, mischance, sudden sorrow, or supposed injustice, she folds him to her breast, or takes him to walk with her alone in the wood; then she reasons with him like any philosopher, and to reason Victor is ever accessible; then she looks at him with eyes of love, and by love Victor can be infallibly subjugated; but will reason or love be the weapons with which in future the world will meet his violence? Oh no; for that flash in his black eye—for that cloud on his bony brow—for that compression of his statuesque lips, the lad will some day get blows instead of blandishments—kicks instead of kisses; then for the fit of mute fury which will sicken his body and madden his soul; then for the ordeal of merited and salutary suffering, out of which he will come (I trust) a wiser and a better man.

I see him now; he stands by Hunsden, who is seated on the lawn under the beech; Hunsden's hand rests on the boy's collar, and he is instilling God knows what principles into his ear. Victor looks well just now, for he listens with a sort of smiling interest; he never looks so like his mother as when he smiles—pity the sunshine breaks out so rarely! Victor has a preference for Hunsden, full as strong as I deem desirable, being considerably more potent, decided, and indiscriminating than any I ever entertained for that personage myself. Frances, too, regards it with a sort of unexpressed anxiety; while her son leans on Hunsden's knee, or rests against his shoulder, she roves with restless movement round, like a dove guarding its young from a hovering hawk. She says she wishes Hunsden had children of his own, for then he would better know the danger of inciting their pride and indulging their foibles.

Frances approaches my library window, puts aside

the honeysuckle which half covers it, and tells me tea
is ready.   Seeing that I continue busy, she enters the
room, comes near me quietly, and puts her hand on my
shoulder.

"Monsieur est trop appliqué."

"I shall soon have done."

She draws a chair near, and sits down to wait till
I have finished.   Her presence is as pleasant to my
mind as the perfume of the fresh hay and spicy flowers, as the glow of the westering sun, as the repose of
the midsummer eve are to my senses.

But Hunsden comes; I hear his step, and there he
is, bending through the lattice from which he has thrust
away the woodbine with unsparing hand, disturbing
two bees and a butterfly.

"Crimsworth!   I say, Crimsworth!   Take that pen
out of his hand, mistress, and make him lift up his
head."

"Well, Hunsden, I hear you."

"I was at X—— yesterday; your brother Ned is
getting richer than Crœsus by railway speculations;
they call him in the Piece-Hall a stag of ten; and I
have heard from Brown.   M. and Madame Vandenhuten and Jean Baptiste talk of coming to see you
next month.   He mentions the Pelets too; he says
their domestic harmony is not the finest in the world,
but in business they are doing "on ne peut mieux,"
which circumstance, he concludes, will be a sufficient
consolation to both for any little crosses in the affections.   Why don't you invite the Pelets to ——shire,
Crimsworth ?   I should so like to see your first flame,
Zoraïde.   Mistress, don't be jealous, but he loved that

lady to distraction; I know it for a fact. Brown says she weighs twelve stone now; you see what you've lost, Mr. Professor. Now, Monsieur and Madame, if you don't come to tea, Victor and I will begin without you."

"Papa, come!"

THE END.

NEW BOOKS

And New Editions Recently Issued by

CARLETON, PUBLISHER,

NEW YORK.

418 BROADWAY, CORNER OF LISPENARD STREET.

N.B.—THE PUBLISHER, upon receipt of the price in advance, will send any of the following Books, by mail, POSTAGE FREE, to any part of the United States. This convenient and very safe mode may be adopted when the neighboring Booksellers are not supplied with the desired work. State name and address in full.

Victor Hugo.

LES MISERABLES.—The only unabridged English translation of "the grandest and best Novel ever written." One large octavo vol., paper covers, $1.00, . or cloth $1.50

LES MISERABLES.—A superior edition in five vols.—Fantine—Cosette—Marius—Denis—Valjean. 8vo., cloth, each, $1.00

LES MISERABLES—In the Spanish language. Fine 8vo. edition, two vols., paper covers, $4.00 ; or cloth, bound, . $5.00

THE LIFE OF VICTOR HUGO.—By himself. "As charming and interesting as a novel." 8vo., cloth . . . $1.75

By the Author of "Rutledge."

RUTLEDGE.—A deeply interesting novel. 12mo. cloth, $1.75

THE SUTHERLANDS.— do. . . do. $1.75

FRANK WARRINGTON.— do. . . do. $1.75

LOUIE'S LAST TERM AT ST. MARY'S.— . · . do. $1.75

A NEW NOVEL.—*In press.*

Hand-Books of Good Society.

THE HABITS OF GOOD SOCIETY; with Thoughts, Hints, and Anecdotes, concerning nice points of taste, good manners, and the art of making oneself agreeable. Reprinted from the London Edition. The best and most entertaining work of the kind ever published. . . 12mo. cloth, $1.75

THE ART OF CONVERSATION.—With directions for self-culture. A sensible and instructive work, that ought to be in the hands of every one who wishes to be either an agreeable talker or listener. . . . 12mo. cloth, $1.50

Mrs. Mary J. Holmes' Works.

DARKNESS AND DAYLIGHT.—*Just published.*   12mo. cl. $1.50
'LENA RIVERS.—   .   .   A Novel.   do. $1.50
TEMPEST AND SUNSHINE.—   .   do.   do. $1.50
MARIAN GREY.—   .   .   .   do.   do. $1.50
MEADOW BROOK.— .   .   .   do.   do. $1.50
ENGLISH ORPHANS.—   .   .   do.   do. $1.50
DORA DEANE.—   .   .   .   do.   do. $1.50
COUSIN MAUDE.—   .   .   .   do.   ·do. $1.50
HOMESTEAD ON THE HILLSIDE.—   do.   do. $1.5c

Artemus Ward.

HIS BOOK.—An irresistibly funny volume of writings by the
  immortal American humorist .   .   12mo. cloth, $1.50

Miss Muloch.

JOHN HALIFAX.—A novel.   With illust.   12mo., cloth, $1.75
A LIFE FOR A LIFE.—   .   do.   .   do. $1.75

Charlotte Bronte (Currer Bell).

JANE EYRE.—A novel.   With illustration.   12mo. cloth, $1.75
THE PROFESSOR.—do.   .   do.   .   do. $1.75
SHIRLEY.— '. do.   .   do.   .   do. $1.75
VILLETTE.— .   do.   .   do.   .   do. $1.75

Edmund Kirke.

AMONG THE PINES.—A Southern sketch.   12mo. cloth, $1.25
MY SOUTHERN FRIENDS.—   do.   do.   . $1.25
DOWN IN TENNESSEE.—Just published.   .   do. $1.50

Cuthbert Bede.

VERDANT GREEN.—A rollicking, humorous novel of English
  student life; with 200 comic illustrations. 12mo. cloth, $1.50
NEARER AND DEARER.—A novel, illustrated. 12mo. clo. $1.50

Richard B. Kimball.

WAS HE SUCCESSFUL?—   A novel.   12mo. cloth, $1.5c
UNDERCURRENTS.—   do.   do. $1.5c
SAINT LEGER.—'   do.   do. $1.5c
, ROMANCE OF STUDENT LIFE.— do.   do. $1.5c
IN THE TROPICS.—Edited by R. B. Kimball.   do. $1.50

Epes Sargent.

PECULIAR.—One of the most remarkable and successful novels
  published in this country.   .   .   12mo. cloth, $1.75

Miss Augusta J. Evans.

BEULAH.—A novel of great power.   12mo. cloth, $1.75

A. S. Roe's Works.

A LONG LOOK AHEAD.— A novel.   12mo. cloth, $1.5c
TO LOVE AND TO BE LOVED.— do. . . do. $1.50
TIME AND TIDE.— do. . . do. $1.50
I'VE BEEN THINKING.— do. . . do. $1.50
THE STAR AND THE CLOUD.— do. . . do. $1.50
TRUE TO THE LAST.— do. . . do. $1.50
HOW COULD HE HELP IT.— do. . . do. $1.50
LIKE AND UNLIKE.— do. . . do. $1.50
A NEW NOVEL.—*In Press.* do. $1.50

Walter Barrett, Clerk.

OLD MERCHANTS OF NEW YORK.—Being personal incidents, interesting sketches, bits of biography, and gossipy events in the life of nearly every leading merchant in New York City. Two series.   . . 12mo. cloth, each, $1.75

T. S. Arthur's New Works.

LIGHT ON SHADOWED PATHS.—A novel.   12mo. cloth, $1.50
OUT IN THE WORLD.— do. . do. $1.50
NOTHING BUT MONEY.—*In Press.* do. . do. $1.50

The Orpheus C. Kerr Papers.

A COLLECTION of exquisitely satirical and humorous military criticisms. Two series.   . 12mo. cloth, each, $1.50

M. Michelet's Works.

LOVE (L'AMOUR).—From the French.   12mo. cloth, $1.50
WOMAN (LA FEMME.)— do. . . . do. $1.50
WOMAN'S PHILOSOPHY OF WOMAN.—By Hericourt, do $1.50

Novels by Ruffini.

DR. ANTONIO.—A love story of Italy.   12mo. cloth, $1.75
LAVINIA; OR, THE ITALIAN ARTIST.— do. $1.75
VINCENZO; OR, SUNKEN ROCKS.— 8vo. cloth, $1.75

Rev John Cumming, D.D., of London.

THE GREAT TRIBULATION.—Two series.   12mo. cloth, $1.50
THE GREAT PREPARATION.— do. . do. $1.50
THE GREAT CONSUMMATION.— do. . do. $1.50
TEACH US TO PRAY.— do. $1.50

Ernest Renan.

THE LIFE OF JESUS.—Translated by C. E. Wilbour from the celebrated French work.   . . 12mo. cloth, $1.75
RELIGIOUS HISTORY AND CRITICISM.— 8vo. cloth, $2.50

Charles Reade.

THE CLOISTER AND THE HEARTH.—A magnificent new novel, by
the author of "Hard Cash," etc.   .   8vo. cloth, $2.00

The Opera.

TALES FROM THE OPERAS.—A collection of clever stories, based
upon the plots of all the famous operas.   12mo. cl., $1.50

J. C. Jeaffreson.

A BOOK ABOUT DOCTORS.—An exceedingly humorous and entertaining volume of sketches, stories, and facts, about
famous physicians and surgeons.   12mo. cloth, $1.75

Fred. S. Cozzens.

THE SPARROWGRASS PAPERS.—A capital humorous work, with
illustrations by Darley.   .   .   12mo. cloth, $1.25

F. D. Guerrazzi.

BEATRICE CENCI.—A great historical novel. Translated from
the Italian; with a portrait of the Cenci, from Guido's
famous picture in Rome.   .   .   12mo. cloth, $1.75

Private Miles O'Reilly.

HIS BOOK.—Rich with his songs, services, and speeches, and
comically illustrated.   .   .   .   12mo. cloth, $1.25

The New York Central Park.

A SUPERB GIFT BOOK.—The Central Park pleasantly described,
and magnificently embellished with more than 50 exquisite
photographs of the principal views and objects of interest.
A large quarto volume, sumptuously bound in Turkey
morocco, ... $25.00

Joseph Rodman Drake.

THE CULPRIT FAY.—The most charming faery poem in the
English language. Beautifully printed. 12mo. cloth, 75 cts.

Mother Goose for Grown Folks.

HUMOROUS RHYMES for grown people; based upon the famous
"Mother Goose Melodies."   .   .•   12mo. cloth, $1.00

Stephen Massett.

DRIFTING ABOUT.—A comic illustrated book of the life and
travels of "Jeems Pipes."   .   .   12mo. cloth, $1.25

A New Sporting Work.

THE GAME FISH OF THE NORTH.—One of the best books on fish
and fishing ever published. Entertaining as well as instructive, and full of illustrations.   .   12mo. cloth, $1.50

Balzac's Novels.
CÆSAR BIROTTEAU.—From the French.　12mo. cloth, $1.25
THE ALCHEMIST.—　　　do.　　　do.　$1.25
EUGENIE GRANDET.—　　do.　　　do.　$1.25
PETTY ANNOYANCES OF MARRIED LIFE.—　　do.　$1.25

Thomas Bailey Aldrich.
BABIE BELL, AND OTHER POEMS.—Blue and gold binding, $1.00
OUT OF HIS HEAD.—A new romance.　12mo. cloth, $1.00

Richard H. Stoddard.
THE KING'S BELL.—A new poem.　.　12mo. cloth, 75 cts.
THE MORGESONS.—A novel.　By Mrs. R. H. Stoddard. $1.00

Edmund C. Stedman.
ALICE OF MONMOUTH.—A new poem.　12mo. cloth, $1.00
LYRICS AND IDYLS.—　.　.　.　.　do.　75 cts.

M. T. Walworth.
LULU.—A new novel.　.　.　.　12mo. cloth, $1.50
HOTSPUR.—　do.　　.　.　do.　$1.50

Author of " Olie."
NEPENTHE.—A new novel.　.　.　12mo. cloth, $1.50
TOGETHER.—　do.　　.　do.

Quest.
A NEW ROMANCE.　.　.　.　12mo. cloth, $1.50

Victoire.
A NEW NOVEL.　.　.　.　12mo. cloth, $1.75

Red-Tape
AND PIGEON-HOLE GENERALS, as seen by a citizen-soldier in the Army of the Potomac.　.　.　12mo. cloth, $1.25

Author " Green Mountain Boys."
OENTEOLA.—A new work,　.　12mo. cloth, $1.50

C. French Richards.
JOHN GUILDERSTRING'S SIN.—A novel.　12mo. cloth, $1.50

J. R. Beckwith.
THE WINTHROPS.—A novel.　:　12mo. cloth, $1.75

Jas. H. Hackett.
NOTES AND COMMENTS ON SHAKSPEARE.—　12mo. cloth, $1.50

Miscellaneous Works.

ALEXANDER VON HUMBOLDT.—Life and travels. 12mo. cl. $1.50
LIFE OF HUGH MILLER, the Geologist. . . do. $1.50
ADAM GUROWSKI.—Diary for 1863. . . do. $1.25
DOESTICKS.—The Elephant Club, illustrated. . do. $2.00
HUSBAND AND WIFE, or human development. do. $1.25
ROCKFORD.—A novel by Mrs. L. D. Umsted. do. $1.00
THE PRISONER OF STATE.—By D. A. Mahony. do. $1.25
THE PARTISAN LEADER.—By Beverly Tucker. . do. $1.25
SPREES AND SPLASHES.—By Henry Morford. . do. $1.00
AROUND THE PYRAMIDS.—By Gen. Aaron Ward. do. $1.50
CHINA AND THE CHINESE.—By W. L. G. Smith. do. $1.00
WANDERINGS OF A BEAUTY.—Mrs. Edwin James. do. $1.00
THE U. S. TAX LAW.—"Government Edition." do. 75 cts.
TREATISE ON DEAFNESS.—By Dr. E. B. Lighthill. do. $1.00
LYRICS OF A DAY—or newspaper poetry. . do. $1.00
GARRET VAN HORN.—A novel by J. S. Sauzade. do. $1.25
THE NATIONAL SCHOOL FOR THE SOLDIER.— do. 50 cts.
FORT LAFAYETTE.—A novel by Benjamin Wood. do. $1.00
THE YACHTMAN'S PRIMER.—By T. R. Warren. do. 50 cts.
GEN. NATHANIEL LYON.—Life and Writings. . do. $1.00
PHILIP THAXTER.—A novel. . . . do. $1.00
LITERARY ESSAYS.—By George Brimley.. . do. $1.50
HAYING TIME TO HOPPING.—A novel. . . do. $1.25
THE VAGABOND.—Essays by Adam Badeau. . do. $1.00
EDGAR POE AND HIS CRITICS.—By Mrs. Whitman. do. 75 cts.
TACTICS; or, Cupid in Shoulder-Straps. . do. $1 00
JOHN DOE AND RICHARD ROE.—A novel. . do. $1.25
LOLA MONTEZ.—Her life and lectures. . . do. $1.50
DEBT AND GRACE.—By Rev. C. F. Hudson. . do. $1.50
HUSBAND vs. WIFE.—A comic illustrated poem. do. 50 cts.
TRANSITION.—Edited by Rev. H. S. Carpenter. do. $1.00
ROUMANIA.—By Dr. Jas. O. Noyes, illustrated. do. $1.50
VERNON GROVE.—A novel. . . . . do. $1.25
ANSWER TO HUGH MILLER.—By T. A. Davies. do. $1.25
COSMOGONY.—By Thomas A. Davies. . 8vo. cl., $1.50
NATIONAL HYMNS.—By Richard Grant White. do. $1.50
TWENTY YEARS Around the World. J. Guy Vassar. do. $3.50
SPIRIT OF HEBREW POETRY.—By Isaac Taylor. do. $2.50